g a r d e n c u i s i n e g a r d e n c u i s i n e g a r d e n c u i s i n e

g a r d e n c u i s i n e g a r d e n c u i s i n e g a r d e n c u i s i n e

g a r d e n c u i s i n e g a r d e n c u i s i n e g a r d e n c u i s i n e

g a r d e n c u i s i n e g a r d e n c u i s i n e

g a r d e n c u i s i n e g a r d e n c u i s i n e

g a r d e n c u i s i n e g a r d e n c u i s i n e

g a r d e n c u i s i n e g a r d e n c u i s i n e

g a r d e n c u i s i n e g a r d e n c u i s i n e g a r d e n c u i s i n e

g a r d e n c u i s i n e g a r d e n c u i s i n e g a r d e n c u i s i n e

g a r d e n c u i s i n e g a r d e n c u i s i n e g a r d e n c u i s i n e

g a r d e n c u i s i n e g a r d e n c u i s i n e g a r d e n c u i s i n e

PAUL WENNER

Garden Cuisine

Heal Yourself and the Planet
Through Low-Fat Meatless Eating

SIMON & SCHUSTER

It's not that long ago that the average American mother would have been more concerned to learn that her son or daughter was becoming a vegetarian than to discover that he or she had started smoking. People who ate vegetarian diets were considered strange creatures who, it was believed, resided on the fringes of society.

Still today, in many parts of the country, people who eat food that damages their cardiovascular systems, that depends on the killing of animals, and that contributes mightily to the destruction of our environment are considered normal—while those who eat healthy foods that are produced with compassion and ecological responsibility are considered weird.

And yet this is all changing, and changing fast.

Part of the reason is due to increasing evidence that meat eating is as damaging to the human body as smoking. Part of the reason is that increasing numbers of people are sick of being sick, and eager to do what they can to take responsibility for their lives. But another part of the reason is that there are certain businesspeople who are recognizing the enormous importance, and financial wisdom, of providing people with food that both tastes great and is good for them.

Paul Wenner, the inventor of the Gardenburger, the world's most popular vegetarian burger, is such a person. I am honored to introduce him, and his story, because I know how many more rain forests remain alive today because of his work, how many fewer heart attacks people have suffered, how much cleaner our air and water remain, how much healthier our society and ecosystems are. Paul says he's not out to change the world, just breakfast, lunch, and dinner. But he *is* helping us to change the world, those of us who have along with him broken the stranglehold of the meat machine—breaking

> "To be vegetarian is to disagree—to disagree with the course of things today. Starvation, world hunger, cruelty, waste, wars—we must make a statement against these things."
>
> ISAAC BASHEVIS SINGER

Apart from the health and environmental horrors engendered by a meat-based diet, there is also the nearly incomprehensible cruelty that is inflicted upon the animals that are bred and grown—like inanimate units—to feed us. John Robbins, in *Diet for a New America,* has created a multitude of new vegetarians who were horrified by his painstakingly accurate portrayal of just how hideously these food animals are treated. No one has a better grasp of this subject than John, but I will review and update a few aspects of this story in part II, particularly where they are relevant to health and environmental issues.

In part III, "The GardenPlan—Your Personal Program for Optimal Health," I'll take you on a tour of my own "garden," that almost magical realm of nutritional healing that is my real passion in life. I'll introduce you to the general principles of vegetarianism, revisiting some old debates about protein complementarity and perhaps introducing some new ones, related, for example, to my personal purification prescription. I'll tell you what I've learned over the years about what it takes to make vegetarianism an integral, joyous, and sustainable part of your life—rather than a challenge and a chore. I'll show you how vegetarianism is evolving and how much easier it is to make the transition today than it was even five or ten years ago.

I'll provide specific goals and guidelines for men, women, and children. I'll introduce you to the "GardenGroups," from which you'll be selecting tasty, filling-but-not-fattening, healthy foods on a daily basis—with emphasis on a wide variety of fresh, *whole* foods.

In a chapter called "The Healing Garden," I'll relate some of the latest scientific and medical data on the preventive and curative powers of meatless cuisine. There are now very sound, long-range scientific studies that are demonstrating the sometimes miraculous-seeming qualities of vegetarian fare. I'll identify some of the superstars of a cornucopia of healing, fresh, whole foods.

In another chapter, "The Lean Green," I'll show you how to structure a *vegetarian weight-loss regimen.* Vegetarianism provides the best possible approach to long-term sustainable weight control. There is absolutely nothing better. Going vegetarian is, without question, the best way to fill up without filling out. And unlike so many other weight-loss programs, mine fills you with the kind of energy that you need to stay on track—because dieting, no matter what form it takes, requires stamina. Too many diet regimens leave their victims either tired and listless or cranky and high-strung.

And for those of you who want to be lean and muscular, there's nothing about vegetarianism that precludes this. You can get all the high-quality, muscle-building nutrients you need from a vegetarian diet. Vegetable protein is far healthier than meat protein, and I'll demonstrate why.

It comes as a surprise to some to learn that being muscular does *not* automatically equate with good health. In fact, though I know I risk making a lot of bodybuilders— and especially those who provide them with expensive concentrated protein supplements—angry, there are significant health risks in the way a great many pursue the "perfect" physique. In other words, muscularity in itself is not the issue—it's how you get there that matters. I'll show you the best path through the garden.

In "Taking the Garden on the Road," I'll share with you what I've learned over the years about sticking with a vegetarian diet, even when you have to spend much of your life traveling. It never ceases to amaze me how many people who have no trouble adhering to sound nutritional practices while at home throw all caution and reason to the winds when they are on the road, eating out on business or with friends, attending celebrations or on other special occasions.

Unfortunately, for many of us, given our busy schedules, those "special occasions" become more the norm than the exception. And excuses, of course, abound, once we are outside our own kitchens. A lot of this simply has to do with not being prepared, not knowing what to ask for in restaurants, not knowing how to deal with meat-eating associates, friends, relatives. Believe me, there are effective ways to meet all of these situations and to create a plan of action to ensure that your optimal nutrition program proceeds without interruption, no matter where you are or who you are with at any given time.

Of course, ultimately, what makes any nutritional program work (or fail) are the recipes that are at the heart of it. Drawing upon my own decades of cooking and relying upon the help and insight of some of the world's best cooks, I have prepared more than 150 vegetarian treats for you. All meet my strict "GardenChef" standards for nutritional content, down to the very most "minor" ingredient, though, in truth, I don't consider *any* ingredient minor; if it's in there, it's got an important role to play. They also meet my equally exacting standards for taste, texture, and consistency. And they've also got to *look* good, in addition to *being* good. Why? Because people eat with their eyes, and good-looking food goes down easier and begs to be repeated.

I've worked with Jennifer Raymond, a top nutritionist, who also happens to be one of the world's great cooks, on these recipes—and she has devoted a great deal of time to what I call "quality control," making sure that these recipes really do deliver what I say they deliver and that they are "reproducible," which means that by following the recipe instructions, you can re-create these dishes consistently. We're all tired of those recipes that look fantastic on TV or in the pages of a magazine and turn out looking like glop on our tables, even though we followed instructions to the letter.

Some of these recipes use my GardenProducts—GardenSausage, GardenChick'n, etc.—but most are vegetarian dishes you can put together using ingredients you pick up at the produce market or pluck out of your own garden. And most are quick, economical, easy to prepare.

One of our mottoes is: *We're not out to change the world—just breakfast, lunch, and dinner.* If you want to experience the change, you can begin right now.

Start out with a Mango Dango Cocktail and some Golden GardenSausage Waffles. At lunch, have a bowl of Barley, Tomato, and Bean Soup and a salad of Wild Rice and Fruit, or perhaps you'd prefer some Broiled Polenta Squares and Tomato Chutney to get you going, followed by our savory Zucchini Onion Pie. For dinner, ease into things with a few pieces of Meditation Sushi before advancing to our favorite Exotic Stir-fry, with side dishes of Garlic-Infused Green Beans and Calcutta Cauliflower. Or maybe you'd rather start with some Gypsy Soup, spicy Wild Rice and Asparagus Salad, and then experience our luscious Garden Lasagna before mellowing into some Poached Pears, Apple Custard Fruit Tart, or our Fruit Compote, a soup made with Almond Dumplings. When you get the munchies, try the pita chips with any of our great dips— Pea Guacamole, Island Salsa made with papayas—or, for those more serious in-between hunger pangs, avail yourselves of some of our "handheld" nutrition rockets—for example, a righteous Reuben Sandwich, a toasty Gardenburger Maui, or a Zucchini Pocket Pizza. For a liquid snack, try some sassy Fruity Sangria or a Banana Frappé.

And now that I've whetted your appetite, let's get started.

PART ONE

Growing the Garden

There is probably no subject more important than the study

of foods in relation to nutrition and health.

GEORGE WASHINGTON CARVER

gardencuisinegardencuisinegardencuisine

gardencuisinegardencuisinegardencuisine

gardencuisinegardencuisinegardencuisine

gardencuisinegardencuisinegardencuisine

gardencuisinegardencuisinegardencuisine

gardencuisinegardencuisinegardencuisine

stands right behind home plate. Joe hit a foul ball that flew back up into the grandstand. My mother was pregnant, a little over seven months, but could still move pretty fast. She saw the ball coming right at her and moved up to get out of the way. My grandmother did the same, but the ball hit her on the leg. As my mother, Frances, lurched out of the way, she lost her balance and fell down the grandstand.

A bit later, she went into premature labor and had to be rushed to the hospital. It would have made a great opening scene in a movie—but it turned out to be the opening scene in my life. And almost the *last* one. My twin sister, Peggy, and I were born that day in 1947, both of us weighing in at about three pounds. My sister apparently looked a lot better than I did, because the doctors told my worried parents, "The girl's going to be okay, but the boy probably won't make it."

Well, there's another trait to which I attribute my success and that's persistence. Despite the negative prognosis, I persisted, lived, and ultimately achieved optimal health. But it was a long, hard battle. I was a wimpy kid, underweight and always sick. I was lacking in energy and soon developed serious asthma and life-threatening chronic tuberculosis, both of which were to plague me for years.

Because I was too weak to go outside much, let alone play sports, I spent most of my time inside. I had an inquisitive mind, undimmed by my illnesses, and whiled away the hours with a chemistry set. When I'd used that up, I started tinkering around in the kitchen, which seemed to me like a giant chemistry set. Consequently, I started cooking at an early age. As you can see, bad health already has me pointed in the right direction.

During my growing-up years, there were the endless bouts with lung disease, the trips to the doctor and the hospital, the shots, the huge pills I gagged on, the tubes down my nose and into my lungs, the other kids ignoring me or making fun of me. I went to an all-boys Catholic school, and the teasing could be pretty merciless at times, especially since I was so weak that I sometimes couldn't carry my books at my side but, instead, had to clutch them to my chest. My health was so fragile that I'd occasionally pass out just from climbing a short flight of stairs.

By the time I was fourteen, my dogged determination had finally earned me enough respect that I was briefly made a center on the eighth-grade football team. I'd just stand there, hike the ball, and then fall down; they didn't expect me to block or do anything else. I was the token center. It was kind of a joke.

My mom felt sorry for me through all this and made excuses for me. My father, of course, was disappointed that his son wasn't an athlete. I had some friends, but I was more of a loner. To survive, I lived inside my own world and developed an independence of spirit.

Meanwhile, my parents' reaction to my situation, and under doctors' directions, was to try to beef me up with more of the great American diet. Mom served meat two or three times a day, minimum. My dad, who could eat a seventy-two-ounce steak, would have considered himself a failure if he couldn't have meat on the table three times a day, 365 days out of the year—not much different at that time from many other American dads.

Unfortunately, my health often seemed to get worse, rather than better, no matter how "well" my parents fed me. By the time I was seventeen, I still had problems with wheezing, couldn't run even a short distance, and had been permanently exempted—banned, I think is more accurate—from high school PE. When other kids had to run up and down the bleachers, I was allowed to walk.

Then, one day, I was watching television, just casually, and I heard someone say, "You don't have to accept disease." If you can imagine those words amplified a thousand times and also visually projected in pulsating, neon colors, you might begin to understand my reaction.

You don't have to accept disease!

My ears became ultrasensitive antennae. The next thing I heard was:

Check into diet!

The rest of it was confusing. Maybe it was because my head was spinning. But I did manage to pick up three more words:

Health-food store

Once this near-psychedelic experience subsided, my first question was: "What's a health-food store?" My mother merely shook her head in deep concern, and my father pushed the meat platter at me. But, finally, persistent as I was, I found someone who said, "Oh, yeah, I think there is one here in Portland." And that was the case. There was exactly one, and it was run by the Seventh-Day Adventists, who were among the first to recognize the value of vegetarianism and so-called "natural foods."

The minute I found out about that store I was single-minded in my determination to get there as quickly as possible. Once there, I was surrounded by what I assumed were "health foods," including bottles of vitamins and minerals. But I didn't have a clue as to what to do with them. I think that up until that point, I had imagined that once I arrived at a "health-food store," everything would magically fall into place. As it turned out, it *did*.

Thank You, Ellen G. White and Paul C. Bragg

As I looked frantically around the place, wheezing, I remembered the words: "Check into diet." My eyes came to rest on a rack of books that were for sale. I breathed a little easier, especially when I spotted a book called *Counsels on Diet and Foods,* by Ellen G. White. This, I thought, must be what they were talking about on television—the key to *checking into diet.*

Another book grabbed my attention as well: *The Miracle of Fasting,* by Paul C. Bragg. It had the subtitle *Proven Throughout History for Physical, Mental and Spiritual Rejuvenation.* I was sure I'd hit pay dirt when I read, in the book jacket copy, that Bragg was the "Father of the Health Movement in America," that he had "named and opened the first health food store in America," that he had "created the first health foods and products and made them available nationwide," that he had opened "the first health restaurants and first health spas in America," and that Olympic Gold medalists, movie stars, and business tycoons were among his disciples, including J. C. Penney, Conrad Hilton, Del E. Webb, Jack LaLanne, and so on.

But what really made my hair stand on end was this passage from the flap copy:

> Crippled by TB as a teenager, Bragg developed his own eating, breathing and exercising program to rebuild his body into an ageless, tireless, painfree citadel of glowing, radiant health. He excelled in running, swimming, biking, progressive weight training and mountain climbing.

At that point, I would have robbed a bank to buy Bragg's book. Fortunately, I had enough money to buy both the Bragg and the Ellen White books. I was about to "check into diet" and rushed home to do just that, feeling an excitement and hope I hadn't felt in years. Little did I know at the time how lucky I had been. There were a lot of bad "health-food" books out at that time, as there are today, but I had stumbled upon two of the soundest ever written—by two self-taught titans in the field of human nutrition—and these books were to change my life, dramatically for the better, forever. In fact, I fully credit these books with the healing that I was soon to begin experiencing.

I quickly learned that White was a strict vegetarian and that Bragg was a near-vegetarian. Both of them said that meat-based diets introduced all manner of toxins and imbalances into our bodies. This came as a shock, but since I was doing so poorly on a meat-intensive diet, it made a certain sense, too. Both authors made impressive arguments for purifying our "systems," both physical and mental (and, where White was concerned, spiritual), through the consumption of natural foods and the avoidance of synthetics, additives, pesticides, refined foods, excessive salt and sugar.

Bragg's book was easier for me to follow, because he had developed a step-by-step program to purge the body of impurities, obtain optimal nutrition, and fight disease. His dietary regimen was supplemented with a program of fasting, drinking purified water, and getting plenty of sunshine and exercise.

Bragg was far ahead of his time in much of his advice; the wisdom of most of his recommendations, however, would later be confirmed by scientific testing. He was among the very first to warn of the dangers of too much salt in the diet, of saturated fats and hydrogenated oils, of smoked foods containing nitrates and nitrites—later found to be carcinogenic—of refined carbohydrates and white flour. He was also among the first to point out that vegetable protein can substitute entirely for animal protein without adverse effect—an idea that was considered dangerous and heretical when first proposed, an idea that it took until 1995 for the medical establishment in the United States to confirm and endorse! Bragg's ideas on exercises also predated what is now one of the givens of preventive medicine—the need for consistent aerobic activity.

Bragg's ideas on "autointoxication" in many ways, decades ago, foresaw our current preoccupation with oxidants and antioxidants. He pinpointed, with stunning accuracy, those substances in our diet that introduce "free radicals" that corrode our systems and contribute to the whole spectrum of degenerative diseases, including the autoimmune diseases—well before science had even begun using the term "free radical." He also pinpointed the "anti-oxidant" components of nutrition, those factors that can defend us from the toxins and poisons of everyday life. He called the autointoxicants "the enemy within our bodies." Said Bragg in *The Miracle of Fasting:*

The worst of autointoxication is that it has been coming on for a matter of years. It takes water-fasting, good natural eating and clean living habits to defeat it. . . . First, make it a habit to take a complete water-fast once a week of from 24 to 36 hours. And on the days you eat, eat natural, unpoisoned foods. Let your mind rule your body. Flesh is dumb. You can feed your stomach anything. But now you are going to use commonsense, eat with intelligence. Always eat foods as close to nature as possible.

"Flesh is dumb." That was one of Bragg's favorite sayings and one that I found particularly illuminating and empowering. I had always assumed I was the slave of my own flesh. Suddenly, I was being told I could make it do what I wanted it to do—through the way I ate, breathed, exercised, and even through the way I *thought* about things. Bragg was also an early advocate of positive thinking. The way we thought about ourselves and visualized ourselves helped define our reality, in Bragg's view. Recent discoveries, properly considered revolutionary, that some of our immune cells come equipped with receptors for brain neurotransmitters, establishing a direct link between "body" and "mind," would not have surprised Bragg at all.

Nor Ellen White, for that matter. Though she substituted religious faith for positive thinking, in essence it came to the same thing. And, like Bragg, she was advocating nutritional approaches to preventing and treating disease. She called diet the "rational remedy." Way back in 1897, she was writing: "It is important to become familiar with the benefit of dieting in case of sickness. All should understand what to do for themselves." And, in 1890, she wrote: "Pure air, sunlight . . . rest, exercise, proper diet, the use of water . . . these are the true remedies." And again in 1905: "Fresh air, exercise, pure water and clean, sweet premises, are within the reach of all, with but little expense; but drugs are expensive, both in the outlay of means, and the effect produced upon the system."

After reading these books, I immediately began to practice what they advised. I decided then and there to no longer eat meat or dairy products, to cut out white flour and eat only *whole* grains. I vowed never to eat anything with a mother, a face, or a heartbeat, and I started Bragg's fasting program, following it like clockwork.

Every week, I'd fast for twenty-four hours on Wednesday; once a month, I'd fast for three full days, and once a year for ten to fourteen days. These were water fasts, and, as

Bragg advised, I used only distilled water. This may sound extreme, but not a fraction so extreme as having suffered most of the days of my life from chronic asthma and debilitating, sometimes life-threatening tuberculosis.

I still strongly believe that fasting, to varying degrees, can benefit nearly everyone, but I insist that all who embark on fasting programs first get the approval of their doctors. I will explain my fasting regimen in part III, where I also expand upon my dietary recommendations and provide the recipes that I am confident will convince you that the proper diet is not only "rational," as Ellen White put it, but that it can also be incredibly delicious and varied as well.

So, hold off on any fasting of your own until you read part III. Done properly, it can be a joyous and life-enhancing experience.

My parents, of course, were curious about this new turn in my life, but they thought it was a phase that I'd soon tire of and drop. I really didn't get into the fasting until after I graduated from high school. I insisted on making my own food, following directions in other books I picked up by Bragg and others.

I noticed the results within a month.

My breathing definitely improved. I was wheezing less and had more energy than I'd ever had before, though I was still very weak. My friends and family refused to believe my new diet and fasting program had anything to do with it. "You're finally growing out of it, that's all," Mom said, though clearly she was delighted to see me doing a bit better.

By the end of the summer, I was feeling so well I told my parents I was going to join the Navy. They didn't quite laugh, but it was obvious my dad didn't think I stood a chance of getting in. By September, I was in the Air Force—when I'd gone down to the recruitment center, the line for the Navy was so long I jumped into the shorter Air Force line. I still had a positive TB reaction when they tested me, so my entry was provisional. They said, "We'll see how you do during basic."

Basic training was tough; there was still a lot I couldn't do, but what I could do were things I had never done before in my life. My progress started to reverse, however, within a few days of going on military chow. Suddenly, I was wheezing again, something I hadn't done for a while. My newfound energy began to slip away. I immediately limited myself to eating canned and frozen vegetables, along with a lot of plain mashed potatoes. I avoided everything else, and that was enough to get me through.

I think my eccentricity actually endeared me to my otherwise bored sergeant and other superiors, who cut me some slack—waiting to see what this persistent "geek" would try next. Once I was out of basic training, I was actually allowed to spend $130 a month on food I obtained off-base. This was in Texas and, fortunately, there was a health-food store in nearby Abilene. It was the mid-1960s, and the whole health-food concept was still considered offbeat and suspect by most.

Once I was able to manage my own diet again, my health improved dramatically and continued to get better—so much so that I was soon holding down *three jobs* during my off-hours from the base. The improvement in my mental energy, as well as my physical energy, was phenomenal.

Up to this point, I'd always been quiet and reclusive. But even as I felt my physical energy expanding, my mental energy began to soar, too. One of my jobs in the Air Force was to order parts for downed aircraft and dispatch them to wherever they were needed in the world. This was all done via phone and computer. I found myself really opening up on the phone. I was communicating with a lot of other people for the first time in my life and I found that I loved it. Before long, I was finding it possible to talk to people face-to-face and actually enjoy it.

In fact, I was enjoying it so much that my first off-base job was selling vacuum cleaners door-to-door. Then I added a second job, working at a library part time, and then a third, working at a Mexican fast-food place that offered a few vegetarian dishes. Pretty soon, I was making enough money to buy not one but two recent-model Corvette Sting Rays. They became my hobby. And, on the side, I even started a bead business. This was the Vietnam War era, and the hippie, counterculture movement was well under way. I'd sell strings of beads to the airmen, who wore them under their uniforms as a form of modest rebellion.

My military stint was up in 1969, and a few months before I got out, I began making the transition to the hippie life I'd been dreaming about. I started to grow my hair six months before my discharge. I had to conceal it under my cap, but by the time I left the Air Force, it was long enough to enable me to fit right into the flower-child scene, then at its peak, in San Francisco, which was my first stop en route back to Oregon. San Francisco was like heaven to me—finally, it was not only acceptable but actually *hip* to be a vegetarian and an environmentalist. For the first time in my life, I felt accepted. Vegetarian and health-food restaurants abounded, and I began to dream of having one of my own some day.

I returned to Portland after a prolonged stay in San Francisco, fired up over the prospect of beginning a new chapter in my life, one that I was certain was going to lead me to greater health and happiness. For the first time, I was actually feeling almost grateful for my prolonged illness, convinced that without it, I would never have been launched on a path that I was confident would lead to something immensely rewarding.

"There are but few as yet who are aroused sufficiently to understand how much their habits of diet have to do with their health, their characters, their usefulness in this world, and their eternal destiny. . . . Physical habits have a great deal to do with the success of every individual."

ELLEN G. WHITE, *Counsels on Diet and Foods*

CHAPTER 2

Failed Crops

From Shining Shoes to Selling Electric Cars

It was 1969, and I wasn't sure what to do with my life. I knew I wanted to do something related to health, and so it seemed logical to start hanging out at a health club. There was a sign on the wall looking for an instructor—someone to show new customers how to use the weights and bodybuilding machines. I had little weight-lifting experience, but I figured it didn't take a bodybuilder to provide basic instruction—and somebody who *didn't* look like Mr. Universe might be less intimidating to new members. The owners of the place bought the argument, and suddenly I was a weight-lifting instructor.

The job was a start and it *did* relate to health, so I was happy about that. But it didn't pay much, barely enough to live on, and I started thinking about other ways of generating income out of the same place. If there was one thing I'd excelled at in the military, it was shining my shoes. I'd always been a neatnik anyway, and I began noticing how many people were coming into the club with scuffed shoes. I cleared a space near the maintenance room and set up shop. I didn't wait for business to come my way. I had a different line for everybody who walked by with a pair of unshined shoes. I made shined shoes the moral equivalent of success, whether it was in business, romance, or bodybuilding. If I told somebody his sex life would improve if his shoes were shinier, I'd generally get a smile and a customer. I was working very hard, but in no time I was making $60 to $70 a day shining shoes.

People who had known me from my childhood couldn't believe the change in me—from extreme introvert to extrovert in just a few short years. What they didn't realize was that the change was a natural reaction to all those years of feeling isolated; without that deeply felt period of deprivation, I seriously doubt I would ever have mustered the energy and enthusiasm that were to make me a superior salesman in later years. So, again, I was reaping the benefits of ill health.

With cash in pocket and some help from the GI Bill, I started attending a community college in Portland and made a down payment on a small house in which I rented a couple of rooms to some other students. I wanted to study nutrition but was appalled at what was being offered. I did not endear myself to the instructional staff when I told them that their curriculum was backward and antiquated. By then, I'd read volumes on nutrition and felt passionately about it. But absent a decent nutrition program, I enrolled in television production.

Meanwhile, after three and a half years, my shoeshine empire collapsed when the health club was sold and the new owner installed his son in my lucrative little slot. The son could shine shoes, but he was no salesman and was out of business in short order—no comfort to me, since they didn't invite me back.

In retrospect, I realize shining shoes taught me more about business than anything I've done before or since. It taught me to do the two most important things people in sales must master if they are to be truly successful. It taught me to *observe* and *listen* to people. A salesperson can and does often sell products and services to people that they don't need or want, but even under such circumstances, he or she is selling to or through *wants and needs* that are observed, perceived, and then addressed. I've tried always to sell things that people *do* want and need, but either way, you have to listen to what people want and offer them something that meets their need.

When I was shining shoes, I secured most of my business through careful listening and observation, if only to a snatch of conversation here, a bit of body language there. From what I saw and heard, I could begin to grasp what *motivates* each prospective customer. Shoe shining was ideal for learning about motivation, because once I had a customer, they would open up to me. You can tell a shoe shiner almost anything without feeling compromised or exposed. People love to unburden themselves under such circumstances. (Years later, when I was addressing an M.B.A. class at Stanford University, the students were more interested in what I learned about business as a shoe shiner than anything else I had to say—and with good reason.)

I quickly realized I was selling something more complicated than just a shoe shine, and that products and services can have "hidden" or inapparent dimensions that are as important or more important than the products or services themselves. These extra dimensions can create "super products." It was this insight that later made me feel so confident that the Gardenburger, which I had not yet even conceived of, would be a super product because it provided something greater than itself—the prospect of good health for both the individual and the environment.

From all of this, I came to believe that poor salespeople focus on product, good salespeople focus on people. You can sing the praises of a product in the voice of a great tenor and still not get anywhere if you don't modulate your pitch so that it resonates in the hearts and souls of those you're singing to at any given time.

Increasingly, I found that I needed to *communicate* with people; maybe that was one reason I went into TV production. But I missed communicating at the more basic, sometimes visceral level that I'd experienced while shining shoes. And I missed my nutritional pursuits, which I continued, of course, at a personal level, but wanted to expand upon. And so I started offering nutritional workshops at community centers. These quickly became so popular that Mt. Hood Community College, Portland Community College, and other institutions with tens of thousands of students invited me to introduce nutritional classes into their curricula.

So, as an undergrad TV major, I was suddenly developing course materials and teaching classes in natural foods, food dehydration, wine tasting, and so on. I eventually developed and/or taught some twenty-four different classes, virtually launching a new department at one large community college. These branched off into other "alternative" courses, such as how to make nontoxic home cleaners. I was Portland's Martha Stewart, Heloise, and Erma Bombeck rolled into one!

By the time I graduated from college, TV jobs were in short supply. I continued to teach, but in 1974 I married and figured I needed a more substantial job. My father-in-law was selling golf carts, and that got me thinking about transportation in general, especially with the gas shortage and the long lines at gas stations that began occurring in 1974.

Given my environmental interest, I was pleased my father-in-law wanted to import electric-powered vehicles from Italy. Here, for sure, I thought, was a product with that "extra dimension" that could provide a real service while, at the same time, make people feel good about themselves. Both my father-in-law, an experienced businessman, and I, an experienced salesman, got tremendous media publicity and all kinds of people who wanted to take our electric cars for a spin. But the cars didn't sell.

I finally realized that, in this case, I'd let myself slip too far into that "extra dimension." People felt great driving around in those little cars for ten or fifteen minutes—but when they turned the key off, they noticed their shoes still weren't shined, in a manner of speaking. The cars, which could only go thirty-five miles per hour and had to be recharged every thirty-five miles, weren't about to replace Henry Ford's invention. I regained a proper respect for product and realized that the adhesion between the product and the dream—the extra dimension of ideas and ideals that some products can project—has to be a tight one. I was learning *balance*. And I'll always be grateful to my father-in-law for providing this opportunity, which became an important learning experience.

My next endeavor was to renovate and sell old houses. (My father, who had become a real-estate agent, helped me find them.) I had a knack for this, it turned out, a design sense that I still use today, creating homes from recycled materials in both Portland and Honolulu, and soon I set off on my own. Portland is blessed with an abundance of Victorian and Craftsman-style homes, and soon I was restoring more houses than I could handle, just as the recession of 1980 set in.

The timing couldn't have been worse because I had also just completed construction on my dream restaurant, in Gresham, a suburb of Portland. At last, I was going to realize my dream—the opening of a gourmet vegetarian restaurant. Or so it had seemed until the bottom fell out of the real-estate market, stranding me with mortgages on houses I couldn't sell. I lost all of the houses and had to scramble to find a partner or I would lose the new restaurant, too.

Birth of the Gardenburger (And the Slow Slide into the Weirdest Period of My Life)

The partner was found and in 1981 I opened the Gardenhouse Restaurant to good reviews. My aim was to dispel the stereotype of the "natural-food restaurant," a funky place with a cuisine of sprouts, soybeans, and rawbits only a concrete mixer could digest. The Gardenhouse featured candlelight dining, attractive decor, courteous waitpersons, and a wide selection of gourmet dishes.

Like all restaurateurs, I was soon faced with what to do with the leftovers. My solution was something I called the "Gardenloaf Sandwich," made of leftover vegetables and rice pilaf. Later, I got the idea of slicing up the loaf into what looked like patties—and suddenly the Gardenburger was born. Grilled and placed in a hamburger bun, it was an instant success.

One out of every two lunches sold was a Gardenburger. I developed a number of variations: teriyaki Gardenburgers (with slices of fresh pineapple and my own special teriyaki sauce thickened with arrowroot starch so it would really stick), a Gardenburger Olé (with jalapeño, jack cheese, and guacamole), and so on. But apart from the seasonings and sauces, the ingredients were about the same: mushrooms, brown rice, onions, rolled oats, part-skim mozzarella, egg white, cheddar cheese, bulgur wheat, and spices. (Cottage cheese curd was added later.) Much later, for those who want to avoid dairy cheeses as well, I developed the Gardenburger Veggie Medley, a zero-fat product, which includes mushrooms, brown rice, onions, nondairy soy cheese, rolled oats, broccoli, carrots, bulgur wheat, squash, bell pepper, and, as with the Gardenburger original, natural seasonings and spices.

I soon discovered that the Gardenburger could be grilled on the stovetop or barbecued, baked in the oven or even in a toaster oven or microwave.

As the Gardenburger original has evolved, a 2.5-ounce patty is only 130 calories, with just 3 grams of total fat and 10 milligrams of cholesterol. There's no added sugar, 6 grams of protein, and 2 grams of dietary fiber in each patty. Cholesterol consciousness was just beginning to build in the country in the early 1980s, and I'd truly found the "food for the times." The new diet trend was toward low-fat, high-complex-carbohydrate diets.

I was thrilled that a product I loved and knew to be a health-packed meal was so popular, but I still hadn't conceived of it as a product that might build a miniempire and launch thousands of Americans on a path away from meat. Caught up in the everyday necessities of running a restaurant—and at this point it was not unusual for me and some of my coworkers to put in one-hundred-hour weeks—I was focused on making a new business fly.

In the summer of 1982, however, I began to get an inkling that there might be life for the Gardenburger outside my little restaurant in Gresham. At the famous annual Mt. Hood Jazz Festival, I set up a small stand and sold eight hundred Gardenburgers in two days—mostly to people who'd never even heard of a meatless burger. And most of them raved about the product. Some ate five or six during the festival. The next year, I sold twice as many.

Another restaurant with a food booth at the festival was so impressed by my sales that its owners asked me if they could sell the Gardenburger at their deli. I consented, and they sold more than I did because they had a much better location. I thought, Wow, if I could get one hundred restaurants to sell Gardenburgers I could live off something I really believe in. At the time, a friend of mine began selling Gardenburgers at his natural-food store. I now had two accounts.

I was encouraged enough by this experience for me to go to the Seventh-Day Adventist Medical Center, where I knew the hospital restaurant served soy burgers, and I got a third account. Pretty soon, people at the hospital were eating the Gardenburgers, and the soy burgers weren't selling. That told me something important, too: a meatless burger doesn't have to have the texture of meat (which soy tries to imitate) in order to succeed; neither does it have to try to taste like a meat burger. What *was* clearly important, however, was *taste*. The product had to taste great—and it seemed important that it *look* sort of like a burger.

About this time, I was beginning to have that "dream too big," that I might actually have a replacement for the most-consumed food in America!

I was on a roll, so to speak, and next tried the delis and restaurants at Mt. Hood Community College. Bingo. I had my fourth account.

But another reality soon asserted itself. In 1984, the Oregon recession was verging on a depression, and my Gresham location—far from the center of things—was beginning to hurt me badly. It was a struggle to keep the restaurant afloat, and my helpers were burning out rapidly. I knew it was all over the day I found a notice on the front door from the gas company warning me they were going to shut me off for nonpayment within a day or two. I couldn't pay the bill, and the restaurant closed in November 1984, about three years after it had opened. I thought it was the end of the world for a short time. In fact, it was the best thing that could have happened.

Remember, at the beginning of this book, I said I owe my success to ill health and business failure. I've explained how ill health influenced me in a very positive way. As for business failure, if the restaurant had succeeded I'd probably still be there today, and Wholesome & Hearty Foods and the tremendous success of the Gardenburger might never have come to be.

But at the time, I was feeling pretty bleak. I was approaching forty and was broke. I was having trouble finding a job because my previous self-employed status, despite all those one-hundred-hour weeks, didn't impress prospective employers. My marriage had ended, and I was at loose ends and feeling a bit desperate. In an effort to keep the restaurant afloat, I'd sold everything I owned, including all of my tools. So I couldn't even do maintenance work.

This was truly a weird time in my life. I remember how odd I felt trying to get a waiter's job in a restaurant, having the prospective employer looking at me as if I were too old for this and feeling the same way myself. Suddenly, I realized how easy it is for people to fall between the cracks in this society and this economy. The experience was to make me more open, later on, to the "nonconforming" employees I would ultimately hire myself—with very good results. But right then I was up against it and too proud to take food stamps.

Old customers from the restaurant called me for a while to commiserate, and almost all of them told me how much they were going to miss my Gardenburgers. Several asked me if there wasn't some way they could still get them.

One of my best customers was a salesman named Allyn Smaaland. Allyn had said on more than one occasion that he would love to help me sell Gardenburgers. Before long, I found myself sleeping in the spare bedroom of Allyn's apartment, doing a little cooking and housework in exchange for my board and room, and we began plotting ways to salvage the Gardenburger.

Enter Harry Merlo (Who Eats the Most Important Gardenburger in History)

Neither Allyn nor I had any money, just a lot of imagination and energy. We put out feelers everywhere, and one day, my sister Linda, who was a top salesperson for Louisiana-Pacific (L-P), then a $2+ billion company in the building industry, said, "You ought to talk to Harry Merlo." I thought maybe my sister was joking. Harry was the CEO of L-P and was a legendary, swashbuckling figure in the Pacific Northwest who brooked no interference from anybody in the running of his company.

"No, I'm serious," my sister said. "Harry's really into this health thing."

Health thing!

That was all I needed to hear. If Harry was into the "health thing," I felt confident that I was enough of a salesman to sell him on the hottest new component of the "health thing"—the Gardenburger. Harry was going to be my angel.

I immediately called the number my sister had given me and then sat back and waited for Harry's return call. And I waited. And waited. And then I called again and again. Nothing. Finally, I complained to my sister. She's as brassy as I am and called Harry up herself. She called me back a few minutes later and said I had failed to point out that she and I have different last names and so Harry didn't have a clue as to who I was. This time when I called him I got right through.

"Can you come into my office tomorrow morning?" he asked.

I already knew Harry had his own chef, an amiable guy named Buzz. I made arrangements with Buzz to bring the fixings for Gardenburgers along and arrived early the next day for my appointment with Harry, in his suite high atop Portland's tallest skyscraper. The stairway leading directly to the roof and Harry's personal helicopter was a little intimidating, but I stayed focused and gave Buzz some quick tips on how to heat a Gardenburger. I knew this was the most important Gardenburger that would ever be grilled.

A few minutes into delivering my crash course in garden cuisine, I was summoned into Harry's office. Harry invited me to talk about myself, and I did. He was knowledgeable about wines and was impressed that I had taught wine-tasting classes.

Then, abruptly, he asked me why I thought Gardenburgers would succeed. I said they'd succeed because they feed a growing hunger people have—to be healthier. "The Gardenburger," I pronounced, without even blushing, "is the future of food, starting *now*."

I could see Harry really perk up.

"I like how you think."

Those were the most important words I'd heard since "You don't have to accept disease," "Check into diet," and "health-food store." The next words were important, too. Harry pushed himself away from his big desk and said, "Let's go into the kitchen and try one of those burgers."

CHAPTER 3

The Golden Harvest

Launching the Company

"These are pretty good," Harry Merlo said, taking another bite as if he really meant it.

"These are *fabulous*," Buzz the chef chimed in, upping the ante.

"Let's do something with this," Harry trumped him.

I don't remember taking the elevator down from the forty-third floor after that meeting, and when I hit the pavement, I still felt as if I were up in the clouds.

The great Harry Merlo was going to help me make Gardenburgers the future of food!

Harry had instructed Allyn and me to develop a business plan and take it to a high-powered venture capital outfit where Harry invested millions every year. Harry gave me the name of someone to contact there, but when I took him my plan, I could sense his disdain. It was clear he had no confidence in this venture and that he would be participating only because Harry asked him to do so. If there was anything I had learned about salesmanship, it was that you can't sell what you don't believe in. So I considered this guy the kiss of death for the Gardenburger and told Harry that. He said, "Okay, let's do it in house," meaning he'd provide the money himself. "How much do you need?"

"Forty-five thousand the first year."

This was the only time I ever saw Harry actually look startled. For a moment, used to economizing as I was, I thought I might have asked for too much, but it was soon evident Harry had expected me to ask for more, a lot more, probably something in the neighborhood of half a million.

Harry composed himself and said, "Let's make it sixty thousand."

I looked relieved, but only for a moment, because Harry quickly froze me with a piercing look and asked, "When will this business make money?"

I knew Harry expected me to have thought out all of this very carefully and that he'd expect me to be definite in my reply. I gulped and said, "Harry, this business will make money in the thirteenth month and from then on will be profitable."

I think Harry may have suppressed a slight smile, but he didn't say anything, just nodded. My answer was based on nothing more than the notion that I'd work my tail off for a year, and if we weren't flying by then, we weren't going to get off the ground. I also knew that Harry wasn't one to throw away money and that he'd most likely hold me to my promise—or close to it.

So I had $60,000 to pay Allyn and myself and buy the raw materials for the burgers. I made arrangements with a local bakery to use their equipment to make them. I paid the bakery about a nickel for every burger we made there.

We incorporated in March of 1985. Wholesome & Hearty Foods, Inc., was a division of L-P. Harry was chairman of the board, and L-P owned 55 percent of the company. I was vice president. Gary Maffei, one of Harry's right-hand men, a top accountant and personnel director, was president. He was my liaison with L-P, and it was clear that he, too, was skeptical at first about Harry's latest little adventure. He was the personnel director in charge of twelve thousand people at L-P, and the added burden of WHFI was no doubt extra work he didn't want. I believe he thought the pittance we were working with would dribble away by the end of the year and we'd be out of the picture.

Though Gary and I didn't always agree, I'm definitely grateful to him for rigorously teaching me how to read and analyze a financial statement, an exercise that taught me some accounting discipline and enabled me to see how major businesses manage their affairs and adjust for all manner of contingencies. This was a vast improvement over my previous toss-the-receipts-in-a-shoebox approach to accounting.

Of the 45 percent control that I retained in the company, I gave Allyn 15 percent and kept 30 percent for myself. Since Allyn was the one who had made his living as a salesman, he was the one who went out in search of new accounts while I made Gardenburgers at the bakery.

Things didn't go well in the beginning. Allyn would go around to fifteen or twenty restaurants some days and still come back with few accounts. It was starting to look grim. I found the situation extremely frustrating. I *knew* people wanted Gardenburgers, and I *knew* I could sell them. So I suggested to Allyn that we switch places for a while.

And, sure enough, I started getting accounts—not in great waves at first, but steadily. Apart from my salesmanship, I had my chef background going for me; I could go into restaurants and show people how to make Gardenburgers so appealing that the next customer who came in couldn't resist them.

The trick, though, was to get through the front door and to the manager and his or her grill before getting thrown out. And more than a few places did toss me out. I wore out several pairs of Birkenstocks trooping around Oregon and up and down the West Coast, using my refrigerator van—and, occasionally, Motel 6—as home base. More than one hardened meat eater literally spit my product, along with several choice expletives, back in my face. Generally, though, if I could get the product into somebody's mouth, the Gardenburger completed the sales job. It was always a pleasure to see the preparatory grimace relax into a broad smile after the first bite.

For every restaurant manager who would say yes to my commandeering his or her grill, another nine would say no. A lot of people asked me how I could stand all that rejection. But I always looked at each no as a positive. I knew it was a numbers game. Each no simply brought me closer to the inevitable yes.

That, I believe, is another key trait of every successful salesperson—always seeing a positive in a negative. I put this attitude into practice whenever I'd enter a restaurant to be told that "we don't get any vegetarians in here." My response was, "Maybe that's because there's nothing vegetarian on your menu." Then I'd give them a little spiel on how you can't grow a market without product. A lot of them got the point—like a lightbulb turning on—but I had to be quick about it and avoid sounding as if I were telling them how to run their businesses.

For some of the most resistant cases, I had to resort to leaving some free product and some of my handmade "table tents"—little folders that sit on the table and tell people to try a low-fat, low-cholesterol, *delicious* Gardenburger instead of a regular hamburger. This approach paid off without any failures. Every time I'd come back after leaving a free case of Gardenburgers, I'd have a new account. Every Gardenburger in the case had sold. No failures.

By the end of 1985, I had seventy-five or eighty restaurants signed up. I was finally doing what I wanted to do, and Allyn was happy back at the bakery. He was a good quality-control man who enjoyed doing a single task to perfection. I'd say, "How are you doing, Allyn?" And he'd reply, "I'm doing what you want me to do, Wenner. I'm making you pretty Gardenburgers." I must have heard him say that a thousand times. The high quality and consistent flavor that Allyn guaranteed was one of the keys to our success.

But despite progress, time was running out on us, as was our money. We still hadn't turned a nickel of profit. We'd already received some favorable local media coverage and that was helping, but we needed to grab some *national* attention.

The big national Natural Food Expo Show was coming up in Los Angeles in March of 1986, and I knew we had to get our product into that show, so health-food retailers from all around the country could learn about us and actually sample Gardenburgers. I wanted to be there pitching them. The fee to get in was $1,200, close to what we had left in our seed money from Harry. I decided to spend it, even though Gary at L-P thought it was a mistake and said this would probably sink us. I was certain we were sunk without it.

The HUGE $300 Profit

Fortified with some new packaging for the product, I headed down to LA. I knew there was a cafeteria at the expo center where the trade show was being held. I had thought every exhibitor would be battling to get their products into the cafeteria and was astounded to discover that not a single one had approached management. Management was lukewarm until I offered them free Gardenburgers. That got me in, along with a sign right at the front of the cafeteria. And it was right at the main entrance of the building—so everybody coming in saw that Gardenburger sign.

Those who missed my booth didn't miss that sign. Retailers started noticing how many people were buying Gardenburgers at the cafeteria and sought me out on the floor. Orders started to pour in from retailers all around the country. Suddenly, the Gardenburger was the talk of the show. (And the next year there was a stampede among manufacturers to get their products onto the cafeteria menu.)

I went back to Portland feeling vindicated. Now Gary was finally talking about how *our* little company was doing real well, whereas, before, it had always sounded and felt more like *your* little company.

And so it was that we arrived at the thirteenth month and, right on schedule, our first profit—$300! Harry had flown his private jet over to Europe on some megadeal, but somehow he got wind of our little triumph and phoned me.

"You said you'd make money in the thirteenth month, Wenner," he boomed, "and, by God, I understand we've got three hundred bucks profit in the bank. Congratulations!"

The best part of it was he wasn't being sarcastic. That $300 was beginning to look like millions.

Meanwhile, we had hired our first food broker, Michael Meek, and he was soon cultivating the lucrative southern California market. Michael was to become a key player in our success. Soon we hired another broker, for northern California. I was still handling the Pacific Northwest. I'd go into health-food stores and let customers taste-test. Many times, I'd sell one hundred boxes or more in five or six hours, making converts and getting new accounts.

I quickly found that only one out of five people who buy Gardenburgers are real vegetarians. The other four (I call them "meat reducers") are looking for a change, something healthier than red meat, low-fat and, of course, tasty. This broadened our marketing considerably.

In Los Angeles, Michael Meek's first restaurant account was Cosmas Kapantzos's Astroburger on Melrose Avenue. Henry Winkler (the "Fonz"), the whole *Cheers* crew, and a lot of people from Paramount Studios would go there and buy Gardenburgers on a regular basis. Cosmas started out selling a case every two or three weeks and today sells up to three cases a day (each case holds forty-eight one-third-pound Gardenburgers). He pitched them as "lite" fare, which caught on fast in LA, and pretty soon he had a whole low-fat, "lite" menu that others began copying.

Other distributors were paying heed. But a lot of them wanted exclusives for their regions. I believe my decision to resist that was very important. Gardenburgers were still in their infancy, and to a giant distributor, handling all manner of foods, they weren't going to be all that compelling once they had the contract. I needed a *lot* of distributors, each doing a *little* Gardenburger business, rather than a *few* distributors doing a little.

By the end of 1986, we had more than two hundred food service accounts supplying restaurants and were in more than one hundred retail outlets, mainly health-food stores. Distribution was increasing rapidly. And we were getting great press.

Still, we needed more money to go into higher gear. To get that money from L-P, we had to give up another 30 percent of our equity. But the infusion of cash enabled us to get our own building and manufacturing equipment. We hired more people. We even had a secretary!

Hiring the right people for the right jobs was also crucial to our success. I seemed to have a knack for this, partly because I didn't dismiss people out of hand on the basis of appearance or quirky job histories. People would walk in whom others might wave away, and I'd interview them.

I even hired a guy in his twenties who had never had a job in his life. That was in 1986, and he's still working for us today. He had some traits that perhaps made other potential employers shy away, but he was able to master repetitive tasks with uncanny ability and put the repetition into high gear. I gave him a job catching Gardenburgers as they came out of the forming machine. They had to be placed twenty-four to a pan, properly spaced. Our new employee took to the job like a duck to water. We calculated that by the time we automated this function years later, he had caught and perfectly placed *27 million* Gardenburgers!

I was never one to look too closely at a résumé. I'm interested in a person's attitude toward life because, given the right attitude, you can train almost anybody to carry out a task. I look specifically for somebody who has a strong desire to do a good job. They have to love what they're doing.

Defining Our Mission

In 1989, my girlfriend, Anita Pati, and I developed a corporate Mission Statement, to help us clarify our objectives and help prospective employees decide whether they would be comfortable with us. I expressed how I felt about the company, and Anita made it coherent:

MISSION STATEMENT

• Wholesome & Hearty Foods pursues visionary ideas that are helping to sustain the health and integrity of our planet. We are committed to offering great tasting, convenient and healthy food choices to the world.

• Our objective is to develop products that are timely, yet futuristic, products that are made with compassion and a caring consciousness for the earth's fragile resources. We believe in the importance of producing only "earth-wise" products for all present and future generations.

• Wholesome & Hearty Foods values its employees. They are the very soul of our company. We know our continuing success depends on respecting every individual's uniqueness and recognizing each person's contributions.

- We strive to promote harmony in the world by developing our dream of a healthy and balanced planet.

I tried to make sure that each new employee understood and embraced our mission. And the following year, I introduced a Vision and Values System that enables employees to critique our performance, make suggestions for changes, and otherwise help ensure that we remain true to our Mission Statement.

By the end of 1988, sales had leaped to $1.7 million, and in 1989, Allyn wanted to try to buy out Harry and L-P. They had 85 percent of the action, and we were doing all the work. Allyn started talking to a business attorney, Nick Goyak. Nick helped us formulate an offer, but L-P turned it down. Nick said, "How bad do you guys want this?" Nick argued that we hadn't been treated the same as other L-P employees, in terms of getting health benefits and so on. He put together a legal filing to use as leverage to get L-P to sell to us but never filed it with the court. I was opposed to suing them and was embarrassed by the mere threat of a lawsuit.

L-P insisted that we come up with $660,000 (they valued the company at about $1 million) to buy them out within ninety days. If we succeeded, we'd own the company; if we didn't, they said they would buy out our stock.

I accepted L-P's challenge. Nick Goyak and I started calling everyone we knew, trying to raise the money. We got some of it from a bank and the rest from an assortment of doctors, dentists, investment bankers, and other investors, some of whom joined our new board of directors.

It literally took until 5:00 P.M. on the ninetieth day to get the money together. Our deadline was 6:00 P.M., and Allyn and I were at the bank to close the deal when our loan officer asked, "And how will you be handling the fees?"

Allyn and I looked at each other blankly.

"Fees?"

The closing costs added up to about $20,000. Both of our accounts were drained, but I managed to compose myself long enough to write a check for the amount due. It was a Friday, and we'd been expecting to celebrate. Instead, it was back to the phones so we could cover my check first thing Monday morning.

Cosmas Kapantzos of Astroburger in LA was our rescuing angel. And so we finally reclaimed the garden. It felt good. With the stroke of a pen, we went from 15 percent ownership to 100 percent. And the prospects for the company had never looked better.

Allyn, who kept everything in his head, would keep track of the dollars we'd make, and I'd try to fall asleep calculating the number of cows we'd save if we sold 100 million Gardenburgers. (I figured about fifty thousand!)

Going VERY Public

By early 1990, cash reserves were growing again. We could see enormous growth ahead, provided we had the capital to increase production dramatically. We were at that stage of growth where the idea of going public began to crop up. My investment banker friend Steve Rosendahl, one of Allyn's basketball buddies, pushed the idea, and in 1992, he found us an underwriting firm run by a bunch of brash, hard-selling kids just starting out. This after some of the bigger guys had turned us away and told us to come back when we had $15 million to $20 million in sales.

Several members of my board were horrified, not only by our underwriter, but also by the very idea of going public. An investment banker on our board was particularly scathing. He asked Steve and me if we were smoking dope and proclaimed that Wholesome & Hearty Foods could never do well enough to stay alive in the market. When we persisted, he called us idiots.

We prevailed and, with several carefully selected new employees, we immersed ourselves in the paper ordeal of preparing a public stock offering. This was a particularly tumultuous time, not only because of the rapid growth of the company and going public, but also because Allyn was leaving the company. A short while after we went public, his stock went in value from a few hundred thousand to many millions.

After months of day-and-night preparation, we went public on June 9, 1992, opening at $4.50 a share. Demand for the stock exceeded supply, driving the stock up to the $6.50 to $7 range. I felt enormous relief. I'd been on what is called "the road show" for the previous two weeks, pitching the company nonstop to investment bankers in fourteen cities, serving Gardenburgers in all of them. In each city, before each group, I told my story, how I'd been sick as a kid, how nutrition had rescued me, how Gardenburgers could improve the health of millions and the health of the planet, too.

I'd been warned that financiers are the most cynical people on earth, but my sense was that they were moved by my story and not just for the money they could see in it.

At the end of my pitch in each of those cities, I'd always look down at the plates we'd served the Gardenburgers on; they were always empty. Not a crumb left on those bankers' plates. Of course, I don't doubt for a moment that all my talk about grabbing a big slice of the $50-billion-a-year hamburger market increased their appetites.

By the end of 1992, we had sales of about $7 million and had set up a bigger production facility in, ironically, an old meat-packing plant. Prior to moving in, we had the placed blessed, invoking the spirits of all the countless cows that had been butchered there. I imagined I saw those spirits rise up and leave the place, after which we sanitized the facility from top to bottom. Our production space went from five thousand square feet to forty thousand square feet.

The move paid off. Sales were strong all through 1993, ending at about $13 million. In January of 1994, I started getting calls from the *Wall Street Journal, Fortune, Forbes,* the television networks, and many others. When the first call came in telling me we had the fastest-growing stock in 1993, I was stunned, even though I thought the reporter meant fasting-growing over-the-counter stock in the food business.

"No," I was told. "Fastest-growing stock on *any exchange anywhere in the world!*"

I think I sat down for five minutes and tried not to panic. The first thing we did after that was to call a meeting of all our employees to tell them not to pay much attention to all the hype that was about to engulf us. We warned that there was no way we could maintain this head of steam indefinitely, that there would be downs as well as ups—and that when you go this high this fast, any reversal will be viewed as particularly disappointing.

I think I believed most of what I said. At the same time, it was one heck of a high. We were now about as public as any business can get. And the publicity was tremendous. *Fortune* called the Gardenburger "a meatless burger that (surprise) actually cures Big Mac attacks." The *Wall Street Journal* declared, "They've got a very good product in the Gardenburger."

In 1994, we knew the investment world was watching us; it seemed unlikely to many that we would be able to double sales again, as we had in 1993. We implemented a series of incentives to help us meet our production goals, avoid injuries, and keep overhead—especially energy—costs within target ranges. These paid off, and we ended the year with sales just a bit under $24 million, an 85 percent increase over the previous year.

"100 Million Sold"

The slowdown we'd been expecting finally came in 1995, a year marked by a lot of personnel changes. In addition to the Gardenburger, we were already producing the

GardenSausage, Gardenburger Zesty Bean, and the Gardenburger Veggie Medley. In 1995, we launched the GardenDog, so similar in taste and texture to meat hot dogs that we told the press it "does everything but bark." In taste tests, many people could not tell the difference between GardenDogs and meat franks.

Despite the slowdown, we still managed to increase our sales in 1995, ending the year at nearly $36 million. We made a number of internal adjustments and corrections, all essential after such rapid growth. I needed more time to devote to the creative and promotional aspects of the business, and so we hired a new, highly professional chairman of the board, Kay Stepp. We also resolved to begin an intensive search for an accomplished CEO, the appointment of whom would free me to become CCO—a new position in the corporate world: chief creative officer.

Perhaps the biggest event of 1995, however, was our 100 millionth Gardenburger sale. When we updated our McDonald's-inspired sign to read "100 million sold!," it grabbed headlines around the world. It took McDonald's about ten years to reach that sales figure, and it took us about the same amount of time—quite a feat for a meatless burger and a sure sign that the dietary times are changing dramatically.

The publicity around the 100 millionth Gardenburger gave the press a new chance to look at us again, and it was widely reported that our products were being sold in nearly thirty thousand restaurants worldwide and in nearly ten thousand retail outlets. By 1995, you could get a Gardenburger at Disney World, at McMurdo Sound Station in Antarctica, at Harvard, Yale, and scores of other colleges and universities, on major airlines and cruise lines, in the biggest hotel chains and in the cafeterias of many of the world's largest corporations. You could also buy them in frozen-food departments of several major grocery chains.

Nineteen-ninety-five was a significant year for me in a personal sense; I was honored to be named Entrepreneur of the Year in the Pacific Northwest in the manufacturing category.

The Future: Moving Toward the Meatless Society

In 1996, we began emphasizing expansion of our retail market and began developing a new line of products based on a research breakthrough that will enable us to closely simulate the texture and appearance of beef, chicken, turkey, ham, even pepperoni and tuna. By mid-1996, total Gardenburgers sold topped 200 million.

Meanwhile, with Subway, the world's second-largest fast-food chain, rapidly adding Gardenburgers to more and more of its 10,500 outlets, we are poised to take an ever-bigger bite of the multi-billion-dollar burger market. The sandwich market as a whole grosses $50+ billion a year. Our goal of capturing $500 million of that per year seems more in reach than ever. We're in more than 40,000 outlets now, and it's not unreasonable to expect that we will be in 100,000 within a few years.

In 1996, we were fortunate enough to secure the services of Lyle Hubbard, a top marketing expert and former Quaker Oats executive, as CEO. Lyle is credited with, among many other things, taking Quaker rice cakes from a $20 million per year (in sales) product to a $200 to $300 million per year product.

We were fortunate in other ways, as well. Wholesome & Hearty Foods was selected by *Oregon Business* as one of the Best Companies to Work For in Oregon, and *Business Ethics* named the company one of the 100 Best Corporate Citizens, placing us on the magazine's coveted roster of "America's most profitable and socially responsible companies." Not only did Wholesome & Hearty Foods make the list, it was *ranked number nine out of the one hundred chosen.*

One of the high points of 1996 was a five-course vegetarian dinner I hosted for Bill and Hillary Clinton and Al and Tipper Gore, in Portland. The main course was grilled Gardenburgers with portobello mushrooms. We also served our zesty Carrot Ginger Soup and our tangy Twins' Fruit Dip, two recipes you'll find in this book.

In 1996, I also began laying the groundwork for a One Percent for Health Foundation, first proposed by Michael Jacobson, director of the Center for Science in the Public Interest. The objective of the foundation will be to secure 1 percent of pretax profits from a number of health-oriented and earth-friendly businesses for the purpose of promoting selected personal- and environmental-health goals. It is my hope that one "product" of this foundation will be a nationally syndicated television show that will aim to become the *60 Minutes*—or, in this case, the *30 Minutes*—of health advocacy.

Just one more step toward the meatless society, my ultimate goal.

PART TWO

Why We Must Reinvent Breakfast, Lunch, and Dinner

To eat the typical American diet is to participate
in the biggest experiment in human nutrition ever conducted. And
the guinea pigs aren't faring so well!

FRANCES MOORE LAPPÉ

gardencuisinegardencuisinegardencuisine
gardencuisinegardencuisinegardencuisine
gardencuisinegardencuisinegardencuisine
gardencuisinegardencuisinegardencuisine
gardencuisinegardencuisinegardencuisine
gardencuisinegardencuisinegardencuisine

CHAPTER 4

Health

The $60 Billion Burger

If there were no other reason to reinvent breakfast, lunch, and dinner, the astounding price we pay in physical and financial suffering for the way we eat today would more than suffice. Fortunately, our knowledge about diet and health is becoming more profound day by day, enabling us to focus more sharply on *why* and *what* we need to change, making the argument ever more accessible and thus more persuasive to more people. (*How* we change is the subject of the last chapter in this section and of part III of this book.)

It has often been demonstrated that economics, more than anything else, is the real engine of change in the world. As Frances Moore Lappé has said: "People can take ever greater responsibility to change the economic ground rules that determine how resources are used, once they understand these rules and can see where to begin. That means we believe in the possibility of genuine democracy."

A wonderful recent example of how continuing research and study are helping us to better understand how our resources are being used—or, in this case, misused—was reported upon in the November 1995 issue of *Preventive Medicine*. In what many already consider a landmark paper, "The Medical Costs Attributable to Meat Consumption," authors Neal D. Barnard, M.D., Andrew Nicholson, M.D., and Jo Lil Howard estimate that the consumption of meat results in *more than $60 billion in health-care costs each year in the United States alone!*

The researchers emphasize that this is a *conservative* estimate and that it includes only *direct* medical costs, those that are incurred for the services of doctors, for drugs, and for hospitalization. The indirect costs—for lost productivity, disability pay, and so on—are incalculable.

By contrast, the medical costs of smoking are widely agreed to be about $50 billion annually. Smoking is now perceived by a significant part of the population to be economically harmful to everybody, not just to smokers. Thus, there is strong support for placing high taxes on smoking, banning smoking in public places, spending tax dollars to educate the public about the dangers of smoking, and so on. And the powerful insurance industry further drives the point home by making smokers pay more than non-smokers for health insurance.

So information does help us make wise decisions. As we begin to understand that the meat-heavy American diet is hazardous to our physical and economic health—to an extent even greater than smoking—we will further discourage the consumption of meat. This is already happening and will accelerate in the wake of additional studies.

Dr. Barnard and his associates analyzed numerous published studies that quantified the differences in the prevalence of various diseases among vegetarians and meat eaters. The researchers adjusted their analyses to control for the effects of other factors, such as smoking, exercise, and alcohol consumption. In this way, they were able to closely calculate the health-care costs directly attributable to meat eating.

Some of the random, controlled studies used, for example, compared Seventh-Day Adventist vegetarians with Mormon meat eaters. Both groups had similar levels of physical activity and equal avoidance of tobacco and alcohol. Both groups had similar salt intake and were controlled for age, sex, and other relevant factors. Hypertension—high blood pressure—was significantly higher in the meat-eating populations studied than in the vegetarian groups. The difference in health-care costs due to treatment of diet-related hypertension is estimated at $12.5 billion annually.

Analyzing similar studies, the researchers found that the enormous costs of meat eating are attributable to seven common conditions, adding up to:

Heart disease	$9.5 billion
Hypertension	$8.5 billion

Cancer	$16.5 billion
Diabetes	$17.1 billion
Gallstones	$2.4 billion
Obesity-related problems	$1.9 billion
Food-borne illness	$5.5 billion
Total	*$61.4 billion*

Dr. Barnard has declared that "it is time to stop scratching our heads about the nation's exploding health-care costs. We can cut those costs by eliminating subsidies for livestock feed and dairy products, and scrapping out-of-date guidelines that encourage traditional, meat-based diets."

His associate, Dr. Nicholson, adds that insurance companies are beginning to take a serious look at diet. He believes vegetarians, like nonsmokers, may soon be charged lower premiums for health insurance. Dr. Barnard adds that the combined health costs of cigarette smoking and meat eating exceed the estimated costs of insuring *all* currently uninsured Americans.

What's Wrong with Meat and Our Diet in General?

Many people can't believe there's anything wrong with a meat-based diet since it is "traditional," the idea being that we have lived with—and thrived on—such diets throughout human history. Even Dr. Barnard, quoted above, refers to the "traditional, meat-based diet." But he is referring to the tradition of the last century—nothing more than that.

As he has pointed out many times himself, there is nothing at all traditional about a diet heavily laden with meat, high in sugars and fats, low in complex carbohydrates and fiber. And there's certainly nothing traditional about foods that are laced with antibiotics, pesticides, herbicides, growth hormones, and dozens of other man-made chemicals.

Americans and most Westerners are, in fact, eating the most radical diet in human history—and one that is exacting a radical toll on health and happiness.

For most of our history, we were hunter-gatherers; we ate meat, but in minuscule quantities compared with what we eat today. We exerted a lot of energy, building cardiovascular strength, in pursuit of elusive meat, and the meat we ate was itself from well-exercised, lean animals that were never exposed to high-fat feeds and synthetic, chemical growth promoters. Most of what we ate for millennia was vegetable in origin, rich in micronutrients and fiber, all of which we now know to be vital for good health.

"Oh, yeah?" say the skeptics. "Then why is it we live so much longer today on our meat-based diets?"

The answer is: *We don't*. A typical American male in his forties today has a life expectancy only a few years longer than a male of the same age had in 1900. That's mind-boggling when you consider the billions that have gone into medical research and all of the "advances" that have supposedly emerged from that effort, not to mention so-called "improvements" in nutrition.

The truth is that those extra five to seven years in life expectancy for the man in his forties have come from lifesaving operations, drugs that fight infections, and improved sanitation. If it weren't for these improvements, our current diet would be exposed for what it is: a *life-shortener,* not a life-prolonger.

With the advent of industrialization and improved means of transport, food production moved from field and farm into factories. Sweet, fatty, highly refined foods and meats, all of which had been scarce or nonexistent before, could now be provided with ever-greater ease. The era of overindulgence was launched—and we've been on a binge ever since. And, concurrently, we've experienced a new wave of diseases—the diseases of overconsumption. Nowhere has this been more evident than in the United States— the country that today spends more of its gross national product on health care than does any other nation in the world.

"Diet-related diseases are responsible for 68 percent of all deaths in the United States."

U.S. SURGEON GENERAL

The biggest changes in our diet have been the doubling and tripling of meat consumption, the vast increases in per capita intake of sugar and salt, along with decreases in consumption of fruits and vegetables. Protein intake has remained roughly constant, but our sources of protein have shifted dramatically—from plant protein to meat protein. For years, we were led to believe that only animal protein was "complete." In fact, during the past few years this deadly myth has been completely debunked—though a significant proportion of Americans are still unaware of this.

Does it really matter where we get our protein—so long as we get it? *Yes.* Meat protein lacks the fiber and many of the vital micronutrients that protect against disease that are found in plant proteins. Meat protein comes in high-fat "packages" that raise cholesterol and contribute to heart disease. When meat is cooked, it forms compounds that are beginning to be implicated in cancer, as are the animal fats already firmly associated with a broad spectrum of malignancies. And meats are, typically, reservoirs of chemicals, bacteria, and other toxins and pathogens.

The radical American diet of today serves up about one hundred pounds of sugar per person per year (half of it concealed in packaged foods), ten pounds of salt per person per year (40 percent of it added at the table, another 20 percent added to packaged foods), only fifteen to twenty grams of fiber per day (whereas the real tradition was to get sixty or more grams a day), and, in a lifetime, *about six thousand pounds of fat per person.* That fat figure is an average. Some Americans consume fifteen thousand pounds of fat or even more in a lifetime. Run that through your arteries and think about it—if you're still breathing.

Most of that fat comes from meat and dairy products. The average American consumes nearly two hundred pounds of meat a year, along with more than two hundred eggs, plus vast quantities of cheese, milk, butter, margarine, cooking oils, ice cream, sour cream, chocolate, and so on. Whereas fats traditionally provided fewer than 30 percent of our total calories, they now constitute more than 40 percent.

Let's see what this radical change in our diet has done to us, looking first at heart disease.

Exploding Hearts

Imagine a terrorist organization so cruel and effective that it would detonate bombs in major American population centers—in office buildings, suburban shopping malls, at amusement parks, wherever people gather—killing an average of two thousand people with each bomb. And imagine that this happens not just a few times, *but every day for years on end*.

Unthinkable, isn't it? Imagine the changes this would effect in our society. Governments would topple, the economy would reel, our civil liberties would be sacrificed. Democracy, as we know it, would be no more.

And, yet, every day in the United States, about two thousand people drop dead from exploding hearts and blood vessels caused by diet-related heart attacks and strokes. Another three thousand are felled each day by nonfatal but often seriously disabling versions of these same "detonations." And the phenomenon goes largely ignored by most of us, despite the fact that the bottom line—the number of dead and wounded—is the same as in the terrorist scenario above, a scenario that would bring the country to its collective knees. And what makes this particularly devastating is that most of these lives could be saved with simple, healthful changes in diet.

Meats and dairy products are laden with cholesterol and saturated fats that clog veins and arteries leading to our hearts, brains, lungs, and other organs. These deposits of fat cause heart attacks when insufficient blood, carrying oxygen and other nutrients, reaches the heart—or strokes when insufficient blood reaches the brain. But fat-clogged vessels also contribute to all manner of other disorders, including hypertension and sexual dysfunction.

Atherosclerosis—the process by which fatty plaques clog arteries—is so prevalent in our society that its earliest manifestations show up in three-year-olds, and, by age thirty-five, about a fourth of all men have distinct atherosclerosis. There is overwhelming epidemiological evidence that this process is related to diet and, especially, to blood levels of cholesterol (which, in turn, are closely related to dietary intake of cholesterol).

In countries where dietary intake of cholesterol is lowest, so is the incidence of heart disease—and vice versa. The United States consistently ranks near the top of the international list for cholesterol consumption and also near the top of the list for heart disease. In Japan, by contrast, where the national diet has long been low in fat and cholesterol, the incidence of heart disease is quite low. But when the Japanese migrate to the United States and adopt our diet, their incidence of heart disease soars—to ten times what it was in their homeland!

Diet, of course, is not the only factor in heart disease. Stress, genetics, tobacco and alcohol consumption, lack of exercise—all of these are contributors. But diet is the most important. And diet is the easiest to change.

In part III, we'll talk about optimum levels of cholesterol and other lipids, and I'll show you how my dietary purification system and vegetarian fare can help *reverse* the ravages of atherosclerosis and give you back years of life that will otherwise be lost or made miserable by disease. You can dramatically decrease your risk of heart disease by making dietary changes—*no matter what your age when you begin.*

Diet and Cancer

Half a million Americans die every year of cancer. One in every five deaths in this country is caused by cancer, the most frequently suffered forms of which are prostate, breast, lung, and colorectal. The relationship between many cancers and meat consumption is overwhelming.

Most people think of lung cancer as strictly smoking-related, and there is no doubt that smoking is a major cause of this dread disease in many people. But studies have now shown that lung cancer rates are significantly lower in vegetarians than in nonvegetarians—*even when the vegetarians smoke as much as the meat eaters.* Clearly, there are powerful factors in vegetarian fare that protect against a wide range of pollutants, including cigarette smoke.

It has been estimated authoritatively that at least 40 percent of all cancer deaths are attributable to the typical American diet, with its emphasis on meats, dairy, and other high-fat foods. Both women and men who consume meat daily, for example, have 2.5 to 3.6 times more colon cancer than do those who eat meat less than once a month. Again, higher concentrations of cholesterol (in combination with bile acids), this time in the intestinal tract, seem to be the source of the problem.

Though the debate goes on about the primary cause of breast cancer, which, in terms of numbers, is the most deadly malignancy in women (one out of eight American women get it), there is more than ample evidence to satisfy many of the world's top researchers that a high-fat diet is the chief culprit. Breast cancer afflicts four to seven times more American women than Asian women—and genetics is not the reason; when Asian women move to the United States and begin consuming the same amounts of meat and other fatty foods consumed by U.S. women, their breast cancer rates soon match American rates.

If you look around the world at meat/fat consumption, you will find a strong direct correlation between diet and breast cancer. Those countries with the highest fat consumption have the highest rates of breast cancer (the Netherlands, Canada, Switzerland, United States, Australia, Austria, Germany). And those with the lowest fat consumption have the fewest cases of breast cancer (Thailand, Ceylon, Japan, Taiwan).

It's not merely what is in animal fat (estrogen-promoting factors that stimulate malignant growth, among other things), but what the animal fats substitute for in diet that is at the root of the problem. When Asian women move to the United States, for example, they begin substituting meat for their traditional soy products. Recent evidence shows that soy produces a form of estrogen that is not only benign but also actually inhibits disease-promoting forms of estrogen. Thus, the change to the American diet delivers a double negative. I'll have a lot more to say about the protective factors in soy and other vegetables in part III.

Meanwhile, in men, the most deadly malignancy in numerical terms is prostate cancer. And, once again, you can see a powerful direct relationship between animal-fat intake and the incidence of this disease. The United States is up near the top of the list again, along with several of its high-fat European allies, and autopsies on American men as young as their early thirties show that perhaps a third of them already had microscopic clusters of cancer cells in their prostate tissues, according to researchers at Memorial Sloan-Kettering Cancer Center in New York.

How such early-stage cancer cells develop likely depends upon diet. When Sloan-Kettering researchers recently injected human prostate cancer cells into mice on diets that varied in fat content, they got some very interesting results. Mice that were on diets that derive 30 to 40 percent of calories from fat (remember, many Americans get 40 percent or more of their calories from fats) got tumors that kept growing. But the mice that were on a diet that derived only 20 percent or less of its calories from fat got tumors that *stopped growing.*

Harvard researchers, meanwhile, have reported that men who get thirty grams of fat a day from red meat are at *twice the risk* of getting prostate cancer than are men who eat almost no red meat. It only takes about five ounces of typical hamburger meat, by the way, to deliver thirty grams of fat.

There are many other animal fat–cancer links. And there are also many additional causes. In part III, we'll look at some exciting new evidence for protective factors in vegetarian fare. One of the most remarkable recent findings has to do with the potent protection *tomatoes* and various tomato products exert with respect to prostate cancer. No wonder Mexico and El Salvador, among other high-tomato–consuming countries, have such low rates of this deadly affliction.

Diabetes, Osteoporosis, and Other Dietary Disasters

Adult-onset diabetes, afflicting more than 7 million Americans, is one of the most serious diseases. It is also one of the most difficult to treat and one of the most costly to society in monetary terms.

Most people think of diabetes as a "sugar problem" unrelated to meat and animal fats. Diabetes can cause blindness, tissue decay (often necessitating amputations), and death. At the base of all this mayhem are cells that are not getting the glucose—sugar fuel—they need to operate properly and survive. Insulin is the hormone that governs glucose metabolism. When insulin can't do its work at cell-surface receptor sites—because those sites are clogged with fat—diabetes is the result.

So, perhaps, instead of calling it *sugar* diabetes, it would be more descriptive of the real problem if we called it *fat* diabetes.

Several studies have shown that vegetarians have a far lower incidence of diabetes than do meat eaters. *The rate among vegetarians is 40 to 50 percent lower.* And when diabetics are put on vegetarian or near-vegetarian diets, the need for medication is greatly reduced and, in some cases, eliminated entirely.

Osteoporosis—thinning of bone—is similarly linked to a high consumption of animal products. Drinking more milk to try to "beef up the bones" is precisely the wrong thing to do. Animal proteins contain a type of amino acid that is not prevalent in plant protein, and this particular amino acid causes excessive excretion of calcium, the mineral that gives substance to bone.

Other factors can also contribute to osteoporosis—especially smoking and alcohol consumption—but dietary animal fat is more significant. To this day, of course, the milk industry would love to have you believe that drinking milk will help prevent or ameliorate osteoporosis. As I've indicated, nothing could be farther from the truth. American women get more calcium in their diets than almost any other group of women—and yet *they have one of the highest rates of osteoporosis in the world.*

I'll have much more to say about calcium and other minerals in part III, but, for now, I want to issue a general warning about milk and milk products, for they, too, are implicated very strongly in all of the diseases we have been discussing. There is enormous misunderstanding about milk, particularly among those who feel good about themselves when they purchase milk products that are advertised, for example, to contain "only 4 percent fat!" What this means is 4 percent fat by weight—but what isn't understood is that nearly everything apart from that 4 percent is water! So the majority of the calories you get from milk are still derived from fat. Even 2-percent-fat milk still delivers a high quantity of fat, about 38 percent of calories from fat.

> "Our goal was to change the kind of milk Americans drink, because whole and 2% milk (which is mislabeled as 'lowfat') increase the risk of . . . disease. Drinking one glass a day of whole milk instead of skim milk over a lifetime adds 400 pounds of fat and 1.6 million calories to your diet!"
>
> CENTER FOR SCIENCE IN THE PUBLIC INTEREST

The list of diseases now strongly associated with diets high in animal fats and animal proteins goes on and on, to include various forms of kidney disease, obesity, gallstones, venous thrombosis (blood clots), constipation, diverticular disease, appendicitis, hemorrhoids, hiatus hernia, and varicose veins of the legs, in addition to the diseases we've already discussed. Some of these illnesses result from the *underconsumption of plant foods* that are eliminated from diet in favor of an excess of animal products.

In addition, there is a growing epidemic of food-borne illnesses related to toxins and pathogens that are polluting meat. These are contributing to cancers, infectious diseases, and, according to alarming new evidence, infertility and reproductive problems. We have known for some time that diets high in animal fats can cause impotence in men by clogging the vessels leading into the penis, a significant problem, given that one out of four American men over the age of sixty is impotent. But the new reproductive problems we'll be discussing below go far beyond this in scope and danger.

"Killer E. Coli," "Mad Cow Disease," and "Silent Sperm"

Unfortunately, meat, hazardous enough even when it is pure, increasingly comes freighted with an abundance of biological and chemical contaminants, most of which are bad for human health. A few years ago, the public first heard about "killer *E. coli*," a superstrain of bacteria that showed up in the hamburgers of some fast-food chains and killed some children and sickened others. Many assumed that this headline-generating story was a once-in-a-lifetime event, and once the media tired of the story, it went away, seemingly confirming that assumption.

In reality, food-borne illnesses, many of them resulting in death, occur with growing regularity. Most go unreported in the media. They have not, however, eluded the attention of the Department of Agriculture. In one recent twelve-month period, the department estimated there were as many as 7 million cases of food-borne illness, of which as many as 5 *million* were from contaminated meat. Some nine thousand Americans died last year from bacterial food poisoning.

Apart from such pathogenic nasties as *E. coli, Salmonella, Campylobacter jejuni, Toxoplasma gondii,* and *Listeria monocytogenes,* there are other "passengers" aboard the meat entrée consumers must worry about, including antibiotics, growth hormones, and a variety of pesticides and other man-made chemicals. Feces is another common pollutant. When Consumers Union tested fish from many different markets over a six-month period, it found that almost 50 percent of the samples were contaminated with human or animal fecal matter!

Antibiotics are pumped into animals destined for our dinner plates in order to keep them alive—and growing—under highly unsanitary, crowded conditions. Growth hormones are fed to the animals to increase "yields," and most of the other contaminants accumulate in ever-greater concentrations the higher up the food chain one goes. The growth hormones, incidentally, make animals more susceptible to disease and thus in need of ever-greater quantities of antibiotics, which also accumulate in the animals, ending up in human consumers. Nearly all cattle in the United States get these hormones, which also find their way into milk products.

"Bovine growth hormone (BGH) makes cows produce more milk. BGH also makes cows sick. BGH injections cause cows' udders to become infected, releasing increased levels of pus into the milk. The FDA doesn't like the word 'pus.' They call it 'somatic cell counts.' The FDA has decided to keep this information 'within the beltway' as they refer to keeping information inside Washington, D.C. The FDA will not require that BGH-tainted products be labeled."

EARTHSAVE HEALTHY SCHOOL LUNCH ACTION GUIDE
(a publication of the environmental group EarthSave)

Pesticides are another major "additive" in meat these days. I'll have more to say about this shortly. But, for now, be aware that more than a dozen pesticides commonly found in meat sold to Americans every day are known carcinogens. Other powerful carcinogens found in meat are the PCBs—polychlorinated hydrocarbons, polluting by-products of various industrial processes.

So meat is literally stewing in chemicals and other contaminants. Fully half of all antibiotics used in this country are fed to or injected into animals that are to be eaten by humans. That's more than *25 million pounds of antibiotics!* Add to this vast quantities of growth hormones and steroids, lace well with fecal matter, bacteria, and other pathogens, pepper liberally with pesticides and PCBs, fold in those "somatic cells," and you've got what some will call "dinner" and others will call "disease."

Do we really need to wonder why one of every three Americans dies of cancer to-day? Can it get any worse? Very possibly. In 1996, the world was horrified to learn about "mad cow disease," which was reported to have infected British herds. After a few well-publicized human deaths some attributed to eating beef contaminated with this almost science-fictionish killer, beef consumption in Britain plummeted. There were no doubt a number of permanent converts to vegetarianism in the wake of this publicity—as there were after the *E. coli* stories appeared—but soon public officials lulled many back into a state of relative complacency.

The agent responsible for "mad cow disease" is something that is neither bacterial nor viral. It is called a "prion," for "proteinacous infectious particle." There is something particularly ghoulish about the prion and its affinity for meat eaters; prions were first found in New Guinea cannibals! And these deadly but slow-acting particles apparently entered cows through sheep entrails that were routinely fed to them—another practice that sounds a bit cannibalistic. The prions "drill" through the brains of their victims and drive them "mad."

No one is sure how many people may be infected with this ghastly disease—and it may be years, possibly even decades, before we know the full story. The first case cropped up in England in 1986 and was linked at that time to the practice of feeding sheep guts to cattle. Yet the practice was not banned in England until 1989.

"In the three years that elapsed between the first official diagnosis of mad cow disease and the 1989 ban, virtually every meat-eating person in Britain—not to mention those abroad who ate British beef—could have been exposed to the disease, according to Stephen Dealler, consultant microbiologist at Burnley General Hospital."

RAY MOSELEY, *Chicago Tribune*

There is considerable evidence that the British government suppressed what it knew about this disease for many years out of fear that publicity would destroy the multibillion-dollar beef industry. That fear is still at work today and will continue to make it difficult to get the full story for some time to come.

What is particularly shocking is that, even after the 1989 ban in England, the United States did not follow suit. Cattle in the United States were still being fed sheep and other cattle remains. It was only in the wake of all the publicity about "mad cow disease" in 1996 that the cattle industry announced it would henceforth stop this practice, though it is not required to do so by law and is not monitored for compliance by any government regulatory agency.

And, yes, people have died in the United States of diseases that closely resemble "mad cow disease." No one is sure of the cause.

Whatever ultimately comes of this situation, it serves to demonstrate, at the very least, how vulnerable we are when we rely for a major portion of our food upon an industry that is so powerful that even governments will shut their collective eyes to situations that potentially threaten millions of lives. Meat, in so many ways, has become at once a magnifier and a microcosm of the ills of our society.

It's hard to trump "mad cow disease," but "silent sperm," another story that began to break wide open in 1996, might do it. The *New Yorker* magazine is not a journal noted for its "end-of-the-world" headlines—but this is what was splashed across the cover of its January 15, 1996, edition:

SILENT SPERM

ALL OVER THE GLOBE, HUMAN SPERM COUNTS ARE DROPPING—
AT A RATE THAT COULD BRING THEM TO ZERO IN A LIFETIME

The title, of course, is a play on Rachel Carson's landmark book, *Silent Spring,* in which she documented the deadly effects DDT and other pesticides were having on birds and other wildlife, taking some of them to the brink of—and others beyond the brink to—extinction.

The article meticulously, and in great detail, analyzed research by numerous independent scientists from around the world, demonstrating that human sperm counts are sharply declining, and sought to understand why this is happening on a global scale.

Author Lawrence Wright discovered that *both the quantity and the quality* of human sperm are on a sharp, downward spiral. He also found numerous researchers reporting on increases in testicular cancer and genital deformities among male infants.

One of these researchers is the highly respected pediatric endocrinologist Niels E. Skakkebaek of the National University Hospital in Copenhagen, Denmark. Dr. Skakkebaek was among the first to note a sharp rise in testicular cancer, genital deformity in infants and young boys, and a significantly increased incidence, in recent years, of undescended testicles. He also reported on an increase in male infertility, after having observed how difficult it was for sperm banks at infertility centers to find donors with adequate sperm counts and quality.

These observations led to Dr. Skakkebaek's first sperm-count study. He selected men who were *not* exposed to hazardous chemicals and pesticides in their jobs, thinking that, in this way, he would be able to establish a "baseline" of healthy men against which he could compare other men who *did* work in hazardous environments. To his astonishment, however, he found that these men had dismally low sperm counts and that about *40 percent of the sperm were abnormal.* Some had two heads, others had no tails, still others were literally bent out of shape.

Many others have made similar findings. Instead of finding sperm counts at 100 million per milliliter of semen, as was common in the 1950s, researchers found that average sperm counts in many countries are *half of what they were* and that, as was the case in Denmark, a very high proportion are abnormal in structure. Researchers in Iowa, Texas, Philadelphia, England, Denmark, Scotland, Paris, etc.—all came up with similar results. Retrospective analyses showed that the declines began in the 1940s in most locales.

There is controversy around all of this, and there are those who have found flaws in these studies. Some have presented contrary studies. The topic will no doubt be debated for some time to come. But there is sufficient evidence to date that this is a real phenomenon that needs to be taken seriously and further investigated.

Possible explanations for these declines have covered a broad spectrum. It is known that antibiotics, widely used and abused for decades, can kill sperm, as can tobacco, alcohol, marijuana, and a host of other drugs. So can venereal diseases, X rays, gasoline fumes, pesticides, and emotional stress.

In one study, at Florida State University, declining sperm counts were associated with synthetic chemical production, meat consumption, fat and alcohol intake. There was no link to climate, altitude, radiation, or population density.

With some hundred thousand synthetic chemicals being used in industry, and another thousand being introduced every year, many believe it would be amazing if we were *not* beginning to see some drastic effects on our reproductive systems. Most of these chemicals have been introduced in just the last fifty years; our bodies have had no chance to adapt to this unprecedented deluge of foreign substances.

How NOT to Fix the Problem

I'll be showing you ways to fix all the problems we've been discussing later in this book. For now, I feel I must say something about one "fix" that is bound to put us in a deeper fix. Rather than encourage people to alter their diets in healthful ways, to reduce meat and fat consumption, one segment of the food industry has come up with a solution it calls "Olestra," an artificial substitute for fat that is now being added to a variety of foods, despite the fact that testing of this product, according to numerous consumer-advocacy groups, has been woefully deficient.

And, in fact, what testing has taken place has turned up some pretty alarming "side effects." Researchers at the Center for Science in the Public Interest and others have found that Olestra robs foods of natural cancer-fighting substances called carotenoids. These caretonoids help protect us against cancers of the lung, prostate, and colon, among others.

"And if that's not enough reason for the Food and Drug Administration to reject Olestra, consider this unpleasant side effect: the amount of Olestra . . . present in a small, one-ounce serving of potato chips sometimes causes diarrhea, 'fecal urgency' and cramps. Larger amounts may even cause an unsavory phenomenon called "anal leakage." Olestra could probably be marketed as a laxative if Procter & Gamble wanted to!

CENTER FOR SCIENCE IN THE PUBLIC INTEREST

What the world needs now is not more *additives* but more *subtractives*. We need to get back to a food supply that is full of only those ingredients nature intended. In part III, I'll show you how to cleanse your body of toxins and then how to ensure that your food supply is clean, too.

CHAPTER 5

Environment

The Last-Gasp Diet

As we've seen in the preceding chapter, our diet is killing millions of us. But the situation is worse than that. Our diet—and all that goes into producing it—is killing our planet, literally threatening to extinguish all life on earth. And at the very center of this killing diet is *meat*.

Meat production is taking a terrible, potentially *terminal*, toll on our vital resources—soil, water, air/atmosphere. Illnesses born of pollution and overpopulation are proliferating at an alarming rate. Ecosystems are collapsing. Nearly all environmental scientists and international policy analysts agree that we are on a collision course with disaster, but long before we succumb to chemical poisoning or mutant viruses, we're going to feel the crunch at the dinner table.

Food, declares the internationally respected Worldwatch Institute, is the "defining issue." There simply isn't enough of it to go around, given the way Americans and Europeans eat—at the vast expense of the rest of the world. And it's going to get much scarcer in the very near future. Many scientists say it is evident that we have already far exceeded the "carrying capacity" of the planet, the earth's ability to sustain us and other living things.

A research team at the University of British Columbia has concluded, from its extensive studies, that as of 1996, it would take two additional planet earths to sustain current populations at the level of consumption present in the United States and much of

Europe. To sustain at the same level the 10 billion humans expected to populate the earth by the year 2040, it would take *five* additional planet earths to do the job. William E. Rees, who headed the studies, notes that the richest third of the world's population must decrease its grotesquely disproportionate use of the planet's resources *fivefold* if anything approaching sustainable development is ever to be achieved.

So how are we doing on that front? Not well. World carryover stocks of grain—essentially our reserves, what stands between "civilization" and chaos—fell to an estimated forty-nine days of consumption in 1996—*the lowest level ever recorded*. This continues a trend several years in the making and is only partly explained by adverse weather conditions (some of which, in any case, are themselves the result of destructive energy and agricultural practices and policies).

Even as populations increase, our soils and other resources increasingly are depleted, worn out by our misuse and overuse of them. What experts call the "horizontal expansion of agriculture" is at an end. In past centuries, increased grain outputs were achieved simply by putting more acreage under cultivation. Now we've used up virtually all of the land capable of sustaining crops. For much of this century, we have achieved increases in output through irrigation, the use of fertilizers and pesticides, the development of new, higher-yielding crop varieties, and other measures.

"We are approaching the end of one of the most remarkable transitions in the history of agriculture," observes Vernon Ruttan, agricultural economist at the University of Minnesota. Worldwatch scientists concur, noting that there are seemingly unavoidable and *imminent* limits to further expansion.

Irrigation can no longer bring arid lands into cultivation. Irrigation has so depleted our groundwater and aquifers that even vast areas of the United States may become uninhabitable within the next few decades, according to Worldwatch authorities.

We've already fertilized to the hilt. Adding more will do no good. And, in fact, the environmental pollution that resulted from the massive fertilization that commenced in the 1970s has, Worldwatch experts say, cost us more than it has saved. The same is true of pesticides. Pests rapidly adapt to pesticides that, at the same time, disorient entire ecosystems, frequently allowing new, more powerful pests to gain dominance. The miserable failure of pesticides is attested to by the U.S. Department of Agriculture, the National Academy of Sciences, and studies by other groups showing that the percentage of crop loss due to pests has actually increased significantly since pesticides were introduced in the 1940s.

As for new "miracle" crop varieties, engineered in the lab, we may still have a few of those to pull out of the hat, but nobody expects these to spell salvation. The World-watch Institute forecasts only "modest opportunities" on that front. Lester R. Brown, in the Worldwatch publication *State of the World, 1996* says:

> Avoiding catastrophe is going to take a far greater effort than is now being contemplated by world leaders. . . . As we move to the end of this century and beyond, food security may well come to dominate international affairs, national economic policymaking, and, for much of humanity, personal concerns about survival. . . . The effort needed to reverse the environmental degradation . . . will require mobilization on a scale comparable to World War II. . . . If we fail, our future will spiral out of control. . . . It will almost guarantee a future of starvation, economic insecurity and political instability.

In the face of all this, we continue to commit unconscionable, irrational quantities of our grains and other vital resources to the production of meat, among the least energy-efficient and most environmentally damaging of all foods—so much, in fact, that this allocation is the primary fuel of our current engine of global destruction. If we continue to consume meat as we have for the past several decades, this truly will prove to be our "last-gasp diet."

Meat: The Food That Literally "Costs the Earth"

I always cringe when I hear people talk about the "overpopulation problem" in Third World countries, adding that if all of "those people" would "just stop breeding," most of our environmental woes would evaporate. Overpopulation is a problem *everywhere* (many experts say the U.S. population should be no more than 200 million, instead of the current 263 million), but the First World countries are, by far, the greatest cause of environmental degradation. A tiny segment of the population consumes most of the world's resources. It feeds itself on meat at the expense of billions.

It would actually be far more appropriate for people in the Third World to complain about the overpopulation problem in the United States than vice versa. I'm talking about the overpopulation of animals raised in the United States for meat—*more than 8 billion annually!* The toll this takes on grain crops and the environment generally is outlandish.

What I call the "meat machine" is a major despoiler of air, atmosphere, water, soil, and forests. The meat machine erodes the soil, sucks up enormous amounts of water and contributes to desertification, dumps billions of pounds of excrement and other wastes onto the land and into the water, creates vast "dead zones" in the oceans, mows down rain forests, contaminates the earth with pesticides and other toxic chemicals, sucks up energy, kills plant and other animal species, intensifies poverty, hunger, and other miseries throughout the world, threatens all life with its contribution to ozone depletion and global warming, and adds mightily to the tax burden on all of us.

Agricultural expert David Pimentel of Cornell University reports that one-third of all the world's agricultural lands have been rendered useless by soil erosion that has taken place in just the last forty years—the four decades that coincide with the explosive growth of the meat machine. Various studies conducted by the United Nations have concluded that 10 to 15 percent of the planet's previously most-productive lands are *permanently* ruined. That's enough land to feed 1.5 billion people—more than 25 percent of today's world population, clearly a loss we cannot afford.

If we were a rational society, we would place a higher value on topsoil than we do on diamonds and gold. It takes, on average, about five hundred years to accrete an *inch* of usable topsoil through natural processes. In some cases, it takes a thousand or more years to produce that single inch of soil. Then, when you take into account the fact that it takes a minimum of *six inches* of topsoil to sustain a crop, you can begin to grasp the depth of the problem. Once we've destroyed our topsoil, *we could be waiting six thousand years for the next crop to come up*—assuming we do nothing further to damage the environment in the meantime!

"Soil—the very foundation of agriculture—is under siege around the world. . . . More than just unsustainable, this loss of topsoil is tragic; in just a few decades, human activity has squandered a natural patrimony that took thousands of years to accumulate."

GARY GARDNER, *State of the World, 1996,* Worldwatch Institute

---

Overuse of land—especially for the production of grain to feed cattle—is what causes soil erosion. Overgrazing by cattle also contributes significantly. One half of the earth's surface is devoted to cattle grazing; fully 70 percent of the western United States is similarly committed to cattle grazing. Cattle consume *half* of the world's grain harvest. (Incredibly, livestock also eat *one-third of the world's fish catch!*)

Not content with the enormous amount of beef and other meat we produce at home, we import still more from other countries, including some 300 million pounds from Central and South America, encouraging the wealthy minorities in those regions to despoil their own lands in pursuit of short-term profits. This is dramatically illustrated by the fact that 30 to 80 percent of many Central and South American rain forests have now been burned to the ground to clear fields for cattle production. The world's tropical forests have shrunk by more than 50 percent in just a few decades.

The tragedy is further compounded when you factor in the loss of literally thousands of species, now extinct as a direct result of deforestation, the loss of miracle medicines that might have been derived from those tropical forests, and the loss of atmospheric cleansing and oxygen regeneration from all that plant life. The rain forests are the "lungs of the world"; at the rate we are destroying them, we are literally suffocating ourselves.

And for what? It has been demonstrated that rain forest soils are too fragile to sustain cattle grazing and other overuse for more than a few years. In the Amazon, the typical cattle operation, built on what was once lush forest, lasts, on average, fewer than eight years. Then the land is so badly eroded that it is abandoned. An ecotapestry of stunning complexity and beauty, one that took nature thousands of years to fabricate, is thus destroyed by a few greedy humans in the blink of a cosmic eye.

Our resource allocations and priorities have become so perverted in the Western world that we continue to import meat even from those countries, such as Ethiopia, that are caught in ever-worsening cycles of hunger, starvation, and death. We create a market so alluring that the elite in those countries rob from their own people, even when they are starving, in order to feed us still more meat.

About forty thousand people starve to death each day around the world, most of them children. More than 20 million people starve to death on the planet each year. *If Americans would cut back just 10 percent on their meat intake, they would free up enough land to grow enough crops to feed all of those 20 million starving people and more. Just 10 percent.*

"It seems disingenuous for the intellectual elite of the first world to dwell on the subject of too many babies being born in second- and third-world nations while virtually ignoring the overpopulation of cattle and the realities of

---

Even while we exploit the Second and Third Worlds, we are also fast consuming all of our *own* resources. Look at all of our major resources, and you will see them being diverted into the meat machine. It has been estimated that one-third of all raw materials used in the United States are consumed in the production of livestock!

Apart from the 21 million acres of agricultural land and the 50 million acres of tropical forests and woodlands that are being lost each year worldwide, losses right here at home are mounting dramatically as a result of our subjection to the meat machine. As previously noted, we're feeding 70 percent of our grain crops to livestock. It takes sixteen pounds of grain to produce just one pound of beef. On the same land that can produce only 250 pounds of beef, we could instead produce 20,000 pounds of apples or 40,000 pounds of potatoes or 60,000 pounds of celery.

But while we devote 64 percent of all our croplands to making feed for livestock, we use only 2 percent to grow fruits and vegetables.

Meanwhile, the water needed to grow one pound of potatoes is 24 gallons, for apples 49 gallons, for tomatoes 23 gallons—and *to produce one pound of beef, it takes 2,500 gallons of water!* A mind-boggling 85 percent of all water consumed in the United States is for farm uses, most of it to water crops to feed livestock.

It has been calculated that the amount of water needed to produce a thousand-pound steer would be enough to float a naval destroyer. The amount of water that goes into the making of ten pounds of steak is enough to meet the household needs of a typical family for an entire year.

This waste proceeds unabated even as many areas of the western United States gear up for "water wars." The livestock industry has already seriously depleted many major aquifers, including the once-massive Ogallala Aquifer that underlies the high plains states. Scientists at Stanford University, the Global Water Policy Project, and elsewhere believe that catastrophe may be no farther out than 2025—when demand for water may match 100 percent of our remaining reserves.

As things stand now, only about 1 percent of earth's water is pure enough and accessible enough to be used by living things, including humans. The meat machine, apart from using an inordinate proportion of this water, is rapidly polluting what is left.

Livestock and related activities are destroying our rivers, streams, wetlands, and even the oceans. Cattle grazing, fertilization, irrigation, the heavy use of pesticides, logging to clear more agricultural land—all result in soil erosion and runoff into our waterways. Sedimentation and pollutants smother the eggs of fish and other aquatic life, block sunlight and promote algal and bacterial growth, and raise water temperatures to levels that cannot be tolerated by salmon and many other fish. Massive amounts of animal excrement add to the problem of agricultural runoff.

In the meantime, meat production is hogging so much of the freshwater supply that what remains is significantly diminished and thus more easily polluted. Forty percent of North America's freshwater fish species are now either extinct or on the brink of extinction, almost all because of habitat degradation and pollution.

In 1880, the salmon and steelhead trout catch in the Pacific Northwest's Columbia River was 19,500 tons. Today, it is 50 tons, and rapidly dwindling below even that meager amount. The same disaster, involving other fish species, is being repeated in virtually every major river basin in the country and the world.

Little wonder that the American Fisheries Society has named the cow the trout's worst enemy. Others have similarly pointed to cattle as the killers of salmon.

But the killing goes far beyond that. The toxic deluge of effluent, a mix of soil, fertilizers, livestock excrement, nitrogen, and phosphorus, that pours from the rivers into the oceans is producing what scientists call "dead zones." Agricultural contaminants are the number-one cause of water pollution in the United States. The pollutants that emerge from the Mississippi River—the principal catch basin of the livestock industry—have created a zone of death in the Gulf of Mexico that has wiped out all life across an area approximately the size of New Jersey—seven thousand square miles, and growing! There are several other massive dead zones in the making.

I'll have more to say about what's happening to the oceans below, but, for now, let's return to land—and the atmosphere above us.

Apart from the sad spectacle of soil erosion, forest clear-cuts, and degraded streams and rivers, we are now confronted with a virtual mountain of animal excrement, the disposal of which is rapidly becoming a political and environmental crisis. All manner of standards have been implemented around the country for the disposal of human waste—while almost nothing has been done to regulate the disposal of animal wastes. This is appalling when you consider that the excrement produced by livestock in California alone is equal to that which would be produced by a city of *73 million humans!*

Livestock produce ten times the amount of waste humans do in the United States, and yet regulations to deal with this are scant to nonexistent. The Natural Resources Defense Council and the International Alliance for Sustainable Agriculture report that nearly two thousand bodies of water in thirty-nine U.S. states have already been seriously polluted by feedlot excrement. Single feedlots produce animal waste equal to small cities of 110,000 people, and taken as a group, U.S. feedlots generate 230,000 pounds of animal excrement *every second*.

Manure spills threaten to challenge oil spills as leading causes of environmental pollution. Five major manure spills in less than a year in the state of North Carolina alone have killed millions of fish and have shut down the shellfish harvest and other commercial fishing in 365,000 acres of coastal wetlands. One of these spills dumped 22 million gallons of waste—twice the volume of oil spilled in the *Exxon Valdez* disaster—into a river, boosting bacterial limits to fifteen thousand times the permissible level, according to the *Baltimore Sun*.

In view of the foregoing, you may have less trouble understanding how livestock make significant contributions to the so-called greenhouse gases—carbon dioxide, nitrous oxide, and methane—that result in global warming. It has been calculated that cattle emit 100 million tons of methane annually, which is 20 percent of the total methane emissions in the world.

Livestock also contribute to the other two major greenhouse gases, all of which trap heat and hold it in the atmosphere. Carbon dioxide is produced when tropical forests are burned to clear new land for livestock. More than 1.5 billion tons of carbon dioxide have already been released into the atmosphere in this way. Still more is produced in the burning of fossil fuels used in the mechanized production of crops and processing of meat.

The Center for Science in the Public Interest, EarthSave, and others have reported that it takes two hundred gallons of fossil fuels to produce one American family's average annual intake of beef; the burning of those two hundred gallons produces two tons of carbon dioxide, about what an average American car emits every six months. They also have calculated that every pound of rain forest beef costs—among other expenditures—about two thousand pounds of carbon dioxide released into the atmosphere.

The other greenhouse gas—nitrous oxide—is generated in large quantities from petroleum-based fertilizers used in agriculture.

The Natural Resources Defense Council reports that greenhouse gases have increased by 25 percent in the last century, raising the surface temperature of earth by one degree Fahrenheit. Scientific projections indicate that, at the current rate of increase, these gases may raise the surface temperature another two to more than six degrees over the next one hundred years. Many experts believe these temperature increases will be enough to submerge ten thousand square miles of American coastline and cause massive shifts in weather patterns, all unfavorable to food production. Some of those changes, many scientists think, are already under way. Unfortunately, even if we slow the production of greenhouse gases—which we *must* do—we will still be stuck with what we have already produced. These gases persist for centuries.

"Some fingerprints of global warming may already be visible in our weather. Since 1980, the world has experienced its ten hottest years in recorded history, perhaps contributing to high heat-related mortality rates from India to the United States, including more than 700 deaths in Chicago. . . . Warming in the Antarctic caused a fifty-mile wedge of the Larsen ice shell to break free. In Northern latitudes, at high altitudes in mountain ranges across the globe, and in the deep ocean waters of the Arctic, temperatures have been rising at a far more rapid pace than before. . . . The Intergovernmental Panel on Climate Change forecasts an average global temperature increase of 3.6 degrees Fahrenheit in the next 100 years . . . the most rapid warming trend in 10,000 years."

NATURAL RESOURCES DEFENSE COUNCIL

Rising seas—from melting ice caps—will wreak havoc with fisheries and disrupt millions of lives in coastal regions. "With as much as 50 to 70 percent of the world's population settled in coastal communities," Colum Lynch of the *Boston Globe* reports, "tens of millions of people could be driven from their homes to roam the earth as environmental refugees."

By 1995, Worldwatch Institute reports, greenhouse gases had reached their highest levels in the past 150,000 years. Cumulatively, they trap an amount of heat equal to that which would be generated by the detonation of 300,000 nuclear bombs!

The livestock industry has also been a villain in the depletion of the ozone layer that helps protect us and other living things from cosmic radiation. Exposure to this radiation is already being called the cause of increased cataracts and skin cancers. Chemical refrigerants used in the cooling of meats and other foods have been one of the main culprits in degrading the ozone layer. These chemicals were banned under the terms of a recent international treaty, but, unfortunately, it takes many years for these gases to dissipate to harmless levels.

"I Don't Eat Meat, Just Fish" and Other Environmental Disasters

I can't tell you how often I've heard people talk about the environmental devastation inflicted by the meat machine, only to add, in self-congratulatory tones, "I don't eat meat—just fish."

Unfortunately, the consumption of fish is neither people- nor planet-friendly. To begin with, overfishing has already turned large areas of the oceans into wastelands, wreaking economic and environmental havoc on a global scale. With 12 million small-boat fishermen and a high-tech industrial fleet of thirty-seven thousand ships on the seas, our remaining fish stocks stand little chance of survival, particularly when you consider the additional assaults they suffer from pollution and wetland destruction.

"If the Earth's oceans were a human being, they'd be rushed to the hospital, admitted to the intensive care unit and listed in grave condition."

EARTHSAVE, Spring 1996

What were once the seventeen most productive fishing areas of the world are all now being harvested at or beyond their full capacity. Stocks of fish in most areas are sharply on the wane, with catches down dramatically, and several, the UN reports, so bereft of life that they are, for all commercial purposes, dead zones. Among these are the once-productive fisheries of the Canadian Grand Banks and the New England Georges Bank.

More than one thousand different types of fish are now heading toward extinction worldwide; many are already extinct, including many Pacific salmon, according to the

CHAPTER 6

Conscience

If Slaughterhouses Had Glass Walls

The meat machine is sickening our bodies and our planet. It is also sickening our minds and souls. It silently and insidiously corrodes our moral fiber the more complicit we become in the mindless cruelty we inflict upon the billions of animals we raise for slaughter. It isn't just the slaughter; it's how we mistreat these animals on the path to slaughter.

It is intriguing to note how often some of the greatest—and most moral—minds in human history have equated the health of a society with the way in which it treats animals. There's an important message here for all of us.

> The greatness of a nation can be judged by the way its animals are treated.
>
> GANDHI

> I care not much for a man's religion whose dog or cat are not the better for it.
>
> ABRAHAM LINCOLN

> Until he extends his circle of compassion to all living things, man will not himself find peace. . . . It is man's sympathy with all creatures that first makes him truly a man.
>
> ALBERT SCHWEITZER

The time will come when men such as I will look on the murder of animals as they now look on the murder of men.

While we ourselves are the living graves of murdered beasts, how can we expect any ideal conditions on this earth?

And thus with their butchering and eating of beasts, they accomplish nothing at all unless it be to degenerate into beasts themselves.

It is apparent that it is not by a true judgment, but by foolish pride and stubbornness, that we set ourselves before the other animals and sequester ourselves from their condition and society.

Sir Thomas More worried that "mercy, the finest feeling of our human nature, is gradually killed off" through the cruelty to which we become accustomed in the mistreatment and slaughter of animals. Shaw echoed this fear: "Custom will reconcile people to any atrocity."

Thoreau, on the other hand, while strenuously objecting to the mistreatment of animals, believed man would evolve to a higher level of behavior: "I have no doubt that it is part of the destiny of the human race in its gradual development to leave off the eating of animals, as surely as the savage tribes have left off eating each other when they came into contact with the more civilized."

I'll throw in with Thoreau, up to a point. I am optimistic that changes are coming. Many are already under way. But this change occurs only when people understand how the meat machine works. When people began to be educated to the real horror of veal production, for example, they responded by buying and eating less veal—so that since 1975 there has been a *65 percent decline* in the consumption of veal in the United States!

There is still a great deal that people don't know about what happens to the animals that finally wind up on their plates and in their fast-food hamburgers, soups, sausages, and Thanksgiving dinners.

A book I wish every child and adult in America could see was recently published by Four Walls Eight Windows. It is called *Dead Meat* and contains text and drawings by Sue Coe. Coe risked a lot (her life was threatened at one point) as she traveled the country for six years, insinuating her way, often with great difficulty, into the feedlots, slaughterhouses, and meatpacking plants of our land. Her sketchbook became the chronicle, at once moving and horrifying, eloquent and damning, of her journey through the hellacious heart of the meat machine.

In his preface to the book, Tom Regan, president of the Culture and Animals Foundation, also envisions at least the possibility of change—if only the public can see for itself the terrible realities of the meat industry.

Only "acts of conscience performed by one person at a time," Regan writes, will lead to the demise of the meat machine. "The only way to stop the supply of meat is to eliminate the demand for meat. And the only way to stop the demand for meat is for people to stop eating it. The morally right means to the morally just ends are that simple."

And that difficult. Many have already become vegetarians for reasons of health, environment, and conscience, but to make further converts, people must first *see,* as Regan understands.

> Many more would join the growing ranks if they knew the horrors of the slaughterhouse "up close and personal"—saw firsthand the terror in the animal's eyes, the . . . organs spilling from the still breathing, convulsive bodies . . . waded ankle-deep in the rivers of fresh, warm blood . . . breathed the fetid odors of life ebbing away. If slaughterhouses had glass walls, would not all of us be vegetarians?

For many, out of sight is out of mind. But as Emerson put it long ago, "You have dined, and however scrupulously the slaughterhouse is concealed in the graceful distance of miles, there is complicity."

Let's close that complicity gap and take a closer look.

The Menagerie of Misery

Cows are typically shipped to feedlots in trucks without food or water and so crowded that significant numbers arrive crushed and crippled and often infected with "shipping fever," a pneumonia that results from the conditions of travel. At the feedlot, they are castrated, dehorned, branded, injected with antibiotics and other drugs, and shuttled into tiny spaces to live out the second halves of their lives, fattening for the market.

In Britain, anesthesia must be used before animals are castrated. In the United States, animals used for food have virtually no protection whatever under existing cruelty-prevention laws. Bulls are castrated, without any anesthesia, in the United States in order to make them more docile and to alter their metabolism so that they put on more fat. They are also dehorned, again without anesthesia, so that they will occupy less space in the feedlots. Both procedures inflict long and intense pain.

All of this pales, however, alongside the conditions in which the animals must live—as noted above, for about half of their lives—in the feedlots. Feedlot operators are proud of how tightly they can pack cattle into small spaces, which quickly become fouled with animal excrement. Currently, many feedlot cattle are provided no more than fourteen square feet of living space each.

John Robbins, whose book *Diet for a New America* has so powerfully documented the agonies of farm animals, writes that "to realize what this means, consider that a typical 12 foot by 15 foot bedroom is 180 square feet. Imagine thirteen half ton steers in your bedroom and you get the picture."

Again, many animals sicken in this environment. The "cripples" and the "downers," as they are called, are simply dragged out of the way and left to die or carted off to the slaughterhouse.

"Several hundred cows are kept in a tiny area . . . which is a couple of feet deep in mud, urine and excrement. There is nowhere for the cattle to walk. I am forced to cover my mouth and nose because of the stench. Many of the cattle have foot and eye infections. The downer is too heavy to get up. She cries as a chain is attached to her leg, and a winch drags her along the ground to a truck. I can see her skin rubbing off, and her bones grinding into the pavement. I can see the white of exposed bone and blood. She can't lift her head up, so her head, ear and eye start to tear on the stone. . . . As she reaches the truck, the cow rolls over, exposing her udders, which are full of milk. This is the total degradation of a life."

S U E   C O E (at a beef feedlot), *Dead Meat*

Then there's the fate of calves destined to become "veal." Veal is prized by some because it is particularly tender and light-colored. To achieve this effect, meat merchants take calves from their mothers at birth and stuff them into cages just twenty-two inches wide by fifty-eight inches long—so small that the calves cannot turn, stretch, or lie down in a natural position. Their heads are chained so that they cannot even lick themselves.

In order to keep the flesh tender for the meat machine, these merchants do not want the calves to develop any muscle tone whatsoever. For the four months these calves will live—if you can call this "life"—they can barely move. And in order to keep their flesh light-colored, they purposely are made anemic. They are fed a liquid diet that leaves them with chronic diarrhea and, generally, respiratory and intestinal diseases. They are not even given drinking water—and so, in order to try to quench their thirst, they eat more and more of their liquid diet, fattening in the process. Many "veals" are "grown" in complete darkness except during brief feeding periods twice a day. Many, of course, die before they reach their target weights. Premature death, however, does not prevent them from reaching someone's dinner plate.

The misuse of toxic drugs in calves destined for veal is particularly rampant, by the way. It is so difficult to keep animals alive under these grotesquely inhumane conditions that some in the veal industry resort to the use of illegal drugs, as if the legal ones weren't bad enough. It often takes extreme "medicine" to keep these animals going even for four months, particularly in light of the fact that they are torn away from their mothers at the most vulnerable stage of their lives.

In 1996, the Humane Farming Association brought criminal charges against some members of the American veal industry, alleging widespread illegal use of the highly toxic, unapproved drug clenbuterol in veal calf feed. The charges involve nearly fifty veal-producing companies. In tests conducted by a highly respected independent laboratory, the exceedingly dangerous clenbuterol was found in more than a third of all veal sampled from a wide range of slaughterhouses. This evidence has now resulted in criminal indictments. But clenbuterol is just one of many highly toxic substances that are pumped into veal.

Okay, you're saying, I've already quit eating veal (millions of previous veal eaters have, in fact, sworn off the stuff), and I'm seriously thinking of going all-out vegetarian, but there's nothing wrong with drinking milk. Is there?

Milk is also a repository for all the pesticides, hormones, and other growth promoters and antibiotics that are injected into and force-fed cattle. And the torture of dairy cows often rivals that of beef cattle. The mechanized, "efficient" milk factory of today is another of the meat machine's chambers of horror.

As John Robbins notes, the milk cow of yesteryear, allowed to roam across open meadows, her calves gamboling along beside her, lived twenty to twenty-five years. Today's "milk machine," as the industry views her, lives so stressful a life that she's lucky to make it to four years of age! Many of these sorrowful animals are kept in milking contraptions that are no more than cages; like "veals," they are so chained and confined inside these devices that they cannot walk or turn around and can barely move. As John Robbins says in *Diet for a New America*:

> Old Bessie may spend her whole life in a concrete stall, or, worse yet for her legs and feet, on a slatted metal floor. She is pregnant all the time, and her nervous system has been made so ragged by breeding practices devoted exclusively to milk production and a lifestyle that affords her no exercise, that this most mellow and patient of animals has become something else. She is today so tense, nervous and hyperactive that she often has to be given tranquilizers.

Pigs are, if anything, treated worse than cows. These acutely intelligent animals suffer unspeakably as they are processed by the meat machine. The "modern" pig factory may "house" tens of thousands of pigs, confining them in cramped cages and, frequently, in darkness. The cages have slats for floors that allow feces and urine to fall into vast pits below, creating an unimaginable stench. Some cages are stacked one on top of the other, so that the excrement falls on the pigs below. Disease is rampant. The air is so bad that the pigs develop lung disease, cough, get chills, and have to be kept on antibiotics.

The pigs' hooves split open and develop painful lesions on the concrete and metal surfaces of their cages and stalls. Their joints weaken and become inflamed. Most factory farms provide no bedding whatever for pigs, not even a little straw.

Pigs thus confined become so frustrated and stressed that they begin to go crazy. Along the way, they begin "tail biting," a perpetual problem much discussed in today's pig-farming circles. Confined in tight cages, the animals have nothing else to do but bite the tail of the pig in the cage ahead of them. This is why some pig "processors" keep their animals in complete darkness. Others simply cut the tails off their pigs, without anesthesia.

John Robbins reports that factory pigs are routinely fed water recycled from their own wastes and laden with antibiotics, heavy metals, and other toxins and that often they are "simply given raw poultry or pig manure" to eat. The animals eat and drink this because they are given nothing else. And, yet, as Robbins observes, the National Pork Council unabashedly claims that pork producers "have historically treated their farm animals with the utmost care and respect." And the council's "American Pork Queen" assures those who worry that pigs are being mistreated that "pigs like the new confinement barns as opposed to living outside in the natural environment, because a herdsman can keep a close eye on us, watch for disease, give us warmth, good feed, and clean air." In assuming the voice of the pig, the Pork Queen, I fear, heaps insult on injury.

"Forget the pig is an animal. Treat him just like a machine in a factory. Schedule treatments like you would lubrication. Breeding season like the first step in an assembly line. And marketing like the delivery of finished goods."

HOG FARM MANAGEMENT

"The breeding sow should be thought of, treated as, a valuable piece of machinery, whose function is to pump out baby pigs like a sausage factory."

NATIONAL HOG FARMER

As for poultry, you should, by now, pretty well be able to imagine what it's like for today's assembly-line chickens. They are raised in 100 percent artificial environments, stacked floor to ceiling in small cages that teem with filth. Like the confined pigs, they go berserk, go into pecking frenzies and attempt to cannibalize one another. To prevent this, poultry farmers cut off the chickens' beaks. The birds are in a constant state of high stress and panic. Some clutch the wire mesh of their cages so tightly and constantly that their tissue actually grows around the wire permanently! This can lead to complete immobility and starvation—so the poultry people simply cut off the chickens' toes as a preventative.

And, again, the animals get a terrible diet heavily laced with antibiotics and other chemicals. Almost all develop cancer. And chicken meat, by the time it reaches the consumer, is very frequently infected with disease-causing bacterial organisms and contaminated with fecal matter. Turkeys, by the way, suffer similar fates.

Unfortunately, for those who want to continue eating chickens, turkeys, and eggs, those poultry products labeled "organic," "free range," and so on are often just flat-out false, as several investigations have revealed. As John Robbins has summarized it, the only way to be sure is to raise the chickens yourself or buy directly from someone you know personally. Or, better yet, stop eating poultry altogether. Your body will thank you for it—and so will a whole lot of chickens.

"The egg factory is a long, bunker-type building, with hen cages stacked three stories high. There are six hens in cages the size of an old-fashioned album cover. They can't stretch their wings, turn around or lie down. . . . Feces from the hens on top fall down on the hens on the second level and so on. The chickens are debeaked before they are put in the battery cage, and sometimes the tongues are burned off. . . . Five hens turn on the sixth and try to peck out her eye. They have difficulty as they are debeaked. . . . Nonetheless, it's relentless pecking, and the hen can't turn around or protect herself in any way. Also, their feathers are all gone."

SUE COLE, *Dead Meat*

CHAPTER 7

What Can We Do?

We Can End "Cowboy Socialism"

When people ask me what they can do, personally, to protect their health, save the environment, and salve their consciences, I tell them the most effective thing they can do is to STOP EATING MEAT. I began this book with a quote from Albert Einstein. It bears repeating here:

> Nothing will benefit human health and increase the chances for survival of life on earth as much as the evolution to a vegetarian diet.

There is nothing I believe in more firmly than that. We are all empowered to make a significant change in the terrible wrongs that have been described in the preceding chapters—simply by eliminating all or most meat and meat by-products from our individual diets. That is what this book is all about—and the next section is devoted to making the transition to a meatless diet easier, while also providing you with the means to cleanse your systems of the impurities that your old ways of eating have deposited.

Before we move on to that next section of the book, however, I wish to pause briefly to point out a few other things we can do, individually and as a society, to alleviate the damage of the meat machine. We discussed the enormous costs to society of livestock overgrazing. Why don't we put a price on that destructive activity instead of doing just the opposite, which is to encourage it through taxpayer subsidization?

Fortunately, people from all walks of life and all political persuasions are finally getting wise to one of the biggest taxpayer rip-offs in the history of this country. Economic analyst Karl Hess, affiliated with the conservative Cato Institute, a Washington, D.C., think tank, calls the taxpayers' subsidization of livestock grazing on 270 million acres of public lands "cowboy socialism." He points out the hypocrisy of conservatives in Congress working to preserve "economic protectionism" rather than fight for free-market principles. Hess and others have calculated the costs of this one subsidy to taxpayers at *$200 million per year.*

Those are direct costs. (One U.S. Department of Agriculture official has acknowledged that annual subsidies and supports total about $25 billion per year for the beef/veal/milk industries as a whole, not counting environmental damage.) Little wonder that a coalition of environmentalists, hunters, antitax activists, true liberals and true conservatives is forming to oppose this and other subsidies.

Hess and Johanna Wald, director of the Land Program at the National Resources Defense Council, propose that:

> First, Congress should put public-land grazing on a market footing: ranchers, not taxpayers, should pay for using federal grass. It should zero a range-budget deficit that amounts to almost $500 million per year on BLM and Forest Service lands (when the costs of planning, resource mitigation and USDA range subsidies are added to the official $70 million grazing shortfall). . . . Second, Congress should bust the cowboy trust on federal lands. All Americans should be free to acquire permits to federal grass and to use the lands to enhance wildlife, stabilize soils, protect endangered species, improve riparian areas. . . . Third, Congress should authorize the secretaries of Interior and Agriculture to engage in an array of range reform experiments that might better protect public lands—such as sustainable land use tailored to the Western rural economy; investing public-land user fees in biological diversity trust funds; and creating non-fee incentives for better land stewardship and effective citizen involvement. . . . Our package will not only tear down fences that divide organizations like ours, but also those that divide East from West and the new West from the old West.

Basically, what we taxpayers are doing is this: we are helping ranchers pay for up to 50 percent of livestock feed so that they can raise a cash (meat) crop that is devastating to both personal and planetary health. So long as we put up with this, each and every one of us is an accomplice in this tragedy. What was intended to be emergency aid to ranchers in periods of natural disasters "has become," observes range-management researcher Jerry Holechek at New Mexico State University, "more of an annual entitlement." The program is poorly monitored and, for the most part, all ranchers have to do to get the public to help them pay for feed is to claim that the growth of grass on their land is 40 percent or more below normal. In view of the fact that some collect as much as $50,000 per year via these subsidies, it should come as no surprise to anyone that this program actually encourages overgrazing, not to mention corruption.

Holechek echoes the sentiments of many when he declares, "I'm convinced that eliminating subsidies would do more for the land and wildlife than anything else that could be done" through changes in government policy. "This program is more destructive of the industry and of wildlife than anything that's out there. The long-term welfare of ranchers will best be served by allowing market forces to function freely."

The same holds true for the fishing industry. It's time to end welfare on the high seas. The United Nations reports that in 1994, the last year for which these data have been calculated, it cost $124 billion to catch fish that were worth only $70 billion in the marketplace. Guess who made up for the $54 billion shortfall—the taxpayers, through subsidies that encourage even more overfishing and destruction of ocean ecology. Between 1970 and 1990, EarthSave reports, "the world's industrial fleet grew at twice the rate of the global catch." This growth was driven entirely by these subsidies. And we continue to swallow this policy hook, line, and *sucker.* How to fix this problem: *Stop eating fish!*

We Can Support Constructive Government Regulations

Even as we end government-mandated subsidies and other support systems for destructive policies, we can support *constructive* government regulations that help protect our health and our environment. *Balance* in government policy, as in most things, is the key. Because some government policies are bad doesn't mean that all government policies are nonproductive.

Recently, I believe, there has been a misconception among some politicians that the public does not want government regulation—in any context—or, at any rate, that is what some politicians would like to believe. Some of these politicians serve interests that would like to see their businesses deregulated—drug companies, meat merchants, pesticide manufacturers, etc.

But public-opinion polls show that Americans not only want regulation of food and drugs, as well as of industries that pollute the environment, but also that they want more thorough and rigorous regulations in these sensitive areas of commerce. Despite this, there are powerful forces lobbying to take away regulations that protect consumers. Those forces must be fought. They must be shown that pollution is actually bad for the very industries that they are trying to protect.

> "Most Americans want to protect the environment. That fact is ignored by 'reform' efforts in Congress and state capitals that would weaken environmental protection. We must strengthen environmental laws and, where possible, make them more flexible."
>
> FRED KRUPP, *Environmental Defense Fund*

After the 1994 congressional elections, there was a movement to weaken environmental protection and the regulation of foods and drugs—and there is still an influential contingent working for that agenda, claiming that these regulations have been costly, ineffective, and unnecessary. Nothing could be farther from the truth.

"Environmental regulations have empowered citizens to protect their own surroundings and have helped create a cleaner environment for millions of Americans," notes Mary Marra, director of the National Wildlife Federation's national office. These same regulations, she observes, have also helped the industries they directly affect. "Regulations have changed economic incentives so that responsible companies are rewarded." These companies become more competitive and thus more profitable.

The Environmental Defense Fund has made similar observations and has acted upon them by working directly with industries to, in Fred Krupp's words, "integrate pollution prevention into core business practices, such as product design, where the most eco-efficiency can be had." EDF is working with General Motors and some other major companies that have begun to see the profits not in pollution but in pollution prevention and the efficiencies thereof.

Vicki Monks, writing in *National Wildlife,* says:

Several recent studies suggest that environmental regulations do not harm the economy and may in fact stimulate economic development. In the Los Angeles area, the "most aggressive air-pollution regulations in history" have not interfered with economic performance. . . . Even the most heavily regulated industries in Los Angeles outperformed their counterparts in regions with looser air-quality rules. The Institute for Southern Studies found similar results in a recent survey: states with the best environmental records had the most productive economies. Conversely, a degraded environment may do considerable harm to businesses.

The World Resources Institute in Washington, D.C., reports that in a study period stretching from 1970 to 1990, those industries in the United States that spent the most on preventing and controlling pollution did significantly better in global competition than those that spent less.

As for what many of these regulations can do for individuals and communities, *books* could be filled with the good news. Thanks to such government policies as those encompassed in the Clean Water Act and the right-to-know laws, for example, millions of Americans are living safer lives today than they were just a decade or so ago.

To cite just one of thousands of examples of the good these regulations have done, consider the Texas Gulf Coast community that was so contaminated by industrial discharges that scientists ultimately demonstrated that if a pregnant woman ate even one fish from those waters, her fetus could suffer serious damage. Had it not been for new government regulations, that community would never have known of the seriousness of this threat until enormous damage had been inflicted.

As things stand now, Alcoa, an aluminum company that was dumping large amounts of toxic methyl mercury into those waters, has entered into a "good neighbor" agreement to try to reduce toxic discharge to zero, in exchange for citizens agreeing to drop lawsuits. Several other major polluters, exposed by these regulations, are taking similar remedial measures.

So, yes, some progress has been made. But there is still much to do. According to a recent study from Harvard University, there are still about sixty thousand people dying every year because of air pollution—and that's just in the United States. Nearly 30 million Americans with chronic respiratory problems are exposed on a regular basis to harmful levels of smog that either contribute to their illnesses or make them worse. The water supplies in thousands of communities throughout the United States are seriously contaminated with dangerous chemicals and bacteria. And we already know that our meat supply, only a tiny fraction of which is ever inspected by government officials, harbors a reservoir of potent hazards.

Who can seriously argue that we need less regulation? Clearly, we need more and better regulations to safeguard our health and our environment.

And let's not forget doing something for our consciences as well. Some seek to trivialize the suffering of farm animals and say that a majority of Americans do not believe that their collective plight is worthy of government regulation and intervention. Again, this is far from the truth. In a random, scientific opinion poll recently conducted by the highly respected Opinion Research Corporation of Princeton, New Jersey, fully 90 percent of adult American respondents voiced their disapproval of the way in which veal, calves, pigs, and laying hens are confined (in filthy spaces so crowded they cannot even turn around to groom themselves). More than 90 percent said they want the United States Department of Agriculture to intervene to make living conditions for these animals better. Only 20 percent were of the opinion that the livestock industry itself could be trusted to alter and improve its current practices.

Perhaps knowing you have a lot of other good people on your side will empower you to speak up, write your congressperson, and otherwise take a more active role in seeking better government protection of the consumer and our environment, including farm animals.

There's much more that can be done. We need to impose "green taxes" on polluters and make sure that people who want to buy energy-inefficient and environmentally costly products pay the full, true costs of those products, with a provision that part of the proceeds go into health care or environmental restoration. Germany and some other countries are already demonstrating that such taxes can be highly effective.

Higher taxes on gasoline in most parts of the world have successfully encouraged better urban planning and public transportation systems, as well as greater use of bicycles and other nonpolluting conveyances. Trash taxes in British Columbia and elsewhere have had dramatic positive impact on recycling and waste management. Taxes on air pollutants in Japan have been used to help the victims of air pollution and curtail further pollution. In Northern Europe, several countries have seen toxic air pollutants diminish dramatically after the imposition of green taxes. In still other areas, tax *deductions* have also served as inducements for industries to clean up their industrial acts, losing the deductions if they fail to meet certain standards.

Others have pointed out that if we would just cut the waste, we could lower taxes across the board and throughout the world. We need to eliminate some $800 billion in global subsidies to activities that degrade the environment and encourage more waste. As David Malin Roodman, writing for the Worldwatch Institute, has observed: "Eliminating the hundreds of billions of dollars of subsidies . . . would allow governments to cut the tax burden on the global economy instantly. . . . In many countries that would do more than any tax or permit change yet to protect the environment."

"A restorative economy is not going to lead to a life of dulling comfort and convenience. We have to recognize that we've reached a watershed in the economy, a point at which 'growth' and profitability will be increasingly derived from the abatement of environmental degradation, the furthering of ecological restoration, and the mimicking of natural systems of production and consumption. Economist Kenneth Boulding described this economy many years ago, one in which an affluent life 'will have to be combined with a curious parsimony . . . every grain of sand will have to be treasured, and the waste and profligacy of our day will seem too horrible that our descendants will hardly be able to bear to think about us."

PAUL HAWKEN, *The Ecology of Commerce*

All right, now let's move on to the meat—or, rather, the *meatless*—of the matter. When it comes to going without meat, I'm going to show you that this is not a state of deprivation but, rather, one of enrichment.

PART THREE

The Garden Plan
Your Personal Program for Optimal Health

*Fresh fruits and vegetables have a medicinal value, and when
wisely prepared and eaten every day will go a long way towards keeping
us strong, vigorous, happy and healthy, which means greater
efficiency and the prolonging of our lives.*

GEORGE WASHINGTON CARVER

Let thy food be thy medicine.

HIPPOCRATES

ardenouisinegardenouisinegardenouisine
ardenouisinegardenouisinegardenouisine
ardenouisinegardenouisinegardenouisine
ardenouisinegardenouisinegardenouisine
ardenouisinegardenouisinegardenouisine
ardenouisinegardenouisinegardenouisine

CHAPTER 8

The Healing Garden

Harvest of Health

Twenty-five years ago, those of us convinced that a diet high in fruits and vegetables and containing little or no animal products could have enormous healing attributes often had to fall back on anecdotal evidence to support our ideas. In my own case, for example, I had no doubt whatsoever that a sudden, "radical" change in diet had resulted in an equally sudden and "radical" change in my health—a change very much for the better. Whenever I would backslide toward my old diet, my old health problems would begin to resurface, and whenever I would make amends, so would my body.

I felt that I had discovered something wonderfully empowering and almost magical. I still feel that way today. And, yet, when I would try to share my enthusiasm over my personal discovery with physicians, the typical response was: "Well, this *may* have something to do with your health, though I doubt it, but you're just one person. Show me long-range studies involving thousands of people and I might be impressed. Meanwhile, I continue to believe, as most of my colleagues do, that animal protein is an important and vital part of our diet. I'm only interested in *scientific* evidence, not *anecdotal* evidence."

The kinds of studies the doctors referred to often cost millions of dollars and involved hundreds of researchers, far beyond anything I could manage. I only wish that, at the time, I had thought to ask these "scientific" skeptics and naysayers where were the long-term studies, involving thousands of people, that established the healthiness of the high-fat, high-animal-protein American diet that prevailed then and, to a lesser extent, still does today. *The fact of the matter is, there weren't any!* But the supposed intrinsic goodness of animal protein was so much a part of our dietary dogma that very few questioned it.

The best I could do was to study every nutritional book and journal I could get my hands on. And I discovered, even three decades ago, that there was, in fact, *some* sound scientific evidence that vegetarians and near-vegetarians were healthier than meat eaters. But somehow, no matter how carefully the studies had been constructed, the forthcoming data had never quite made it into the "mainstream." The prevailing dogma was so strong that anything to the contrary seldom came to the surface.

The next best thing I could do was to teach what I had learned to others and to *listen* to what others, who ate as I did, had to say about their own health. One thing was certain about the anecdotal evidence: there was an awful lot of it. And I saw an abundance of it unfold before my own eyes. Many of the people who enrolled in my earliest food courses were suffering from one ailment or another, and so far had received little help from conventional sources. As the popularity of my courses grew and other colleges asked me to participate in their food curricula, I had the opportunity to see many of my earlier pupils at various later dates in different classes. And so there was continual feedback in many cases, and I could see for myself how well many of these individuals were doing on their new diets.

In the course of several years of teaching, I saw very dramatic healings that closely followed significant dietary change—away from animal products and toward vegetarianism. These involved a broad spectrum of conditions that I saw improve, including acne, psoriasis, and other skin disorders, bleeding and infected gums, asthma and several other respiratory ailments, allergies, infectious diseases and immune disorders, arthritis, osteoporosis, obesity, constipation, hemorrhoids, diverticulosis and various problems of digestion and assimilation of nutrients, chronic fatigue and lack of endurance, moodiness and depression, nervous disorders, high blood pressure, diabetes, heart disease, blood-clotting disorders, some forms of cancer, even hair loss and sexual dysfunction.

I would never claim that every improvement I saw was due to nutritional change; nor do I ever suggest that people should ignore the advice of their doctors. There are many drugs and therapies that are highly beneficial—but I can't think of a single ailment that can't benefit, often dramatically, from optimum nutrition.

In any case, the times are now rapidly changing. The same medical journals that once largely ignored and sometimes openly scorned vegetarianism are now increasingly extolling the virtues of diets that are meatless or meat-reduced. The reason: There are now a growing number of those long-range, scientific studies demonstrating the preventative and healing elements of the kind of diet I and many others have been following for decades.

In this chapter, I will summarize some of the most important findings related to the health benefits of what I call "GardenCuisine." In subsequent chapters of this section of the book, I will introduce you to the goals and guidelines of my own "GardenPlan," which incorporates diet, fasting, exercise, and meditation. And I will show you how you can effectively apply this plan to both weight loss and bodybuilding ("The Lean Green") and utilize it no matter where you go ("Taking the Garden on the Road").

Science Confirms the Amazing Benefits of Vegetarianism

I'm not going to attempt to summarize every study that has now demonstrated the benefits of a vegetarian diet; they are far too numerous. Instead, I will give you a sampling of some of the key findings related to vegetarian (and near-vegetarian) fare and various diseases and disorders.

HEART DISEASE

In a number of long-range studies involving thousands of vegetarians and equal numbers of nonvegetarians, matched for age, gender, smoking status, and so on, dramatic differences in the incidence of heart disease were noted. In one of these studies, involving individuals in the thirty-five–to–sixty-four age range, meat eaters were found to have nearly 30 percent more heart disease. Even greater differences have been found in some other very large studies.

And in a twelve-year study that followed the eating habits of natural-food-store customers, researchers noted a significant overall reduction in mortality from coronary heart disease compared with the general population. But within this subgroup, those who were strictly vegetarian had a coronary heart disease death rate that was 29 percent lower than those health-food patrons who sometimes ate meat.

Not surprisingly, in view of the above, vegetarians are consistently found to have levels of both total cholesterol and LDL cholesterol (the so-called "bad" cholesterol that is strongly implicated in heart disease) that are markedly lower than those found in the general population. LDL levels, in fact, are generally 30 to 40 percent lower!

The longer you continue to eat meat and a lot of dairy products, the greater your risk of heart disease and stroke. Fatty deposits gradually build up in your blood vessels and block blood and oxygen flow to your hearts and brains. Even young children, fed the typical American diet, show early signs of arterial blockage (atherosclerosis), and many teens already have significant blockage.

The good news is that moving toward a plant-based diet can not only help prevent heart disease but can also help *reverse* it. Studies have shown that after as few as six weeks on a vegetarian diet, even long-term carnivores can lower their total cholesterol by 3 to 4 percent and their LDL cholesterol by 11 to 17 percent. Lowering your cholesterol by 3 or 4 percent may not sound like much—but, remember, this was achieved in just six weeks, and medical scientists now agree that for every 1 percent you lower your cholesterol you reduce your risk of heart disease by 2 percent. By persevering on a vegetarian diet, many people lower their cholesterol levels by 20 percent and sometimes more, resulting in a reduced risk of coronary heart disease of *40 percent!*

Dr. William and Sonja Connor, in their highly praised book *The New American Diet,* have reported on experiments in which animals are purposely given very high-cholesterol diets, so that, in fairly short order, their blood levels of cholesterol go up to 700 and their coronary arteries are 60 percent blocked. Then, after thirty-six months on a diet that is very low in cholesterol, the same animals have been shown to have blood cholesterol levels of only 140 and blockage reduced to 20 percent. The Connors are quick to point out that not *all* the damage is undone—but even if you have abused your body for years with a diet high in fat and animal products, you can still achieve significant healing through alteration of your diet.

My friend Dr. Dean Ornish, who has written a superb book called *Dr. Dean Ornish's Program for Reversing Heart Disease* (as well as the equally useful best-selling book *Eat More,*

Weigh Less), has conducted a number of very important scientifically controlled clinical studies showing that even individuals with very severe coronary heart disease can achieve remarkable healing through dietary change, stress management, moderate exercise, and cessation of smoking. Dr. Ornish's largely vegetarian fare derives no more than 10 percent of calories from fat, 15 percent from protein, and 75 percent from complex carbohydrates. This is very close to the diet I have been following for the past thirty years.

Another friend of mine, Dr. John McDougall (author of the best-selling books *The McDougall Plan, The McDougall Program,* and others), also treats his heart patients, with excellent results, through a no-cholesterol, low-fat, high-complex-carbohydrate vegetarian diet. He reports that he is often able to reduce total cholesterol levels in these patients by 25 to 37 percent in six weeks.

It is important to understand that the heart-protective quality of a vegetarian diet does not accrue simply from a reduction in animal fat in the diet. That is a very important factor, but vegetables—and fruits—are rich sources of what scientists call *antioxidants.* These antioxidants include such vitamins as beta carotene, vitamins A, C, and E, but also include a number of other substances found in fruits and vegetables, many of which work synergistically and in ways that we do not fully understand to prevent cellular damage.

With heart disease, vegetable antioxidants are especially important in quelling the "fires" that are set off by toxic oxygen molecules (often called "free radicals"), a by-product of metabolism and exposure to oxidizing substances. Fats and cholesterol particles are particularly vulnerable to free radical attack; and once damaged by free radicals, these particles get deposited in arterial walls as part of the "plaque" that can ultimately block vessels and result in heart attacks, strokes, impotence, etc.

Virtually all fruits, vegetables, grains, beans, and nuts are loaded with antioxidants, and there is now an explosion of research in progress trying to sort out their various antioxidant components, not only in the war against heart disease but also against cancer and many other disorders. Many attempt to get antioxidants through nutritional supplements, and this can be helpful in some cases, but there is no substitute for *whole foods* as a source of antioxidants. There are almost certainly a great many antioxidants we have not yet discovered, and it is clear that they work best together, in the proper combinations—as nature uniquely provided by "packaging" them in whole foods, especially in fruits, vegetables, grains, legumes.

CANCER

When you examine the large number of studies that compare vegetarians with nonvegetarians, the cancer rates among those who avoid animal products are consistently lower—about 40 percent, in many studies. (See part II for more details.) Again, the chief culprits appear to be animal fats, excessive animal protein, and the contaminants that are often found in meat, most of which are oxidants.

There is little doubt that antioxidants and various nutrients found in fruits, vegetables, and grains can help *prevent* many cancers—but there is now also evidence that increased vegetarian fare can also help slow down and even stop cancer progression in some individuals. Antioxidants and other substances in these foods help "mop up" cancer cells as soon as they begin to appear, eradicating them or at least keeping them in control.

Typical of the kind of scientific findings that are being made these days are those that recently revealed that a substance in tomatoes may protect against prostate cancer. This substance is an antioxidant called lycopene, which, among other things, helps impart the red color to tomatoes. In a Harvard Medical School study, involving forty-eight thousand men, a diet high in tomato products (ten servings or more per week) was associated with a 35 percent reduction in the risk of prostate cancer. A lower rate of tomato consumption—four to seven servings per week—still resulted in a 22 percent reduction in risk.

I have previously (see part II) discussed the overwhelming link between high intake of animal fats and breast and prostate cancer—so this provides yet another reason why vegetarian fare has a preventative and healing role in cancer.

If you look at the data on almost *any* cancer, you can find some link to diet. The *American Journal of Epidemiology,* for example, has reported recently that individuals who develop a particularly deadly form of skin cancer called melanoma have significantly lower levels of antioxidants derived from fruits, vegetables, grains.

IMMUNE SYSTEM DISORDERS

Some of today's most exciting dietary research relates to our immune systems. Without strong immune systems, we can't expect to have any significant healing of any disorder. Whether we're talking about cancer, heart disease, infection, or trauma, it takes a fully functioning immune system to restore us to good health.

Animal fats and cholesterol have been shown in numerous recent studies to damage the membranes of our immune cells. In one of these studies, natural killer cells, key soldiers in the body's defensive forces, were found to be far more effective at knocking out cancer cells when human subjects cut their intake of fats in half—going from 40 percent of calories derived from fat to 20 percent. Here is strong evidence that even some cancers can be aborted or otherwise reversed through relatively simple dietary modification.

> "Fat in the foods you eat can harm immunity. White blood cells swim through the blood stream looking for bacteria and cancer cells. They cannot work in an oil slick. For them, a cheeseburger and fries is like the *Exxon Valdez* tanker disaster."
>
> NEAL BARNARD, M.D.

German researchers have compared the immune systems of vegetarians with those of meat eaters by analyzing the relative strength of the immune cells of the two groups in destroying cancer cells. Immune cells from the vegetarians were *two times more effective* in this role than were the same cells from nonvegetarians. Since many of these immune cells decline in number and activity as we age, some medical observers have argued that it is particularly important to eat more fruits and vegetables as you get older. Of course, the sooner one converts to a meatless diet, the better. But findings such as this certainly undermine the complaint I sometimes hear from the elderly, who say, "It's too late for me to change my diet and do any good."

OTHER DISORDERS

I previously have discussed (see part II) a number of other diseases that can be ameliorated or reversed through diet. These include arthritis, osteoporosis, diabetes, gallbladder diseases, obesity, and many others. Nonvegetarians are 40 to 50 percent more likely to be overweight than are vegetarians.

HEALTH-CARE COSTS—VEGETARIANS VS. MEAT EATERS

An additional factor in favor of vegetarianism is health-care costs. Dr. Barnard and his colleagues have reported (*Preventive Medicine*) that, in one long-term study, researchers found that nonvegetarians were hospitalized twice as often as vegetarians. Additionally, the nonvegetarians were using prescription medicines at twice the rate of the vegetarians. It is true that the nonvegetarians were far more likely to be smokers, but this particular population was quite young and thus not likely yet to be significantly impacted by smoking (average age: twenty-six years). Similar results have been found in other studies, some of which have controlled for the smoking factor.

When you consider all the above, it's little wonder that the highly regarded Consumers Union, publisher of *Consumer Reports*, issued this statement in late 1995: "Judging by the ever-growing number of scientific reports confirming the health benefits of a vegetarian diet, it's the devoted meat eaters who look a little out of touch these days."

Consumer Reports on Health, another publication of Consumers Union, noted that vegetarian diets are safe and have numerous health advantages; that because animal protein interferes with the assimilation of calcium into the body, vegetarians may need less of that mineral than do meat eaters; that meat eaters produce higher levels of various stomach acids implicated in colon cancer; and that the amino acid homocysteine, linked to some forms of heart disease, is present in lower quantities in vegetarians than in meat eaters.

The Medical Establishment Embraces Vegetarianism—Finally

After years of ignoring or deploring vegetarian fare, the American medical establishment has finally done a dramatic about-face. In 1993, the American Dietetic Association published a paper that was favorably disposed toward vegetarianism. Still, this wasn't quite the ringing endorsement that was forthcoming from the ADA in late 1995, when it became so enthusiastic about fruits and vegetables that it took out a full-page ad in *Time* magazine to sing the praises of "going vegetarian":

> Choose a vegetarian diet for health or environmental advantages; economic and world hunger concerns; compassion for animals or belief in nonviolence; food preferences or spiritual views. . . . Heart disease, high blood pressure, adult-onset diabetes and some forms of cancer tend to develop less often in vegetarians than in non-vegetarians. Studies also show that vegetarians are at lower risk of osteoporosis, kidney stones, gallstones and breast cancer.

Important and influential as the ADA is, this still didn't quite amount to an *official* endorsement of vegetarianism. But that seems now to be forthcoming. The Dietary

Guidelines Advisory Committee, the scientific panel that recommends the federal government's dietary policies, issued a report, also in late 1995, declaring that vegetarians "enjoy excellent health" and that "vegetarian diets are consistent with the Dietary Guidelines and can meet Recommended Dietary Allowances for nutrients. Protein is not limiting in vegetarian diets."

This is a historic statement. Never before have the government's nutritional panelists even *mentioned* vegetarian diets in their official pronouncements, let alone *endorsed* them. The panel attached no caveats whatever to "lacto-ovo" vegetarianism, that is, to diets that avoid meat but allow dairy and egg products. For "vegans," those who eat no animal products whatever, the committee recommended supplementation with vitamins B_{12} and D and the mineral calcium. (More about this below and in the next chapter.)

The government panel previously had heard exhaustive testimony from numerous medical experts, including Drs. Dean Ornish, Neal Barnard, Benjamin Spock, and William Roberts, who edits the *American Journal of Cardiology.* They said that vegetarian fare can provide all the nutrients we need. They also said that the government's long-standing position that we need meat on a daily basis is not founded in scientific fact and, in reality, is harmful. These medical experts issued a statement, noting that:

> The current recommendation of 2–3 servings of meat every day (or any recommendation for meat consumption) contrasts with the preponderance of scientific evidence showing that meat consumption contributes to several serious illnesses and that those who avoid meats are generally healthier than those who consume them.

The idea that you couldn't get enough protein from vegetarian diets died hard, despite the fact that there is—and has been for some time—overwhelming evidence to the contrary. And, in fact, as you will see when we discuss protein in the following chapter, there is gathering evidence that Americans and most Westerners get far too much protein and protein of the wrong kind from meat consumption.

Then there was the similarly false idea, helped along by the meat industry, that vegetarian diets were "dangerous," not only because they deprived you of supposedly "vital" animal protein, but also because they would leave you with vitamin B_{12}, vitamin D, and calcium deficiencies. There is no such risk whatever for lacto-ovo vegetarians, and numerous studies of vegan diets, in both adults and children, have shown that the risks are small even in these groups, provided a wide range of foods is consumed. Nonetheless, vitamin B$_{12}$ supplementation is highly recommended for strict vegans, especially for vegan children. Again, see the following chapter for more discussion on these issues.

The Vegetarian Wave—Have You Caught It Yet?

The thing to remember about vegetarianism is that it needn't be an "all-or-nothing" proposition. For some, the most effective approach is to change in one fell swoop. But for others, a more gradual approach works best. Being even "a little bit vegetarian" is better than not being vegetarian at all. Every time you choose to avoid meat, you help your health *and* the health of the planet.

There is a vegetarian wave and it is cresting higher all the time. By 1992, there were 12.5 million full-time vegetarians in the United States—double the number in 1985, according to the research firm of Yankelovich Clancy Shulman. It is estimated that at least 1 million Americans are converting to vegetarianism annually. Far more are converting to part-time vegetarianism, that is, reducing their meat consumption and eating more vegetables and fruit.

Here are some other key findings related to the "wave":

• A 1991 Gallup Poll found that 20 percent of Americans regularly seek out restaurants that serve vegetarian entrées. The Gallup organization also found that 88 percent of those who avoid meat do so for health reasons.

• "Demand for vegetarian products is growing among people in their early 20s, who consider vegetarianism a hip way to eat, and seniors, who want to cut their fat intake for health reasons. A growing contingent of African-American consumers, who are more likely to be lactose intolerant than the general population, also accounts for some of the growth" (*Vegetarian Times*).

• "College campuses are hotbeds of veggie eaters. Cornell University's director of dining services, Peg Lacey, says one of four hot entrees at every campus meal is vegetarian" (*The Wall Street Journal*).

• Retail sales in products that provide alternatives to meat and dairy products have enjoyed double-digit growth every year since 1990—with a 500 percent jump in growth over ten years projected (Packaged Facts, a New York research firm).

Recent surveys conducted by the Grocery Manufacturers of America, HealthFocus, and others, show that:

- Up to 80 percent of Americans have now tried meatless burgers.

- Forty-six percent of Americans now agree that it is not necessary to include meat in their daily diets, and 60 million Americans are reducing their red-meat intake.

- Some 60 percent of Americans are increasing their purchase of vegetables and more than 40 percent are buying more grain products.

- Sales of organic foods have doubled since 1990, to currently more than $2 billion per year.

- Natural-food products are growing in double digits each year, to more than $6 billion annually at this time.

- Women are twice as likely as men to be vegetarian.

- Forty percent of Americans now put nutritional value ahead of price and taste in making food choices.

- Thirty-six percent of all Americans say they would purchase meatless entrées, if available, when eating out.

- Seventy-five percent of all Americans now say they refuse to buy from certain companies for two primary reasons: poor service and/or business practices that are perceived to be unethical or harmful. Right after "safety," Americans say they want products that do not pollute air and water. Seven of fifteen Americans say they have judged companies and their products by the way they relate to environmental issues (Walker Research).

So how about it? Are you riding the good-health wave yet? Proceed to the next chapter and I'll help you get your feet wet.

CHAPTER 9

The GardenPlan for Optimal Health

A Wide Variety of Whole Fresh Foods

After thirty years of studying diet and nutrition, I've come to the conclusion that variety and whole foods are two concepts that are of paramount importance in designing a diet for optimal health and weight.

My GardenPlan frees you from counting calories (unless you're trying to lose weight, and you will still be able to eat until you're full), grams of fat, and milligrams of cholesterol. If you follow the GardenPlan, you can eat as much as you want without fear of either caloric or fat overload. And you will be getting the most nutritious cuisine anyone has ever created—because you start out with the culinary creations of the ultimate chef, Mother Nature. Whole foods are the products of millions of years of evolutionary fine-tuning; they are literal "symphonies" of nutrients, compositions so complex and integrally synergistic that we have only begun to understand how they interrelate with one another. They are little universes of undiscovered nutrients, all working together to create healthy plants, which, in turn, become the healthiest foods we know.

We are beginning to divine the often miraculous "ingredients" of these foods—including disease-fighting and disease-preventing antioxidants—but it would be naïve to assume that we have discovered all or even most of them. And it is presumptuous—and often dangerous—for us to assume that we can "improve" these foods by breaking them down, throwing out certain parts, and, in general, refining them to mere ghosts of their original, natural selves. But that, alas, is what we too often do, depriving ourselves of nature's ultimate gifts.

If you consistently eat several servings a day of whole foods, selected from a variety of GardenGroups that I will define shortly, you will be getting the best possible diet that anyone can provide. It is also the diet that is most likely to enable you to lose weight and *keep the weight off permanently.* (I'll have more to say about weight loss in a subsequent chapter.)

In this chapter, I will provide you with the best and latest information on both *macro-* and *micro*nutrition. Macronutrition relates to fat, protein, carbohydrate, fiber. Micronutrition deals with vitamins, minerals, and other "hidden" or undiscovered components in food that contribute to health. You will discover that the stars of GardenCuisine are a variety of natural foods that even science has labeled "superfoods."

GardenCuisine is the key to purifying and healing your body, your mind, and your spirit. To help things along, I also offer an optional program of gradual, gentle fasting that clears the body and the mind.

Finally, I conclude the GardenPlan with a program of simple exercise, breathing, and meditation for aerobic health and mental fitness. As with diet itself, I try to get down to the real basics. A good exercise program, like a good diet, should be simple to grasp, easy to adapt to, and, above all else, immediately rewarding. (We will explore fasting, exercise, and meditation in the following chapter.)

So let's begin by both learning and *unlearning* a few crucial things about nutrition.

The BIG Picture: Macronutrition

FATS

Think of how many books, articles, and television reports have been devoted to fats and cholesterol in the past decade. The verbiage, like the fat itself, is staggering. It would seem that, by now, everybody should know that people in the developed world consume far too much fat and cholesterol and that this is very detrimental to health and weight control. And, to some extent, the message has begun to sink in. Heart attack rates are going down in the United States as moderation in consumption of fat begins to pay off.

Still, it's clear from the fact that fat-promoting diets can climb onto the best-seller lists that people are still willing to let themselves be deluded in order to justify self-destructive diets.

The situation with fat is somewhat analogous to the one that prevailed for so long with cigarette smoking. The evidence was overwhelming that smoking was a killer long before the surgeon general succeeded in placing a warning to that effect on the pack of cigarettes itself. For years, those with vested interests in smoking kept insisting, "We need further study before we can say anything definitive." This same self-serving approach continues to be used by those with vested interests in the meat and dairy industries—and by those authors who know how to make a quick buck by trying to reassure the public that "fat is okay."

The evidence that fat *isn't* okay is indisputable. Yes, some fats are worse than others—but *all* fats, beyond very small quantities, are harmful. People who substitute olive oil, for example, for saturated animal fats and then consume large quantities of it in the sadly mistaken belief that this is "healthy" are seriously deluding themselves. Even those few fats that don't directly contribute to heart disease *do* contribute to weight gain and obesity. *All added fats are bad except when used in extreme moderation.* Remember, nature has included just the right amount of fat in fruits, vegetables, grains, and legumes.

The only real question is: How low should we go? The typical Westerner gets about 40 percent of calories from fat—and the evidence is clear that this produces significant disease and millions of premature deaths annually. The American Heart Association and several other organizations have recommended a diet of no more than 30 percent fat, but a great many leading heart and cancer doctors believe this is still too high. In fact, science has now determined that our bodies require only 4 to 8 percent of calories in the form of fat.

The GardenPlan delivers cuisine that reduces fat intake to under 15 percent—and only a little bit of this is from dairy fat. Moreover, this reduction is achieved without requiring that you cut down on your food portions to the point where you feel deprived. If you are on a typical meat- and dairy-dominated diet, in order to cut caloric intake of fat to 15 percent or lower, you would have to eat such small portions of your normal fare that you would feel as if you were starving. And this is precisely why so many ordinary diets fail. On the GardenPlan, you can eat to your heart's content—and to its health. And with the culinary "tricks" I have learned from nature, GardenCuisine will make your palate forget it's "missing" the fats.

Similarly, cholesterol is another thing you won't have to worry about if you follow the GardenPlan. I invite you to have your cholesterol levels measured before you start the GardenPlan and then again six months or a year after you have embraced GardenCuisine. You'll be thrilled by the results, though I predict you won't need these tests to tell you how much better you will be feeling and how much better you will be functioning.

Here's another dietary component about which mythology has overtaken fact. In general, Westerners have long bought into the idea that there's no such thing as "too much protein." This, of course, naturally follows from those who want to justify a diet glutted with meat and dairy products. Certainly, we need protein—it's vital for all growth and for bodily maintenance—but fruits, vegetables, and grains are rich sources of high-quality protein and, in any event, the best evidence now tells us that we don't need nearly as much protein as we have long been led to believe. In fact, excessive protein can produce serious health problems.

The first thing you need to know is that the scientific community has, as discussed earlier, given its official blessing to vegetarianism and has declared that a broad selection of vegetarian foods can provide more than adequate protein. The old myth that you couldn't get the proper "complement" of proteins from a vegetarian diet finally has been laid to rest.

Now the medical establishment is going farther and is beginning to admit that the typical Western diet most likely includes *too much protein.* Here's a quote from a recent issue of the University of California, Berkeley, *Wellness Letter,* reflective of mainstream nutritional science:

> Many of us grew up thinking only good things about protein. Indeed, we can't live without it. But the trouble may be too much of a good thing. Indeed, some researchers have linked a high intake of animal protein to heart disease and other chronic disorders . . . and some cancers (such as colon and prostate) . . . osteoporosis and kidney damage . . . In carefully controlled studies, animals fed large amounts of isolated animal protein develop higher levels of blood cholesterol (especially LDL, the "bad" kind) than those fed vegetable protein. This suggests something about the composition of animal protein boosts cholesterol.

To give you just one example of how excess animal protein is believed to inflict serious damage, let's look at the protein-osteoporosis link. There is increasingly strong evidence that the more protein you consume, the more calcium you lose through excretion in urine. With high calcium loads, this effect can be so pronounced that it results in thinning of bone—osteoporosis. The milk industry, of course, doesn't like this and continues to tout the calcium- and bone-*building* quality of milk and other dairy products. In fact, the evidence points the other way, especially when the intake of these foods is high. This is one reason we treat dairy products as condiments (sparingly used here and there) in the GardenPlan.

The most recent support for the calcium-osteoporosis link was a long-term (twelve-year) study at Harvard involving eighty-six thousand nurses. There were significantly more bone fractures among the women who consumed the highest quantities of animal protein than among those who consumed lesser amounts. Protein from red meat was found to have the highest association with fractures.

Nutritional experts at Berkeley—and throughout the country—have confirmed that vegetarians who eat a wide variety of foods get more than ample protein, and don't need to carefully mix their plant proteins in order to insure that they are getting the right combination or "complement" of proteins. Even weight lifters and endurance athletes, these scientists confirm, can get adequate protein from vegetarian fare. Loading up with protein supplements is unnecessary and perhaps harmful.

Protein supplements or isolated amino acids won't stimulate muscle growth—only exercise, specifically strength training (such as weight lifting), does. "Excess protein is simply broken down in the body and burned for energy or turned into fat," states the *UC Berkeley Wellness Letter.* You heard it right: *Excess protein is often converted to fat!*

The current U.S. Department of Agriculture Recommended Dietary Allowance for protein is now calculated to be only about 8 percent of total caloric intake. We need a little more as we get older. Americans currently get about 20 percent of their calories from protein. This considerably exceeds the government's RDA, but this would not be unhealthy in and of itself if more of the protein came from plant sources. The GardenPlan delivers about 13 to 15 percent protein, most of it from plant foods.

To give you an idea of how easy it is to overload on animal protein, consider the following. A 175-pound man needs sixty-four grams of protein a day to meet the RDA. A one-pound steak—the sort of steak on the menu in many restaurants—delivers a whopping one hundred grams of protein by itself. Add protein from other sources, and it's easy to see how many people in the developed world get a couple of hundred grams, or more, of protein per day—definitely a significant health hazard, especially when you factor in all the fats that typically are associated with animal protein.

CARBOHYDRATES

Things have become very interesting these days with regard to carbohydrates. To listen to the authors of several recent best-selling books, carbohydrate intake among Americans has soared to "dangerous" levels; indeed, some of them treat carbohydrates on a par with "poisons" and counsel their readers on how to sharply restrict these dreaded substances.

Before we deal with this notion that carbohydrates are bad for you, let's look at the evidence to the contrary, which, by contrast, is both overwhelming and overwhelmingly supported by the best scientific evidence. It was Bill and Sonja Connor, mentioned earlier in this book, who pioneered the low-fat, high-complex-carbohydrate diet. Decades ago, the Connors studied peoples from all over the world, actually living, for example, with the Tarahumara Indians in the Sierra Madre Occidental Mountains of Mexico. The Tarahumaras eat a diet exceptionally high in unrefined carbohydrates and exhibit some of the most remarkable physical endurance ever seen.

These hardy people are noted for their remarkable abilities as long-distance runners. Many of them run races of two hundred miles, yet the Connors found they derive only 12 percent of their calories from fat and almost all of the rest of their calories from complex-carbohydrate-rich plant foods such as beans and corn (which also deliver ample protein). The Tarahumaras, incidentally, have cholesterol levels of about 125 milligrams per 100 milliliters of blood, whereas the typical American adult has a cholesterol level of 200 or more. Heart disease among the Tarahumaras is virtually unknown.

The best sources of complex carbohydrates are the whole foods recommended in the GardenPlan: fruits, vegetables, whole grains, beans and other legumes. About 70 percent of calories derive from complex carbohydrates in the GardenPlan. Many Americans get only about 40 percent of their calories from carbohydrates—and often from refined carbohydrates such as white-flour products. Refined foods are stripped of many of their most important nutrient components and quickly can become "empty calories," as is the case with refined sugar.

Some recent diet books claim nearly the opposite, saying that high-fat, high-protein diets are desirable. The *Tufts University Diet and Nutrition Letter,* which emanates from an institution noted for having one of the world's leading academic nutritional programs, has been highly critical of the high-protein diets and the books that promote them. In its May 1996 issue, the publication reiterated the need for Americans to embrace a high-complex-carbohydrate diet. It points to one population after another that has benefited from such diets, including the Japanese, whose primary staple is carbohydrate-rich rice (and who live on the average several years longer than Americans) and the Seventh-Day Adventists, vegetarians who "suffer heart disease and other life-threatening chronic illnesses at a lower rate than most Americans, as well."

FIBER

You won't have to worry about getting enough fiber on the GardenPlan. Most Americans consume far too little dietary fiber, a particular category of largely indigestible carbohydrates. Fiber is present only in plant foods, such as whole grains, fruits, and vegetables. Fiber, though not digested, is vital to good health. Fiber components act like internal cleansers, helping to speed the passage of wastes through the body and, in the process, helping to prevent certain cancers, constipation, diverticulosis, and other disorders. Because fiber provides "bulk" to the diet, it makes us feel "full" and thus helps prevent overeating and weight gain. There is also evidence that some forms of dietary fiber help reduce cholesterol levels in our blood.

Americans often eat only fifteen or twenty grams of fiber a day. On the GardenPlan, you'll easily increase that to sixty grams or more—and this is precisely what many dietary experts have defined as "optimal." This isn't difficult to achieve once you switch to whole foods. While it takes nearly seven slices of white bread to deliver five grams of fiber, you get that same amount in just two slices of whole-wheat bread. A single bowl of whole-grain cereal will give you another five grams, as will just one-third of a cup of beans.

One of the benefits of following the GardenPlan is that it helps ensure a steady intake of fiber throughout the day—not all at one meal. Fiber works best when it is present in the system on a continual basis—and when you have sufficient water to make full use of it. If you eat a heavy load of fiber without ample water to help activate and disperse it, you will not get the full benefits.

SUGAR

Sugar is another form of carbohydrate. As always, I strongly recommend getting sugar, to the extent that you use it at all, in its whole- or nearly whole-food form. In fact, I recommend sugar in only four forms: pure maple syrup, Sucanat, molasses, and fruit juice concentrates. Sucanat is granulated sugarcane juice and is about as close to a whole sugar food as you can get. You can use Sucanat wherever white sugar is called for—but in sharply reduced amounts. (Remember, sugar is a source of highly concentrated calories.) It may astonish you to learn that Americans get 20 percent of their total calories from refined sugars—much of it concealed in soft drinks and packaged foods, all of which are eliminated under the GardenPlan. Refined sugars are everywhere—and often in foods you wouldn't even suspect. Some salad dressings, for example, are 30 percent sugar, "frosted" cereals are up to 80 percent pure sugar, and so on. On the GardenPlan, you will cut back dramatically on your sugar consumption.

CAFFEINE, ALCOHOL, SALT

I believe that most people will benefit by avoiding caffeine entirely. If you continue to drink caffeinated beverages, try to restrict them to three cups or glasses or fewer per day, and try substituting black or green tea for coffee and colas.

As for alcohol, if you must consume it, go for a good wine or microbrew and limit yourself to no more than three average servings *per week*. That means no more than a maximum of three regular-size bottles of beer per week or three small glasses of wine. There is some evidence that very moderate alcohol consumption, in the amounts specified above, can have some health benefits. But more is definitely not better.

When it comes to salt, the situation is rather like that of sugar. In general, we get far too much salt, and much of it comes hidden in packaged foods. The best solution is to gradually stop adding salt at the table and cut down on the amounts you add to your recipes. Salt, fortunately, is a fairly easy habit to kick. After a few weeks of moderation, you'll begin to notice how unpleasantly salty many prepared foods are—but, by then, you won't be eating those prepared foods, anyway. You'll be on the GardenPlan, where salt is held in check without sacrificing flavor. The higher volume of food consumed in the GardenPlan, along with the plan's scrupulous attention to water intake, helps handle any excess salt.

Micronutrition: Do You Need Supplements?

Most mainstream nutritional experts have long told the public that it doesn't need vitamin/mineral micronutrient supplements, that "you get everything you need in your food." Well, given the way most Americans eat, I can't agree with that. When you add in cigarette smoking and/or polluted air, polluted water, contaminated food, and the general stress of today's way of living, most people need supplementation.

On the other hand, there is no question that the *best* way to get your micronutrients *is* through diet, because nature has combined these nutrients in ways that we are only now vaguely beginning to understand. When we combine micronutrients in vitamin/mineral tablets, we are only guessing at what is optimal and we are almost certainly leaving out many nutrients we have not even discovered yet. We are also guessing about the best quantities and combinations. There is some evidence that if we guess wrong, we may actually do more harm than good sometimes.

Fortunately, the GardenPlan utilizes *whole foods* the way nature made them. By eating a broad selection of these whole foods, you maximize your chances of getting all the micronutrients you need and in just the right combinations. So I do *not* believe that if you follow the GardenPlan, you will need supplements. I don't object to them, though, provided you don't use them as an excuse to deviate significantly from the GardenPlan.

And, in some cases, supplementation is in order. Those who are under unusual environmental stress, perhaps in their workplaces, those who are elderly, those who have had surgery recently or have some chronic illness, those who smoke, may benefit from regular supplementation. In this case, I recommend a well-balanced "insurance" formula, preferably one derived from whole foods. Yes, there are such products on the market. Ask for them. One of the best sources of information about sensible vitamin/mineral supplementation, based on the soundest scientific evidence, is *The Doctors' Vitamin and Mineral Encyclopedia,* by Sheldon Saul Hendler, M.D., Ph.D. (Fireside Books).

As for vegans—those who avoid all animal products—the evidence is mixed on the need for supplementation. Provided they eat a wide variety of plant foods, even vegans probably don't have to take supplements, but, to be on the safe side, I join most others in recommending a supplement that includes calcium, vitamin D, and vitamin B_{12}.

B_{12} supplementation is of particular importance in vegan children. Contrary to some claims, soy products are *not* rich in B_{12}, so don't try to use soy as a source of this vitamin. The same is true of some of the sea vegetables that have previously been touted as good sources of B_{12}. There are some B_{12} analogues in sea vegetables, but they don't do the same job. A supplement of even 5 micrograms of B_{12} a day is adequate—and up to 50 micrograms daily is entirely safe.

Again, lacto-ovo vegetarians get completely adequate amounts of B_{12} from even relatively small daily amounts of eggs or dairy products.

The calcium issue is a bit more complicated, as previously discussed. People on high-animal-protein diets—that's not the GardenPlan—need more calcium, as do those who use a lot of aluminum-based antacids. Alcoholics also often have calcium deficiencies. Most people need about 800 to 1,200 milligrams of calcium daily. The richest sources of calcium are dairy products, but many vegetables also contain significant amounts of calcium, and thus even vegans can get adequate calcium in their diets if they carefully select a high volume of whole foods. (If they don't, they should supplement.)

A glass of milk contains 300 milligrams of calcium, a cup of yogurt 415 milligrams. And note that calcium is not related to the fat content of dairy products; skim milk delivers just as much calcium as an equivalent amount of cream. By comparison, two cups of cooked broccoli deliver 356 milligrams—still quite a lot. An orange will give you 50 milligrams, half a cup of cooked soybeans provides 90 milligrams, one cup of cooked collards contains 360 milligrams, a couple of slices of whole-wheat bread give you another 45 milligrams, and several whole-grain cereals and many commercial orange juices, as well as some tofu products, come fortified with extra calcium (frequently in the 100- to 350-milligram-per-serving range). Check labels.

The GardenGroups

These are the food groups from which you will select your daily fare. With the exception of the "condiments," about equal weight should be given to each group. You don't have to keep track of daily servings from each group, but if you begin to notice, for example, that you are consuming far more fruits than vegetables, make a correction. Things don't have to balance out on a daily basis, but you should achieve a rough balance over longer time periods, such as weekly.

FRUITS

All edible fruits, including dried fruits. Fresh juices are not the whole fruit but can still serve important functions; they should not, however, serve as a substitute for whole fruits. Dried fruits I like include apples, apricots, cranberries, dates, figs, peaches, pears, prunes, golden raisins, mangoes, papayas, and pineapples.

VEGETABLES

All edible vegetables. I recommend that you get your vegetables from each of three primary groups: vegetable greens (such as celery, cabbage, kale), vegetable roots (such as beets, carrots, yams), and vegetable flowers (such as artichokes and broccoli). See the Shopping List (chapter 13) for a list of vegetables in each of these three categories. Again, it is important that you try to select from each category daily, and that you achieve a balance over the course of the week.

LEGUMES

All edible beans, green beans, peas, other legumes. See Shopping List.

GRAINS/CEREALS

All edible whole grains and cereals, including whole-grain breads, muffins, bagels, tortillas, whole-grain pastas, hot and cold cereals, made with no egg yolks, and with no (or only very small quantities of) nuts and seeds added and with no added oil, or only minute quantities. Avoid any prepared food that delivers more than 3 grams of total fat per serving or more than 5 grams of added sugar per serving.

CONDIMENTS

Condiments are those things you add to foods to give them a little extra flavor or texture. With the exception of spices, which you can use freely, condiments are to be used in strict moderation. I include in condiments all fats and oils, nuts and seeds (which are themselves very high in fat). You should add no more than one to two teaspoons of oil to your foods per day. The four oils I recommend are flaxseed oil, canola oil, olive oil, and toasted sesame oil. Include peanut butter, tahini, and the other nut butters in this category. All other fat-containing foods, including cheeses, should be limited to two to three level tablespoons per day. Egg whites, skim milk, and other nonfat dairy products can be used on a very limited basis, never as a substitute for selections from the other GardenGroups, from which most of your calories should derive. The same is true of nonfat sweets.

WATER

That's right. I put water in its own GardenGroup. Water, along with air, is the most important "nutrient" we consume. I emphasize this because water is so often overlooked and underconsumed. Most of us, in fact, don't get water that is optimal either in quantity or quality. It is vital that you get eight to ten glasses of pure water (distilled and/or filtered) a day. GardenCuisine, with its high fiber content, works best with lots of water. But, in any event, we all need this amount of water to keep our metabolism optimal and to cleanse our systems regularly. Start out each day with a glass of water and end each day with a glass of water. And distribute the rest of your intake as evenly as possible, so that you're never "running on empty."

Now let's look at these GardenGroups in a little more detail.

The Super Fruits

When the Center for Science in the Public Interest rated some of nature's—and my—favorite foods, the fruits, for their micronutrient and fiber content, which, do you suppose, topped the list? *Papaya!* And papaya, plentiful in Hawaii, where I live part of each year, just happens to be one of my favorites. Other high ratings went to cantaloupe, strawberries, oranges, tangerines, kiwis, mangoes, apricots, persimmons, watermelon, raspberries, grapefruit, and blackberries.

It's interesting to see what happens when you look at fresh fruits versus canned fruits. The nutrients in fresh pears rate a "48," while canned pears drop to a "16." Fresh peaches go from a "77" down to a "43." So fresh is always better—but even canned fruits, if fresh aren't available or practical, are better than no fruit at all. Frozen is the second-best choice after fresh.

Most fruits have a lot of fiber and significant quantities of various vitamins, especially vitamin A and vitamin C, both of which have important antioxidant and other health-promoting properties.

When it comes to fruits and vegetables, it pays to use all of nature's palette in painting your personal culinary landscape. Those brilliant colors are imparted by chemical components that are, in themselves, disease fighters and preventers. We're only now beginning to learn just how helpful these vegetables and fruit "phytochemicals" are, but the news just keeps getting better. So don't be shy about mixing those colors, to ensure that you're getting a sampling of all nature has to offer. (More on this below.)

A few words about fruit juices. I love them, but, remember, they are extracts of fruits and not the whole food. They can provide concentrated forms of various nutrients and can be used therapeutically. This is a big subject in itself. For those interested in using juices to cleanse themselves and to address specific ailments, I highly recommend *The Juiceman's Power of Juicing,* the best-selling "bible" on this topic by my friend Jay Kordich.

The Vegetable Kings

And how do the vegetables stack up? Again, the vegetables (and some fruits that are commonly considered vegetables, such as tomatoes) were rated for fiber and micronutrient content by the Center for Science in the Public Interest. Many vegetables are rich sources of minerals and vitamins. And how sweet it is for the sweet potato, which comes in at the head of the GardenClass, followed by those stalwart standbys carrots and spinach. Then: collard greens, raw red peppers, kale, dandelion greens, broccoli, Brussels sprouts, potatoes, winter squash, Swiss chard, snow peas, mustard greens, kohlrabi, romaine lettuce, cauliflower, asparagus. Others rank lower but are still valuable sources of fiber and nutrients. Iceberg leaf lettuce, by the way, gets only about one-third the score that romaine lettuce gets.

Again, try to get a mixture of vegetables by the different colors. There are different protective substances in the red, yellow, orange, and green vegetables. The blue/purple ones also have some unique beneficial properties. Here are a few examples of the protective elements in these plant foods: Substances in beets have been shown to have antibacterial and anticancer properties; substances in both beets and broccoli may help protect against radiation damage; some components of the blue/purple fruits and vegetables (for example, eggplant) may help lower the risk of heart disease and stroke; substances in many of the green-pigmented vegetables fight cancer; the antioxidant that gives corn its yellow color helps prevent macular degeneration, the leading cause of blindness as we age; many of the orange pigments appear to protect against some forms of cancer and heart disease. The red pigment of tomatoes and watermelons, among other plant foods, may be one of the most powerful antioxidants ever discovered; preliminary studies indicate that those who consume a lot of these foods have far less colon, stomach, bladder, and prostate cancers.

The Bean Barons

When the CSPI rated legumes, all of which it calls "nutritional powerhouses," these were the types that packed the most punch: Soybeans topped the list, followed closely by pinto beans, chickpeas (also called garbanzos and ceci), lentils, cranberry beans, black-eyed peas (cowpeas), pink beans, navy beans, black beans (turtle beans), white beans, baby lima beans. Most other categories were similar. It's hard to go wrong with a bean or a pea—so indulge freely and, again, mix them up to get maximum benefits.

Grain/Cereal Grandees

The top-ten grains, rated for their nutritional content, are, in order: quinoa, amaranth, bulgur, pearl barley, wild rice, millet, brown rice, triticale, and wheat berries. Other high-ranking grain foods include whole-wheat macaroni and whole-wheat spaghetti. Instant white rice, by the way, has a nutritional score that is only about one-third that of wild rice and less than half of brown rice.

As for cereals, the CSPI gives its "Best Bites" award only to those packaged cereals that list as their *first* ingredient (always check labels) a whole grain or bran. Each serving of a "Best Bite" can contain no more than 3 grams of fat, nor more than 350 milligrams of sodium, no more than 5 grams of added sugar, and each serving must deliver at least 2.5 grams of fiber. Here are some of the "Best Bites": Kellogg's All-Bran, Nabisco Shredded Wheat 'N Bran, Health Valley 100% Natural Bran with Apples and Cinnamon, U.S. Mills Skinner's Raisin Bran, Erewhon Wheat Flakes, Golden Temple Low Fat Muesli, Post Bran Flakes, New Morning Raisin Bran, Health Valley Fat-Free Granola, Erewhon Raisin Bran, Nabisco Shredded Wheat, New Morning Bran Flakes, LifeStream Fruit and Nut Müesli, Health Valley Real Oat Bran, Barbara's High 5, Post Grape-Nuts, Familia No Added Sugar Swiss Müesli, Erewhon Fruit 'N Wheat. For those of you who love Kellogg's Frosted Flakes, you're getting zero grams of fiber and 13 grams of sugar per serving, compared with 11 grams of fiber and 5 grams of sugar in Kellogg's All-Bran. Frosted Flakes and similar cereals do not rate "Best Bites" status.

The Fats of Life: Making Wise Choices

I don't delude myself that everyone is going to follow GardenCuisine to the pea and cucumber. But any movement away from a high-fat, animal-food diet toward GardenCuisine is going to promote better health, both for you and the planet. So you don't have to feel you have "failed" if you backslide from time to time and indulge in occasional high-fat foods or snacks.

As you make the gradual transition toward a vegetarian diet, it might help you to know that not all fats are alike. As I've said, all are bad in excess—and it doesn't take much to achieve "excess"—but some are definitely worse than others. Many people find it effective to begin not by cutting out all fats, but by substituting lower-fat choices for higher-fat selections.

If you continue to drink milk, for example, be aware that what is advertised on the milk carton as "low fat" may not be that. Many, for example, believe that they are getting almost no fat when they drink "2 percent milk fat." Milk is mostly water, so that 2 percent (which is by weight) is highly misleading. Still, 2 percent is better than the 3.5 percent milk fat found in whole milk, which translates to a caloric content that is 50 percent fat! If you must drink milk, work your way down to 1 percent or, better yet, skim milk. (Or try an unfiltered apple juice on cereal.) The same holds true for yogurt and ice-cream products. There are many delicious, rich-tasting nonfat yogurts and ice creams. Frozen sorbets are also generally fat-free.

There is a variety of tasty nondairy frozen desserts on the market, as well as some nondairy ice creams and many nondairy milk drinks. Try some of the soy and rice milks or almond milk. At least one of these is likely to be to your taste. They are also good on cereals.

You should eliminate all egg yolks from your diet, period. They are cholesterol bullets. Egg whites, by contrast, have no fat. There are also a number of commercial egg substitutes available in most supermarkets that have very little fat. Avoid both butter and margarine. Margarines typically contain trans-fatty acids, which are not heart-friendly.

Regular mayonnaise and Miracle Whip are both an artery-choking *two thirds pure fat!* If you are addicted to these, check out some of the nonfat versions. You'll be surprised at how much they taste like "the real thing." Peanut butter, though it contains no cholesterol, is still about 50 percent fat—just like most nuts and seeds. So use peanut butter, nuts, and seeds only as condiments, in tiny quantities—and infrequently.

As far as packaged crackers, snacks, and so forth go, just stick to the rule—no more than 3 grams of fat per serving. And stick to the whole-grain variety. Don't eat more than a couple of servings of these products each day. Avoid snacks that have any cholesterol. Anytime you put a cracker or other snack on a paper towel and it leaves even the slightest greasy imprint, you can be sure the food is too high in fat for good health. Similarly, I often tell people that when they wash a plate, if room-temperature water won't clear everything off it, your food has too much fat.

Finally, we come to cheese and salad dressings. First of all, I advise you to make your own salad dressings. You'll find recipes for several in this book. And when it comes to cheeses, there are definitely some choices that are better than others.

I use cheese in a few of my recipes, but in very small amounts. Treat cheese as a condiment rather than as a main ingredient. Be aware that there are now many nondairy cheeses that contain no cholesterol. Also be aware, however, that the casein that is included in a lot of so-called "nondairy" cheeses is, in fact, derived from dairy products. For a complete list of the cheeses I use in my recipes, see Dairy/Dairy Substitutes on the Shopping List.

As for commercial salad dressings, mayonnaise has a lot of cholesterol and saturated fat, as do the Roquefort and blue cheese dressings. Thousand Island and Russian dressings are way up there as well, as are dressings made with Miracle Whip, including even Light Miracle Whip. Ranch with buttermilk and mayonnaise is in the cholesterol/saturated fat midrange, as is French. Lower yet is ranch with buttermilk and imitation mayonnaise or low-fat yogurt. Lemon juice and vinegar have neither cholesterol nor fat. (Check out my nonfat dressings in the recipe section.)

"The Whiter the Bread, the Sooner You're Dead"

I don't know who first said that about bread, but it's one of my favorite quotations. It summarizes the need to stick to *whole* foods. Make sure your whole foods are fresh foods whenever possible—and eat a wide variety of these mostly plant foods. That's the key. The rest of dietary advice is just fine-tuning.

Remember, when you eat foods like this, you're eating them the way nature designed them, each in the proper proportion of both macro- and micronutrients. Every time we try to make a natural whole food better through one form or another of "refinement," we fail miserably; we manage only to concoct foods that are richer in price and poorer in substance.

CHAPTER 10

The GardenFast, Exercise, and Meditation

The Miracle of Fasting

For me, Paul Bragg's book *The Miracle of Fasting* really did help produce a miraculous turnaround in my health. Most of the evidence for fasting, I readily admit, is anecdotal. But the anecdotal evidence is voluminous and highly positive.

Fasting is an optional part of the GardenPlan. I don't think fasting is for everyone, but I do believe that it can benefit a majority of us. Before beginning any program of fasting, consult your physician. Some people, such as diabetics, should not fast. Other conditions may require medical monitoring. Most people, however, will find brief fasts helpful.

Fasting is like housecleaning—inside the body and the mind. Fasting gives your body a rest and allows for the expulsion of toxins that have built up over a period of time. Fasting is not a new or radical concept; it is as old as mankind. Of course, some of our distant ancestors were sometimes forced to fast from lack of a ready food supply, but others, recalling stories of the beneficial side effects of forced fasting, undertook this activity voluntarily. Fasters often comment on the clarity with which they see (both inward and outward) after going without food. The quest for clarification and purification has kept people fasting for aeons.

The ancient Greek scholars and warriors, as well as the Biblical patriarchs, advocated and practiced fasting. In more recent times, various spiritual and health-oriented groups around the world have similarly fasted. The practice, obviously, gets good "word of mouth" to persist for so long a time.

Combining periodic fasting with GardenCuisine is an excellent way to keep your body in top shape, especially if you add the aerobic exercise recommended later in this chapter. I recommend starting with a twenty-four-hour fast, during which time you will consume nothing but pure, distilled water. This is called a "water fast." There is also the so-called "juice fast," but this is really a liquid diet and not a true fast.

I personally do a twenty-four-hour fast once a week for three weeks and then, in the fourth week, I do a three-day fast. And once a year, I do a one-week fast. But let's look first at the twenty-four-hour fast.

First, be aware that when you begin fasting, others may react with alarm or think that you've "gone off the deep end." That's why Paul Bragg always advised, "Don't tell anyone you are going to fast, because the average person is ignorant of the facts on fasting and they are not qualified to criticize your fasting program." Bragg noted that he always went about his normal business, even when fasting for a week or more, often going on extended lecture tours, never mentioning to anyone that he was fasting.

"Fasting is a very personal thing," Bragg wrote. "It is something that belongs to you. . . . If you have faith in it, that is all that is necessary. You are putting your faith in Nature's oldest and most respected way of purifying, renovating, and rejuvenating the body!"

"When thou fastest appear not unto men to fast, but unto thy Father which is in secret; and thy Father, which seeth in secret, shall award thee openly."

MATTHEW 6:17–18

With the twenty-four-hour fast, you shouldn't encounter much resistance from others, especially if you keep it low-key. Plan the event with a positive attitude and then just do it. Start out with a big GardenCuisine breakfast; eat until you are full but not stuffed. Then stop eating for twenty-four hours. Go about your normal business—or, if fasting makes you nervous in the beginning, plan your first twenty-four-hour fast for a weekend or when you do not have to go to work.

During the fast, consume nothing but *distilled water.* Make sure you always have access to distilled water. If you go out for any extended period of time, take distilled water with you. You can put a little fresh lemon or lime in it, but this is optional and is strictly for flavoring, not to provide calories. During the twenty-four-hour period, you should consume a lot of water, about sixteen glasses or more.

It was Bragg's idea that people who are fasting should drink only distilled water, and, from my own experience, I agree. Distilled water is free of the inorganic minerals that themselves often become impurities in our bodies, adhering to arterial walls and other tissue. During a period of fast, the idea is to give the body a rest from all these substances.

If you think that it is somehow "unnatural" to drink distilled water, consider the fact that for most of the time mankind has roamed this planet, we have consumed mostly distilled water. Most of mankind has depended upon rainwater—nature's own distilled water—as its source of water. Of course, now that much of the atmosphere is polluted, rainwater is no longer a reliable or safe source—but for millennia it was.

Most people experience no difficulty whatever with a twenty-four-hour fast. They may suffer a few hunger pangs and light stomach turbulence. Many, by dinnertime, have a distinct desire to eat. This is the point at which you need to stay away from food. Take a walk. Do some exercise. Watch a film. And keep sipping water throughout the day and evening. It can be hot or cold.

When you awaken the next morning, you will be hungry again. Break the fast with another breakfast of GardenCuisine. A fruit smoothie is the smoothest way to end your fast and the healthiest. And you'll swear it's the best-tasting fruit you've ever had. Just don't gorge.

Even after a one-day fast, most people report some benefits. Most say they think more clearly. Others observe that they see things more distinctly—both literally and figuratively. Fasting has cumulative effects—after you have done several twenty-four-hour fasts, one each week, you will notice a further intensifying of these positive effects. If you have chronic health problems, in many cases you are likely to note some improvement; I would be surprised if you didn't.

"The instinct that leads us to fast when the body is sick or wounded resides in the cells of every living being. The reason why sick or wounded animals refuse to eat is because the instinct of self-preservation takes away their hunger so they will not eat. In this way the vital energy (which would otherwise have to be used in the digestion of food) is concentrated at the seat of injury to remove waste products, thus purifying the body."

PAUL BRAGG

Don't rush your fasting program. Some are so impressed by what they experience after fasting just once or twice, on a twenty-four-hour schedule, that they decide to leap into a ten-day or two-week fast. This is not a good idea. Let your body become used to the once-a-week twenty-four-hour fast for a couple of months before trying anything more ambitious.

Your next logical step is a forty-eight-hour fast. Some athletes fast for two or three days a week before a big event, claiming that this helps them with both focus and energy—provided they leave a few days between fast and event. Others, facing special mental or psychological challenges, also prepare themselves with two- or three-day fasts.

As I said, make the forty-eight-hour fast your next stop if you want to go farther with fasting. There is nothing wrong, however, with just sticking to the twenty-four-hour fasts. For the two-day fast, proceed as you did with the twenty-four-hour fast, again consuming nothing but distilled water. A weekend is a good time to try your first two-day fast. As before, come off the fast without immediately gorging. Stick to nutrient-rich, easy-to-digest GardenCuisine.

After you are comfortable with the forty-eight-hour fast—space several of them a month apart for a few months—you can move on to the three-day fast, where the rules remain the same.

You will lose some weight on the three-day fast—but if you stick to GardenCuisine, you will gain it back without experiencing the "yo-yo effect" that so often plagues dieters. But don't fast while on a weight-loss program. Fasting and weight-loss programs don't mix. When you are on a weight-loss program, your body faces a set of challenges that can be confounded by fasting.

Some very thin people who are trying to gain weight, as well as bodybuilders, often fear fasting. They shouldn't. There have been many reports of slender people actually putting on weight through a program of gentle fasting. There's nothing particularly surprising about this. If a person has a metabolic or digestive problem that makes weight gain difficult, fasting allows the digestive system to rest and heal itself. Similarly, many athletes have fasted regularly for years with only beneficial results.

On two- and especially three-day fasts, many people report striking "clarifications," new and clearer ways of seeing things. Many report having "breakthroughs" in resolving difficulties in their lives and coming to resolutions for effective change.

Sometimes, however, because of the elimination of toxins, some experience a bitter or bad taste in their mouths or a bad odor emanating from their perspiration. As toxins exit the body, they sometimes coat the tongue. This is natural. Those with more toxic buildup of substances will have more difficulty with fasting in the beginning, but this difficulty will abate with time and repeated fasting, as well as adherence to GardenCuisine.

The first time you try a three-day fast, make sure you will not be under a lot of pressure. If you have a three-day weekend or can time the event for a vacation period, that is best. After the first day, hunger pangs will begin to abate. As toxins are eliminated, you may feel a little nauseated at times, though only some people experience this. If you exercise, keep it light—and make sure that you can rest when you want to. After your first three-day fast, you will gain considerably in confidence and will have a much better idea of what you are capable of. As always, keep drinking that distilled water, with or without the lemon or lime.

Many of you have no doubt heard about fasts that are used in conjunction with laxatives and enemas. *Avoid those.* They put unnatural stress on your body. If your bowel movements change or cease during a fast, don't worry about it. They will normalize again when you break the fast. Indeed, many who have suffered for years from bowel irregularity or constipation report normalization after a program of fasting.

I can't tell you how many times I've seen a combination of GardenCuisine and GardenFasting help people with irregularity, chronic bad breath, and body odor. These are indelicate things to discuss, but they are serious problems for many people. The solution, for the majority, I am convinced, is readily at hand. But, again, remember, things may get worse before they get better as your body eliminates the toxins that are the cause of your problem.

Break two- and three-day fasts as you break the shorter fasts. Stick to fresh fruits and other GardenCuisine and don't overindulge in food when you first come off the fast. Eat lightly several times a day and keep on drinking plenty of water (going back to eight to twelve glasses a day).

There are some good ways to monitor your progress as you continue with your fasts. One is to watch your tongue. If you have a lot of toxins in your body, your tongue will become coated, especially during a two- or three-day fast. But with each successive fast, particularly if you adhere to GardenCuisine, you will note that this effect diminishes as your body purifies itself. Another "sign" to monitor is the color of your eyes. As your body expels toxins, you will notice the "whites" of your eyes becoming whiter and the colored part of your eye—the iris—more intense. In my experience, this is almost universally noted by fasters.

If you want to try longer fasting, up to seven days, you will need supervision. These longer fasts can have amazing effects, in my experience, but it is important that you work with a fasting expert or fasting center before attempting one of these. (See the Resources section of this book.)

I once calculated that if people fasted just once a week for fifty years of their lives, they would give their bodies what amounts to a *seven-year rest.* That's seven years in which their bodies do not have to process the food they would otherwise be exposed to; that's a highly significant physiological fact—and one that I believe is bound to have health-improving and, most likely, life-extending benefits. There is already a lot of scientific data showing that the most likely way to extend life is to restrict calories.

And, incidentally, you'll save $15,000 to $20,000 in food costs during that "seven-year rest."

Meditation and Exercise

Fasting is an ideal time to intensify any program of meditation you may want to follow. The clarity of mind many experience during fasting makes it easier to focus on your inner self and to shut out the stressful, conflicting signals of everyday life. If you have a health problem, you can incorporate a meditative program of healthful "visualization," in which you "see" yourself in a whole and vigorous state, into your fasting regimen. But even if you choose not to fast, I believe you will find that gentle GardenCuisine is conducive to a more contemplative state. Not only does it make you feel better physically—but it should also enable you to feel better about your relationship to other animals (including humans), the environment and the planet as a whole.

I strongly recommend that, as a minimum, you incorporate simple breathing exercises into your daily routine. Pick up any beginner's book of yoga, and you will learn all that you need to know about proper breathing. There is an epidemic in our country of "bad breathing." We are a nation of stressed-out "shallow breathers." We quickly fill only the upper portion of our lungs and then quickly exhale. We end up in a state of chronic oxygen deprivation. You will need to learn all over how to breathe properly—

breathing "into your stomach" and then up into your lungs. This is called diaphragmatic breathing. See the Resources section of this book for some recommendations on books about this vital subject.

You can start right now, though, by simply lying down on an exercise mat or other comfortable but firm surface. It helps if you are in comfortable clothing—or no clothing at all—especially when you first learn the proper breathing technique. Try to clear your mind of everything but your present activity. Place the palm of one hand on your abdomen and the palm of the other on your chest. Now breathe as you normally do.

Most of you will feel the hand on your chest rise and fall. Most of you won't feel the hand on your abdomen moving much at all. Now purse your lips as if you are about to suck water through a straw. But, instead, suck in air—way down into your abdomen area, so that you feel the hand on your stomach begin to rise and fall. Now you are using your abdominal diaphragm muscle to get oxygen deep into your lungs as you were meant to before you became a modern-day shallow breather.

At first, you may find this exercise awkward. Breathing in your stomach may feel unnatural and forced. That's because your lungs and diaphragm are out of shape. But as you continue to practice over a period of days, you will begin to experience the rewards of this new way of breathing (actually, the old way relearned). Sucking the air through pursed lips accentuates the exercise and makes it easier to learn.

Now refine the technique. Continue as above, but when you are able to, fill your abdominal area with air so that your hand lifts way up; continue with the intake of breath so that now air also fills your upper lungs. Then, when you can't draw in any more air, hold your breath for about two seconds and exhale—again through pursed lips.

When you exhale, feel your upper chest "deflate." Then feel your lower lungs—in the abdominal area—deflate. This is the rhythm you want. You inhale from the stomach *up* and exhale from the upper chest *down*. As this begins to feel more natural—it may take a week or two—start breathing through your nose when you do these exercises. Then combine your breathing exercises with your meditation. Some find soft light or even darkness and soothing music, played at low volume, helpful.

If you are tense, focus on the part of the body from which your tension seems to emanate, and as you breathe in and out, imagine that part of your body fully relaxing. Imagine that there is a warming, tingling, or cooling in that area, whichever sensation seems most conducive to relaxation or pain reduction. If it is your mind that is troubling you, visualize something particularly soothing—a tropical beach, a field of wild-flowers, the face of a loved one. Shut out all other thoughts. If possible, immerse yourself in the rhythm of your breathing, making your mind otherwise "blank." This takes practice but can be done. Clearing the mind of stressful thoughts and "noise" is rather like fasting. Meditation allows the mind to rest and heal itself.

There is a large and growing body of data on the benefits of proper breathing. Breathing correctly has been shown to dispel everything from panic attacks to some forms of heart disease in some people. Air, like water, is one of those vital "nutrients" we too often overlook and underutilize. For an in-depth look at how dramatically proper breathing can improve health, I recommend a book called *The Oxygen Breakthrough,* by Sheldon Saul Hendler, M.D., Ph.D.

Try to set aside five or ten minutes a couple of times a day for your breathing exercises. And any time you are under stress, whether at your office desk or behind the wheel of your car, consciously switch to diaphragmatic breathing while simultaneously expelling stressful thoughts from your mind.

Meditative Aerobics

As for other exercises, weight lifting and muscle toning are desirable but optional. Aerobic exercise, on the other hand—the kind of exercise in which we strengthen our hearts and lungs—is crucial for everybody. This doesn't mean you have to become a marathon runner or crack-of-dawn lap swimmer. In fact, many studies are showing that overexercising can be as bad for you—taxing your immune system, among other things—as underexercising.

Walking is the ideal aerobic exercise. You can do it almost anywhere—on a beach, in the woods, at a mall, on a city street, inside your own home or apartment, up and down stairs, at a gym, or on a running track. If you have a choice, of course, select an outdoor location where you can "connect" with nature, the ultimate tranquilizer. Dress comfortably and wear shoes that properly support you without inflicting pain or discomfort. I've been wearing Birkenstocks for most of my adult life. After a while, you get hooked on them. Sooo comfortable!

Dr. Kenneth Cooper, "the father of aerobics," used to think that "more is better" when it comes to exercising the heart and lungs. But he changed his mind as more data on exercise accumulated. He and others found that overexercising increases exposure of athletes to oxidant stress, to those "free radicals" we talked about earlier. These toxic molecules do cellular damage to immunity, can increase the risks of heart disease, cancer, cataracts, etc.

Walking just two miles in thirty minutes three times a week—something most of us can manage with little difficulty—is all we need. If all of us did this, Dr. Cooper has calculated, there would be a *55 percent reduction in the premature death rate.* (You might want to read that last sentence again!) Inactivity and a high-fat, animal-based diet are the two biggest killers of our time.

Start out walking slowly for short distances if you have been sedentary for some time. Let your muscles and joints, as well as your heart and lungs, become accustomed to walking. Over a period of weeks, *gradually* work toward the goal of walking two miles in thirty minutes—that's one mile per fifteen minutes. For some this will be easy, for others more difficult.

Any physical activity will be helpful—whether it's gardening, walking up and down stairs, swimming, golfing, building something, doing housework. But, again, walking is ideal. You can pace yourself and monitor your progress.

And walking meshes nicely with meditation, especially if you walk outdoors in a park or other peaceful setting. As you walk, clear your mind of past regrets and fears about the future. Concentrate on the present moment. You might even chant, inwardly or outwardly. Some are so bedeviled by stressful thoughts that they have difficulty clearing their minds. Even counting your steps may help you, as my friend Ram Dass counsels us, to "be here now." Or count the flowers or specific types of plants you pass as you walk; that will force you to begin focusing on your immediate environment. And it's okay to stop and literally "smell the flowers."

If you choose to do more strenuous aerobic exercise, you should read *Dr. Kenneth Cooper's Antioxidant Revolution.* I share Dr. Cooper's belief that many high-performing athletes need extra antioxidant protection, especially if they eat a fairly typical American diet. On the other hand, athletes who consume GardenCuisine may need only a little extra antioxidant supplementation. Dr. Cooper himself notes that there is no substitute for eating the right foods:

> You just can't supplement with vitamins what you can get from food. I strongly recommend that you consume a minimum of five to seven servings

of fresh fruit and vegetables a day, or seven to nine, depending on the size of the serving.

And so, as usual, it all comes back to eating the right things. Exercise is a useful and very important supplement to the right diet—but diet comes first.

There's more on exercise in the next chapter. For those who want to lose weight, exercise is even more crucial.

CHAPTER II

The Lean Green:
Natural Weight Loss

Losing Weight Nature's Way

Not all calories are created equal when it comes to putting on weight. This might surprise you. After all, a calorie is a calorie, just like a pound is a pound. But it turns out that some calories are more likely to stick with us and produce those excess pounds we all dread.

It has been calculated that the average American consumed more calories early in this century than the average American does today. Yet today's American weighs distinctly more. Similarly, Dr. Dean Ornish and others report, the average person in Mainland China consumes 30 percent more calories than the average American—yet the Chinese weigh notably less than Americans.

How can this be so? Researchers in China and at Cornell University, in an ambitious study of sixty-five hundred Chinese distributed throughout China, found that those who stuck to the traditional diet of rice and other vegetables had the lowest weight and that those who had the highest intake of animal products had the highest weight, irrespective of caloric intake. Similarly, scientists at Stanford University, in a study of overweight and lean men in the United States, found that the heftier men consumed more fat, while the lean ones ate less fat and more complex carbohydrates. Caloric intake was equal in both groups.

These studies help to explain why our American ancestors ate more and weighed less. They also ate the "natural way," making fruits, grains, and vegetables their daily staples, with fats and meats only occasional indulgences. In the early part of this century, Americans were getting 60 percent or more of their calories from complex carbohydrates and only 20 percent from fat.

So, in fact, fat makes you fat—not calories per se. You can eat more and actually weigh less!

As noted in chapter 9, a number of authors have recently tried to revive the high-fat diet for weight loss, claiming that it is carbohydrates that lead to weight gain. I've already quoted several nutritional authorities and cited a number of studies that solidly refute these authors, none of whom have any worthy evidence to back their claims.

All of the best studies come to the same conclusion: The only weight-loss regimen that stands a chance of working on a permanent and healthful basis is one that utilizes a wide range of low-fat, high-complex-carbohydrate foods in quantities adequate to avoid the constant feeling of hunger.

This precisely describes GardenCuisine or what I call, in this context, the "Lean Green." If you eat as nature intended you to eat, you will not feel hungry and you will not be fat.

Why Most Weight-Loss Diets Are Actually Fattening

Many of you who have dieted have come to the conclusion, after frustrating years of trying to cut back on calories, that diets don't work. This isn't precisely true. What is true is that *most* diets don't work. Your conclusions are based on the fact that after years of dieting, you now weigh more than ever! You had your successes, but they were brief and temporary. For every pound you lost, you ultimately gained back more. So it is easy to understand why you would conclude that dieting simply doesn't work.

The fault, however, is not in dieting per se but in the type of diet you follow. The degree of caloric restriction and composition of most diets doom them—and you—to failure. Because protein and fat are more calorically dense than complex carbohydrates, you don't get to eat much on a diet that utilizes standard American fare. Thus high-fat, high-protein diets leave you feeling hungry and frustrated most of the time. The "fall-off" rate on such diets is huge.

Going on and off diets—so-called "yo-yo" dieting—is highly destructive. You can lose weight rapidly on a calorically restricted high-fat, high-protein diet, but you tend to lose the weight more from your lean body mass than from your existing fat stores. Then, when you fall off the diet—and almost everybody does, as study after study has demonstrated—you regain the lost weight, which is bad enough, but, worse, you gain it back mostly in the form of fat. There are complex reasons why fat fills in for lost lean mass that I won't go into here—but this is an undisputed scientific fact.

So now you end up with more fat cells than ever before. Lean body mass (muscle) is more metabolically active than fat and requires more calories for its maintenance. (In other words, muscle burns more calories than fat.) And so the fatter you become, the fewer calories it takes to make you fatter still! That's why each time you lose and regain weight, it becomes more difficult to lose it again.

This will also help you to understand why some very lean, active people can eat far more than you and still not gain weight.

Nutritional pioneers Sonja Connor and William Connor, M.D., authors of *The New American Diet,* have presented data comparing the composition of different diets and their effects on percent of weight lost as either lean body mass or fat. On the so-called ketogenic, high-fat, low-carbohydrate diets that allow fewer than 1,000 calories per day, 65 percent of weight loss is in lean body mass and only 35 percent in fat. On mixed food diets, including lots of complex carbohydrates and more than 1,000 calories, 68 percent of the weight loss is in fat and only 32 percent in lean body mass. And when you add mild exercise to this last regimen, you increase the loss in the form of fat to 79 percent and reduce the loss in the form of muscle to 21 percent!

Which would you choose?

"We have found that the diet program which promotes maximum weight lost as fat is one that is made up of a variety of foods, is 800 to 1200 calories for women and 1200 to 2000 calories for men. Our diet programs are always accompanied by increased physical activity. This can take the form of walking for 30 minutes per day, swimming, jogging, bicycling, rowing, tennis, etc.

The purpose of the increased exercise is twofold: 1) The loss of muscle tissue (lean body mass) is lessened during weight loss if the muscles are put to work and 2) exercise tends to inhibit the appetite and the desire for food."

SONJA L. CONNOR, M.S., R.D., AND WILLIAM E. CONNOR, M.D.,

The New American Diet

The Connor diet—like GardenCuisine—is rich in fruits, grains, and vegetables, and restricted in fats and reduced in animal protein. And it is combined with moderate exercise. This is the way we lived for millennia—keeping physically active and eating a largely vegetarian diet. It is thus not surprising that, until recent times, obesity was rare.

If you follow my Lean Green weight-loss program, you will lose weight—in a controlled, gradual, natural way. This is not a "starvation" or "crash" diet—so don't expect to lose fifty pounds in a few weeks. If you value your health, that's the last thing you want to do, anyway. With the Lean Green, both men and women will lose one to two pounds each week—which can add up to fifty or more pounds in a year. And the best part is, if you proceed at this rate, you vastly improve your chances of keeping the weight off for good.

Tips for Permanent Weight Loss

1. Cut the fat and increase the complex carbohydrates; in other words, cut fat, not food—you can diet and still feel full.
2. Eat a wide variety of foods.
3. Avoid very low-calorie diets (under 1,000 calories per day for women; under 1,200 calories per day for men).
4. I believe it is healthier to eat your largest meal in the morning, medium in the afternoon, and smaller in the evening; you'll sleep better and feel more "alive" when you awaken.
5. Several small meals throughout the day are better than two or three big ones. You should never feel hungry or deprived.
6. Drink a lot of water and avoid all sugary and alcoholic beverages. Ten to twelve eight-ounce glasses of distilled water should be consumed daily.
7. Don't undo the benefits of your high-carbohydrate foods by adding

high-fat toppings to them. Your taste buds will gradually learn to appreciate whole-grain flavors and fresher, low-fat or no-fat toppings.

8. Be aware that as you age, you are more likely to gain weight; stopping or slowing weight gain before it gets out of hand is easier than losing weight once it's firmly entrenched.

9. Be aware that abdominal weight can be the most dangerous (fat from this part of the anatomy gets into the bloodstream more easily than fat from other areas). So when you start to notice a paunch, it's time to begin trimming the fat from your diet while simultaneously increasing your physical activity. Many believe that stomach fat is the most difficult to shed but, in fact, it is often the easiest.

10. You don't need to begin dieting with the idea that "it's going to take a lot of willpower" or the idea that "dieting will leave me weak and depressed." Very low-calorie, high-fat diets will justify these assumptions, but the Lean Green—and similar diets—will not have these effects. Making these assumptions at the beginning helps set the stage for failure—no matter what diet you follow. Slower, more gradual weight loss, on a high-complex-carbohydrate diet of fruits, grains, and vegetables leads to more energy and less depression. Researchers at Tufts University School of Medicine found that women following a gradual-weight-loss program reported significant reductions in anxiety and fatigue and a heightened sense of self-worth.

My Twenty-One-Day Weight-Loss Menu

The three weeks of Lean Green meal plans are summarized below. They are fully illustrated in tabular form. The twenty-one-day menu provides the percentage of calories derived from fat in each menu selection and provides total average daily percentages of calories derived from fat. You'll find the recipes for these selections in part IV. Note that these meal plans provide women with between 1,000 and 1,300 calories per day, men between 1,600 and 2,000 calories per day. Some selections provide more calories from fat than the 15 percent or less that we are aiming for, but these are individual selections. Overall, fat intake is reduced to well under 20 percent. The Day One meal plan, for example, derives only about 10 percent of calories from fat, whether you are following the plan for men or for women.

Even though the meals are on the traditional three-a-day plan, you can divide them up as you see fit. As noted earlier, several small meals a day are as good or better than three larger meals. The idea is to avoid hunger and keep your energy and spirits high at all times.

The Twenty-One-Day Meal Plan

Day One

BREAKFAST

Manoa Sunrise Smoothie

Mighty Multigrain Cereal

Almond, Rice, or Skim Milk (wherever included, use ½ cup of lowest-fat product available)

Hot or Iced Herbal Tea with Lemon or Lime

LUNCH

All-American Gardenburger

Confetti Cole Slaw

Apple Custard Fruit Tart

Hot or Iced Herbal Tea with Lemon or Lime

DINNER

Pan-Roasted Portobello Mushrooms over Broiled Polenta

EssentialSalad

Citrus Vinaigrette

VeggiePack

Hot or Iced Herbal Tea with Lemon or Lime

Day Two

BREAKFAST

Fresh Fruit Toss

Hot and Hearty Five-Grain Cereal

Almond, Rice, or Skim Milk

Ice Water with Fresh-Squeezed Lemon or Lime

LUNCH

Vegetarian Reuben Sandwich

Potato, Apple, Cabbage Salad

Ice Water with Fresh-Squeezed Lemon or Lime

DINNER

Tostada Grande

Low-Fat Fried Rice

Hot or Iced Herbal Tea with Lemon or Lime

BREAKFAST

Very Strawberry Smoothie

Golden GardenSausage Waffles

Pure Maple Syrup

Hot or Iced Herbal Tea with Lemon or Lime

LUNCH

Barley, Tomato, and Bean Soup

EssentialSalad

Raspberry Vinaigrette

Spice Cake

Ice Water with Fresh-Squeezed Lemon or
   Lime

DINNER

Roasted Vegetable Enchilada

VeggiePack

Hot or Iced Herbal Tea with Lemon or Lime

Day Four

BREAKFAST

Surfers' Favorite Beverage

Tropical Granola

Orange Wedges

Almond, Rice, or Skim Milk

Hot or Iced Herbal Tea with Lemon
   or Lime

LUNCH

Chili Non Carne

Whole-Grain Bread

Citrus Salad with Lime Dressing

VeggiePack

Ice Water with Fresh-Squeezed Lemon or
   Lime

DINNER

Shepherd's Pie

EssentialSalad

Balsamic Vinaigrette

Whole-Grain Roll

Hot or Iced Herbal Tea with Lemon or Lime

Day Five

BREAKFAST

Fresh Fruit Toss

Mighty Multigrain Cereal

Almond, Rice, or Skim Milk

Ice Water with Fresh-Squeezed Lemon or
   Lime

LUNCH

Healthy Caesar Salad

French Onion Soup

Whole-Wheat Roll

Ice Water with Fresh-Squeezed Lemon or
   Lime

DINNER

Shrimp-Free Tofu Cocktail

Parsley Pesto with Soba Noodles

VeggiePack

Hot or Iced Herbal Tea with Lemon or Lime

Day Six

BREAKFAST

Mango Dango Cocktail

Home-Fried Potatoes

Banana Slices

Ice Water with Fresh-Squeezed Lemon or
 Lime

LUNCH

Linguine with Broccoli and Roasted Garlic

VeggiePack

Fabulous Fruited Bread Pudding

Ice Water with Fresh-Squeezed Lemon or
 Lime

DINNER

Stuffed Eggplant

Broccoli with Dijon Sauce

Ice Water with Fresh-Squeezed Lemon or
 Lime

Day Seven

BREAKFAST

Surfers' Favorite Beverage

Hot and Healthy Five-Grain Cereal

Orange Wedges

Almond, Rice, or Skim Milk

Ice Water with Fresh-Squeezed Lemon or
 Lime

LUNCH

Black Bean Hash

EssentialSalad

Thousand Island Dressing

Healthy Brownies

Ice Water with Fresh-Squeezed Lemon or
 Lime

DINNER

Spinach and Onion Turnovers

Spaghetti Squash Veggie Salad

Whole-Grain Roll

Ice Water with Fresh-Squeezed Lemon or
 Lime

Day Eight

BREAKFAST

Fresh Fruit Toss

Mighty Multigrain Cereal

Almond, Rice, or Skim Milk

Hot or Iced Herbal Tea with Lemon or Lime

LUNCH

Broiled Tofu in Sweet Ginger Marinade

Chinese Noodles and Cabbage

Ice Water with Fresh-Squeezed Lemon or
 Lime

DINNER

Soft Tofu "Chicken" Tacos

EssentialSalad

Citrus Vinaigrette

Hot or Iced Herbal Tea with Lemon or Lime

Day Nine

BREAKFAST

Banana Frappé

Breakfast Barley Pudding

Orange Wedges

Hot or Iced Herbal Tea with Lemon or Lime

LUNCH

Gardenburger Olé

EssentialSalad

Balsamic Vinaigrette

Ice Water with Fresh-Squeezed Lemon or
Lime

DINNER

Fettuccine and Roasted Vegetables

EssentialSalad

Citrus Vinaigrette

Whole-Grain Roll

Ice Water with Fresh-Squeezed Lemon or
Lime

Day Ten

BREAKFAST

Manoa Sunrise Smoothie

Golden GardenSausage Waffles

Fresh Fruit Syrup

Hot or Iced Herbal Tea with Lemon or Lime

LUNCH

Yammin' Ginger Soup

Savory Spinach Bread Pudding

EssentialSalad

Balsamic Vinaigrette

Whole-Grain Roll

Ice Water with Fresh-Squeezed Lemon or
Lime

DINNER

Mom's Tamale Pie

EssentialSalad

Citrus Vinaigrette

Green Beans with Toasted Almonds

Ice Water with Fresh-Squeezed Lemon or
Lime

Day Eleven

BREAKFAST

Fresh Fruit Toss

Hot and Hearty Five-Grain Cereal

Almond, Rice, or Skim Milk

Hot or Iced Herbal Tea with Lemon or Lime

LUNCH

Vegetable Pita Pizza

VeggiePack

Ice Water with Fresh-Squeezed Lemon or
Lime

DINNER

Black Beans and Tofu "Chicken" over Soba
Noodles

VeggiePack

Whole-Grain Rolls

Hot or Iced Herbal Tea with Lemon or Lime

Day Twelve

BREAKFAST

Very Strawberry Smoothie

Home-Fried Potatoes

Whole-Grain Toast

Spreadable Fruit

Hot or Iced Herbal Tea with Lemon or Lime

LUNCH

Border-Town Burritos

EssentialSalad

Thousand Island Dressing

Ice Water with Fresh-Squeezed Lemon or
    Lime

DINNER

Roasted Vegetable Enchiladas

VeggiePack

Citrus Vinaigrette

Hot or Iced Herbal Tea with Lemon or
    Lime

Day Thirteen

BREAKFAST

Banana Frappé

Brunch Fruit Compote with Whole-Grain
    Dumplings

Whole-Grain Toast

Spreadable Fruit

Hot or Iced Herbal Tea with Lemon or Lime

LUNCH

Tofu "Chicken" Teriyaki Sandwich

EssentialSalad

Thousand Island Dressing

Hot or Iced Herbal Tea with Lemon or
    Lime

DINNER

Tostada Grande

Guacabonzo

Whole-Grain Roll

Ice Water with Fresh-Squeezed Lemon or
    Lime

Day Fourteen

BREAKFAST

Surfers' Favorite Beverage

High-Fiber French Toast

Orange Wedges

Ice Water with Fresh-Squeezed Lemon or
    Lime

LUNCH

All-American Gardenburger

Home-Fried Potatoes

EssentialSalad

Hot or Iced Herbal Tea with Lemon or Lime

DINNER

Sweet and Sour Szechwan Tofu "Chicken"

Wild Rice and Asparagus Salad

Hot or Iced Herbal Tea with Lemon or Lime

Day Fifteen

BREAKFAST

Fresh Fruit Toss

Hot and Hearty Five-Grain Cereal

Almond, Rice, or Skim Milk

Hot or Iced Herbal Tea with Lemon or Lime

LUNCH

Middle Eastern Pita Sandwich

Artichoke Hearts and Fava Beans

Hot or Iced Herbal Tea with Lemon or
    Lime

DINNER

Pan-Roasted Portobello Mushrooms over
    Broiled Polenta

VeggiePack

Ice Water with Fresh-Squeezed Lemon or
    Lime

Day Sixteen

BREAKFAST

Banana Frappé

Tropical Granola

Orange Wedges

Hot or Iced Herbal Tea with Lemon or Lime

LUNCH

Garden Lasagne

EssentialSalad

Ice Water with Fresh-Squeezed Lemon or
    Lime

DINNER

Bombay Potatoes, Tomatoes, and Chickpeas

Calcutta Cauliflower

EssentialSalad

Hot or Iced Herbal Tea with Lemon or
    Lime

Day Seventeen

BREAKFAST

Very Strawberry Smoothie

Mighty Multi-Grain Cereal

Almond, Rice, or Skim Milk

Hot or Iced Herbal Tea with Lemon or Lime

LUNCH

Gardenburger Maui

Baked Potato Skins

Hot or Iced Herbal Tea with Lemon or
    Lime

DINNER

Thai Peanut Noodles

String Beans with Ginger

Ice Water with Fresh-Squeezed Lemon or
    Lime

Day Eighteen

BREAKFAST
Fresh Fruit Toss
Hot and Hearty Five-Grain Cereal
Almond, Rice, or Skim Milk
Ice Water with Fresh-Squeezed Lemon or
    Lime

LUNCH
Vegetarian Reuben Sandwich
VeggiePack

Hot or Iced Herbal Tea with Lemon or
    Lime

DINNER
Tostada Grande
Citrus Vinaigrette
Healthful Homemade Sour Cream
Gypsy Soup
Hot or Iced Herbal Tea with Lemon or
    Lime

Day Nineteen

BREAKFAST
Banana Frappé
Tropical Granola
Orange Wedges
Almond, Rice, or Skim Milk
Hot or Iced Herbal Tea with Lemon or Lime

LUNCH
Broiled Polenta Squares and Tomato Chutney
EssentialSalad

Balsamic Vinaigrette
Mango-Apricot Bread Pudding
Ice Water with Fresh-Squeezed Lemon or
    Lime

DINNER
Wonderful Russian Borscht
Wild Rice and Asparagus Salad
Hot or Iced Herbal Tea with Lemon or
    Lime

Day Twenty

BREAKFAST
Manoa Sunrise Smoothie
Yamcakes
Fresh Fruit Syrup
Ice Water with Fresh-Squeezed Lemon or
    Lime

LUNCH
Roasted Vegetable Pizza
EssentialSalad

Thousand Island Dressing
Fruit Cake
Hot or Iced Herbal Tea with Lemon or Lime

DINNER
Healthy Caesar Salad
VeggiePack
Whole-Grain Roll
Hot or Iced Herbal Tea with Lemon or
    Lime

BREAKFAST

Very Strawberry Smoothie

Hot and Hearty Five-Grain Cereal

Almond, Rice, or Skim Milk

Hot or Iced Herbal Tea with Lemon or Lime

LUNCH

Middle Eastern Pita Sandwich

Whole-Grain Satay Salad

Barley Succotash

Ice Water with Fresh-Squeezed Lemon or Lime

DINNER

Exotic Stir-fry (without cheese)

EssentialSalad

Raspberry Vinaigrette

Hot or Iced Herbal Tea with Lemon or Lime

Construct Your Own Meal Plan and Enhance It with Exercise

For many, these meal plans will suffice for the duration of a weight-loss program. Others will want to experiment with different combinations. Just keep your caloric intake in the ranges recommended above and eat a wide choice of whole foods, following my advice on utilizing the GardenGroups, as discussed in chapter 9.

If you want to get lean faster and stay lean longer—permanently—then exercise is crucial. Remember, on my Lean Green weight-loss program, 68 percent of the weight you lose will be fat and 32 percent will be lean body mass. That's about as good as it gets on diet alone. If you want to get better results, you'll need to do mild to moderate exercise on a regular basis, thus boosting the amount of weight you lose in the form of fat to 79 percent, while reducing lean body mass loss to 21 percent.

Actually, everybody who diets should exercise regularly. It's the key to keeping the weight off once you've lost it and to maintaining proper body weight on a permanent basis. The proof of this has appeared in numerous studies.

In one of these studies, conducted by researchers at Boston University Medical Center, dieters on the same weight-loss regimen were divided into two groups. One group followed the diet only, the other group followed the diet *and* an aerobic exercise program. At the end of eight weeks, both groups had lost weight. Those who exercised had, on average, lost four pounds more than the nonexercisers.

This was not a huge difference—but when the two groups were examined eighteen months later, there was a startling divergence. The nonexercisers had gained back about 90 percent of the weight they had lost, while the exercisers hadn't gained back any weight at all!

How much exercise? As discussed in the preceding chapter, it doesn't have to be a lot. Almost any exercise is better than none at all, but walking two miles in thirty minutes three times a week (building up to this goal gradually) will have a definite effect on the permanence of your weight loss.

You may find it effective to walk four or five times a week—or to walk three miles three times a week. More, as I pointed out earlier in this book, is not always better. A variety of studies suggests that mild to moderate exercise is actually more effective than strenuous exercise in helping people lose weight and keep it off. There are good reasons for this. For one thing, short bursts of highly intensive exercise have been found to burn more carbohydrate than fat. Slower, steady exercise tends to dip more into the excess fat stores of your body. And strenuous exercise often increases hunger, while mild to moderate exercise has the opposite effect, especially if it is extended for thirty to sixty minutes per session.

Obviously, you don't have to limit yourself to walking; you can swim, ride a bicycle, or engage in many other activities, either singly or in combination. Even walking around inside your home or inside a mall can provide good aerobic workouts if sustained. Whenever possible, take stairs, not the elevator. There are all kinds of great aerobic exercise devices you can use in your home, including rowing machines, cross-country skiing simulators, stationary bikes, treadmills, stair-steppers, minitrampolines, and so on. There are numerous books on aerobic exercise that will provide you with details about various forms of exercise. Of course, if you have any physical condition that might make exercise risky, consult with your doctor before beginning your exercise program.

	SERVING SIZE WOMEN	CALORIES	% FROM FAT*
Day One			
BREAKFAST			
Manoa Sunrise Smoothie	8 oz	122	2%
Mighty Multigrain Cereal	1 cup	137	10%
Almond, Rice, or Skim Milk (43 calories or more)	½ cup	43	0%
LUNCH			
All-American Gardenburger	1 sandwich	250	14%
Confetti Cole Slaw	1 serving	67	14%
Apple Custard Fruit Tart	¾ slice	132	19%
DINNER			
Pan-Roasted Portobello Mushrooms over Broiled Polenta	1 serving	208	8%
EssentialSalad	2 cups	20	0%
Citrus Vinaigrette	1 tablespoon	12	0%
VeggiePack	1½ cups	60	0%
Total:		1,051	
Day Two			
BREAKFAST			
Fresh Fruit Toss	¾ cup	67	4%
Hot and Hearty Five-Grain Cereal	1 cup	227	17%
Almond, Rice, or Skim Milk (43 calories or more)	½ cup	43	0%
LUNCH			
Vegetarian Reuben Sandwich	1 sandwich	257	14%
Potato, Apple, Cabbage Salad	1 serving	169	20%
DINNER			
Tostada Grande	1 serving	276	10%
Low-Fat Fried Rice	1 serving	145	12%
Total:		1,184	
Day Three			
BREAKFAST			
Very Strawberry Smoothie	8 oz	126	2%
Golden GardenSausage Waffles	1 waffle	218	19%
Pure Maple Syrup	1 tablespoon	53	0%
LUNCH			
Barley, Tomato, and Bean Soup	1 serving	146	5%
EssentialSalad	2 cups	20	0%
Raspberry Vinaigrette	2 tablespoons	8	0%
Spice Cake	1 serving	275	0%

* The daily average % of calories from fat assumes the use of a nonfat milk product. 21-day average % calories

CALORIES FROM FAT	SERVING SIZE MEN	CALORIES	% FROM FAT	CALORIES FROM FAT	AVERAGE DAILY % FROM FAT	
					MEN	WOMEN
2.44	16 oz	244	2%	4.88		
13.70	2 cups	274	10%	27.40		
0.00	1 cup	86	0%	0.00		
35.00	1 sandwich	250	14%	35.00		
9.38	3 servings	201	14%	28.14		
25.08	1 slice	175	19%	33.25		
16.64	1 serving	208	8%	16.64		
0.00	3 cups	30	0%	0.00		
0.00	3 tablespoons	36	0%	0.00		
0.00	3 cups	120	0%	0.00		
102.24		1,624		145.31	8.94%	9.72%
2.68	2 cups	180	4%	7.20		
38.59	2 cups	454	17%	77.18		
0.00	1 cup	86	0%	0.00		
35.98	1 sandwich	257	14%	35.98		
33.80	2 servings	338	20%	67.60		
27.60	1 serving	276	10%	27.60		
17.40	1 serving	145	12%	17.40		
156.05		1,736		232.96	13.41%	13.18%
2.52	16 oz	252	2%	5.04		
41.42	2 waffles	436	19%	82.84		
0.00	3 tablespoons	159	0%	0.00		
7.30	1½ servings	219	5%	10.95		
0.00	3 cups	30	0%	0.00		
0.00	3 tablespoons	12	0%	0.00		
0.00	1 serving	275	0%	0.00		

from fat (men) = 13.94%. 21-day average % calories from fat (women) = 14.42%.

	SERVING SIZE WOMEN	CALORIES	% FROM FAT
Day Three (cont.)			
DINNER			
Roasted Vegetable Enchiladas	1 serving	224	17%
VeggiePack	2 cups	80	5%
Total:		1,150	
Day Four			
BREAKFAST			
Surfers' Favorite Beverage	8 oz	149	20%
Tropical Granola	½ cup	219	32%
Almond, Rice, or Skim Milk (43 calories or more)	½ cup	43	0%
Orange Wedges	1 orange	64	1%
LUNCH			
Chili Non Carne	1 serving	135	3%
Whole-Grain Bread	1 slice	70	13%
Citrus Salad with Lime Dressing	1 serving	69	42%
VeggiePack	2 cups	80	5%
DINNER			
Shepherd's Pie	1 serving	217	2%
EssentialSalad	2 cups	20	0%
Balsamic Vinaigrette	2 tablespoons	10	0%
Whole-Grain Roll	1 roll	70	13%
Total:		1,146	
Day Five			
BREAKFAST			
Fresh Fruit Toss	1 cup	90	4%
Mighty Multigrain Cereal	2 cups	274	10%
Almond, Rice, or Skim Milk (43 or more calories)	½ cup	43	0%
LUNCH			
Healthy Caesar Salad	1 serving	157	19%
French Onion Soup	1 serving	177	48%
Whole-Wheat Roll	1 roll	70	13%
DINNER			
Shrimp-Free Tofu Cocktail	1 serving	106	37%
Parsley Pesto with Soba Noodles	1 serving	138	30%
VeggiePack	2 cups	80	5%
Total:		1,135	

CALORIES FROM FAT	SERVING SIZE MEN	CALORIES	% FROM FAT	CALORIES FROM FAT	AVERAGE DAILY % FROM FAT	
					MEN	WOMEN
38.08	1 serving	244	17%	41.48		
4.00	3 cups	120	5%	6.00		
93.32		1,747		146.31	8.37%	8.11%
29.80	16 oz	298	20%	59.60		
70.08	1 cup	438	32%	140.16		
0.00	1 cup	86	0%	0.00		
0.64	1 orange	64	1%	0.64		
4.05	2 servings	270	3%	8.10		
9.10	1 slice	70	13%	9.10		
28.98	2 servings	138	42%	72.90		
4.00	2 cups	80	5%	4.00		
4.34	1 serving	217	2%	4.34		
0.00	3 cups	30	0%	0.00		
0.00	3 tablespoons	15	0%	0.00		
9.10	1 roll	70	13%	9.10		
160.09		1,776		307.94	17.33%	13.96%
3.60	2 cups	180	4%	7.20		
27.40	3 cups	411	10%	41.10		
0.00	1 cup	86	0%	0.00		
29.83	2 servings	314	19%	59.66		
84.96	1 serving	177	48%	84.96		
9.10	2 rolls	140	13%	18.20		
39.22	1 serving	106	37%	39.22		
41.40	2 servings	296	30%	88.80		
4.00	2 cups	80	5%	4.00		
239.51		1,790		343.14	19.16%	21.10%

	SERVING SIZE WOMEN	CALORIES	% FROM FAT
Day Six			
BREAKFAST			
Mango Dango Cocktail	8 oz	140	1%
Home-Fried Potatoes	1 serving	164	8%
Banana Slices	1 banana	105	8%
LUNCH			
Linguine with Broccoli and Roasted Garlic	1 serving	154	32%
VeggiePack	2 cups	80	5%
Fabulous Fruited Bread Pudding	1 serving	197	9%
DINNER			
Stuffed Eggplant	1 serving	246	46%
Broccoli with Dijon Sauce	1 serving	62	0%
Total:		1,148	
Day Seven			
BREAKFAST			
Surfers' Favorite Beverage	8 oz	149	18%
Hot and Hearty Five-Grain Cereal	1 cup	227	17%
Almond, Rice, or Skim Milk (43 calories or more)	½ cup	43	0%
Orange Wedges	1 orange	64	1%
LUNCH			
Black Bean Hash	1 serving	202	11%
EssentialSalad	2 cups	20	0%
Thousand Island Dressing	2 tablespoons	40	21%
Healthy Brownies	1 brownie	111	8%
DINNER			
Spinach and Onion Turnovers	1 turnover	59	24%
Spaghetti Squash Veggie Salad	1 serving	192	25%
Whole-Grain Roll	1 roll	70	13%
Total:		1,177	
Day Eight			
BREAKFAST			
Fresh Fruit Toss	1 cup	90	4%
Mighty Multigrain Cereal	2 cups	274	10%
Almond, Rice, or Skim Milk	½ cup	43	0%
LUNCH			
Broiled Tofu in Sweet Ginger Marinade	1 serving	114	40%
Chinese Noodles and Cabbage	1 serving	156	23%

CALORIES FROM FAT	SERVING SIZE MEN	CALORIES	% FROM FAT	CALORIES FROM FAT	AVERAGE DAILY % FROM FAT	
					MEN	WOMEN
1.40	16 oz	280	1%	2.80		
13.12	2 servings	328	8%	26.24		
8.40	1 banana	105	8%	8.40		
49.28	2 servings	308	32%	98.56		
4.00	3 cups	120	5%	6.00		
17.73	1 serving	197	9%	17.73		
113.16	1 serving	246	46%	113.16		
0.00	2 servings	124	0%	0.00		
207.09		1,708		272.89	15.98%	18.04%
26.82	16 oz	298	18%	53.64		
38.59	1½ cups	340	17%	57.80		
0.00	1 cup	86	0%	0.00		
0.64	1 orange	64	1%	0.64		
22.22	2 servings	404	11%	44.44		
0.00	3 cups	30	0%	0.00		
8.4	3 tablespoons	60	21%	12.6		
8.88	1 brownie	111	8%	8.88		
14.16	2 turnovers	118	24%	28.32		
48.00	1 serving	192	25%	48.00		
9.10	1 roll	70	13%	9.10		
176.81		1,773		263.42	14.85%	15.02%
3.60	2 cups	180	4%	7.20		
27.40	3 cups	411	10%	41.10		
0.00	1½ cups	129	0%	0.00		
45.60	2 servings	228	40%	91.20		
35.88	2 servings	312	23%	71.76		

	SERVING SIZE WOMEN	CALORIES	% FROM FAT
Day Eight (cont.)			
DINNER			
Soft Tofu "Chicken" Tacos	2 tacos	350	34%
EssentialSalad	2 cups	80	0%
Citrus Vinaigrette	2 tablespoons	24	0%
Total:		1,131	
Day Nine			
BREAKFAST			
Banana Frappé	8 oz	213	11%
Breakfast Barley Pudding	1 serving	271	4%
Orange Wedges	1 orange	64	1%
LUNCH			
Gardenburger Olé	1 sandwich	330	23%
EssentialSalad	2 cups	20	0%
Balsamic Vinaigrette	2 tablespoons	10	0%
DINNER			
Fettuccine and Roasted Vegetables	1 serving	91	20%
EssentialSalad	2 cups	20	0%
Citrus Vinaigrette	2 tablespoons	24	0%
Whole-Grain Roll	1 roll	70	13%
Total:		1,175	
Day Ten			
BREAKFAST			
Manoa Sunrise Smoothie	8 oz	122	2%
Golden GardenSausage Waffles	1 waffle	218	19%
Fresh Fruit Syrup	2 tablespoons	12	0%
LUNCH			
Yammin' Ginger Soup	1 serving	170	14%
Savory Spinach Bread Pudding	1 serving	155	26%
EssentialSalad	2 cups	20	0%
Balsamic Vinaigrette	2 tablespoons	10	0%
Whole-Grain Roll	1 roll	70	13%
DINNER			
Mom's Tamale Pie	1 serving	250	21%
EssentialSalad	2 cups	20	0%
Citrus Vinaigrette	2 tablespoons	24	0%
Green Beans with Toasted Almonds	1 serving	70	33%
Total:		1,141	

CALORIES FROM FAT	SERVING SIZE MEN	CALORIES	% FROM FAT	CALORIES FROM FAT	AVERAGE DAILY % FROM FAT	
					MEN	WOMEN
119.00	2 tacos	350	34%	119.00		
0.00	2 cups	80	0%	0.00		
0.00	2 tablespoons	24	0%	0.00		
231.48		1,714		330.26	19.27%	20.47%
23.43	16 oz	426	11%	46.86		
10.84	2 servings	542	4%	21.68		
0.64	1 orange	64	1%	0.64		
75.90	1 sandwich	330	23%	75.90		
0.00	3 cups	30	0%	0.00		
0.00	3 tablespoons	15	0%	0.00		
18.20	1½ servings	137	20%	27.40		
0.00	2 cups	20	0%	0.00		
0.00	2 tablespoons	24	0%	0.00		
9.10	1 roll	70	13%	9.10		
138.11		1,782		181.58	10.18%	11.75%
2.44	16 oz	244	2%	4.88		
41.42	2 waffles	436	19%	82.84		
0.00	4 tablespoons	24	0%	0.00		
23.80	2 servings	340	14%	47.60		
40.30	1½ servings	233	26%	60.58		
0.00	3 cups	30	0%	0.00		
0.00	3 tablespoons	15	0%	0.00		
9.10	1 roll	70	13%	9.10		
52.50	1 serving	250	21%	52.50		
0.00	3 cups	30	0%	0.00		
0.00	3 tablespoons	36	0%	0.00		
23.10	1 serving	70	33%	23.10		
192.66		1,778		280.60	15.78%	16.88%

Day Eleven

BREAKFAST

Fresh Fruit Toss	2 cups	180	4%
Hot and Hearty Five-Grain Cereal	1 cup	227	17%
Almond, Rice, or Skim Milk (43 calories or more)	½ cup	43	0%

LUNCH

Vegetable Pita Pizza	1 pizza	233	14%
VeggiePack	2 cups	80	5%

DINNER

Black Beans and Tofu "Chicken" over Soba Noodles	1 serving	291	27%
VeggiePack	2 cups	80	5%
Whole-Grain Roll	1 roll	70	13%
Total:		1,154	

Day Twelve

BREAKFAST

Very Strawberry Smoothie	8 oz	126	2%
Home-Fried Potatoes	1 serving	164	8%
Whole-Wheat Toast	2 slices	140	13%
Spreadable Fruit	2 tablespoons	100	0%

LUNCH

Border Town Burritos	1 serving	331	12%
EssentialSalad	2 cups	20	0%
Thousand Island Dressing	2 tablespoons	40	21%

DINNER

Roasted Vegetable Enchiladas	1 serving	244	17%
VeggiePack	2 cups	80	5%
Citrus Vinaigrette	2 tablespoons	24	0%
Total:		1,269	

Day Thirteen

BREAKFAST

Banana Frappé	8 oz	213	11%
Brunch Fruit Compote with Whole-Grain Dumplings	1 serving	145	7%
Whole-Grain Toast	1 slice	70	13%
Spreadable Fruit	1 tablespoon	50	0%

CALORIES FROM FAT	SERVING SIZE MEN	CALORIES	% FROM FAT	CALORIES FROM FAT	AVERAGE DAILY % FROM FAT	
					MEN	WOMEN
7.20	2 cups	180	4%	7.20		
38.59	2 cups	454	17%	77.18		
0.00	1 cup	86	0%	0.00		
32.62	1½ pizzas	350	14%	49.00		
4.00	2 cups	80	5%	4.00		
78.57	1½ servings	436	27%	117.72		
4.00	3 cups	120	5%	6.00		
9.10	2 rolls	140	13%	18.20		
174.08		1,746		279.30	15.99%	15.08%
2.52	16 oz	252	2%	5.04		
13.12	1 serving	164	8%	13.12		
18.20	3 slices	210	13%	27.30		
0.00	3 tablespoons	150	0%	0.00		
39.72	2 servings	662	12%	79.44		
0.00	3 cups	30	0%	0.00		
8.4	3 tablespoons	60	21%	12.60		
41.48	1 serving	244	17%	41.48		
4.00	3 cups	120	5%	6.00		
0.00	3 tablespoons	36	0%	0.00		
127.44		1,928		184.98	9.59%	10.04%
23.43	16 oz	426	11%	46.86		
10.15	2 servings	290	7%	20.30		
9.10	2 slices	140	13%	18.20		
0.00	3 tablespoons	150	0%	0.00		

	SERVING SIZE WOMEN	CALORIES	% FROM FAT
Day Thirteen (cont.)			
LUNCH			
Tofu "Chicken" Teriyaki Sandwich	1 serving	271	21%
EssentialSalad	2 cups	20	0%
Thousand Island Dressing	2 tablespoons	40	21%
DINNER			
Tostada Grande	1 serving	276	10%
Guacabonzo	2 tablespoons	29	33%
Whole-Grain Roll	1 roll	70	13%
Total:		1,134	
Day Fourteen			
BREAKFAST			
Surfers' Favorite Beverage	8 oz	149	20%
High-Fiber French Toast	2 servings	184	16%
Orange Wedges	1 orange	64	1%
LUNCH			
All-American Gardenburger	1 sandwich	250	14%
Home-Fried Potatoes	1 serving	164	8%
EssentialSalad	2 cups	20	0%
DINNER			
Sweet and Sour Szechwan Tofu "Chicken"	1 serving	206	27%
Wild Rice and Asparagus Salad	1 serving	126	5%
Total:		1,163	
Day Fifteen			
BREAKFAST			
Fresh Fruit Toss	1 serving	90	4%
Hot and Hearty Five-Grain Cereal	1 serving	227	17%
Almond, Rice, or Skim Milk (43 calories or more)	½ cup	43	0%
LUNCH			
Middle Eastern Pita Sandwich	1 sandwich	269	17%
Artichoke Hearts and Fava Beans	¾ serving	171	14%
DINNER			
Pan-Roasted Portobello Mushrooms over Broiled Polenta	1 serving	208	8%
VeggiePack	2 cups	80	5%
Total:		1,088	

CALORIES FROM FAT	SERVING SIZE MEN	CALORIES	% FROM FAT	CALORIES FROM FAT	AVERAGE DAILY % FROM FAT	
					MEN	WOMEN
56.91	1 serving	271	21%	56.91		
0.00	3 cups	30	0%	0.00		
8.40	3 tablespoons	60	21%	12.60		
27.60	1 serving	276	10%	27.60		
9.57	4 tablespoons	58	33%	19.14		
9.10	1 roll	70	13%	9.10		
154.26		1,765		210.71	11.93%	13.60%
29.80	16 oz	298	20%	59.60		
29.44	4 servings	368	16%	58.88		
0.64	1 orange	64	1%	0.64		
35.00	1 sandwich	250	14%	35.00		
13.12	1 serving	164	8%	13.12		
0.00	3 cups	30	0%	0.00		
55.62	2 servings	412	27%	111.24		
6.30	1 serving	126	5%	6.30		
169.92		1,712		284.78	16.63%	14.61%
3.60	2 servings	180	4%	7.20		
38.59	2 servings	554	17%	94.18		
0.00	1 cup	86	0%	0.00		
45.73	1 sandwich	269	17%	45.73		
23.94	1 serving	227	14%	31.78		
16.64	1 serving	208	8%	16.64		
4.00	3 cups	120	5%	6.00		
132.50		1,644		201.53	12.26%	12.18%

	SERVING SIZE WOMEN	CALORIES	% FROM FAT
Day Sixteen			
BREAKFAST			
Banana Frappé	8 oz	213	11%
Tropical Granola	⅝ cup	274	32%
Orange Wedges	1 orange	64	1%
LUNCH			
Garden Lasagne	1 serving	226	12%
EssentialSalad	2 cups	20	0%
DINNER			
Bombay Potatoes, Tomatoes, and Chickpeas	1 serving	236	8%
Calcutta Cauliflower	2 servings	104	25%
EssentialSalad	2 cups	20	0%
Total:		1,157	
Day Seventeen			
BREAKFAST			
Very Strawberry Smoothie	8 oz	126	2%
Mighty Multigrain Cereal	1 cup	137	10%
Almond, Rice, or Skim Milk (43 calories or more)	½ cup	43	0%
LUNCH			
Gardenburger Maui	1 sandwich	329	10%
Baked Potato Skins	1 serving	198	19%
DINNER			
Thai Peanut Noodles	1 serving	181	32%
String Beans with Ginger	2 servings	104	53%
Total:		1,118	
Day Eighteen			
BREAKFAST			
Fresh Fruit Toss	1 cup	90	4%
Hot and Hearty Five-Grain Cereal	1 cup	227	17%
Almond, Rice, or Skim Milk (43 calorie or more)	½ cup	43	0%
LUNCH			
Vegetarian Reuben Sandwich	1 sandwich	257	14%
VeggiePack	2 cups	80	5%

CALORIES FROM FAT	SERVING SIZE MEN	CALORIES	% FROM FAT	CALORIES FROM FAT	AVERAGE DAILY % FROM FAT MEN	WOMEN
23.43	16 oz	426	11%	46.86		
87.68	1 cup	438	32%	140.16		
0.64	1 orange	64	1%	0.64		
27.12	2 servings	452	12%	54.24		
0.00	3 cups	30	0%	0.00		
18.88	1 serving	236	8%	18.88		
26.00	2 servings	104	25%	26.00		
0.00	3 cups	30	0%	0.00		
183.75		1,780		286.78	16.11%	15.88%
2.52	16 oz	252	2%	5.04		
13.70	3 cups	411	10%	41.10		
0.00	1 cup	86	0%	0.00		
32.90	1 sandwich	329	10%	32.90		
37.62	2 servings	396	19%	75.24		
57.92	1 serving	181	32%	57.92		
55.12	2 servings	104	53%	55.12		
199.78		1,759		267.32	15.20%	17.87%
3.60	2 cups	180	4%	7.20		
38.59	1½ cups	340	17%	57.80		
0.00	1 cup	86	0%	0.00		
35.98	2 sandwiches	514	14%	71.96		
4.00	3 cups	120	5%	6.00		

	SERVING SIZE WOMEN	CALORIES	% FROM FAT
Day Eighteen (cont.)			
DINNER			
Tostada Grande	1 serving	276	10%
Citrus Vinaigrette	2 tablespoons	24	0%
Healthful Homemade Sour Cream	2 tablespoons	18	32%
Gypsy Soup	¾ serving	140	10%
Total:		1,155	
Day Nineteen			
BREAKFAST			
Banana Frappé	8 oz	213	11%
Tropical Granola	½ cup	219	32%
Almond, Rice, or Skim Milk (43 calories or more)	½ cup	43	0%
Orange Wedges	1 orange	64	1%
LUNCH			
Broiled Polenta Squares and Tomato Chutney	1 serving	178	14%
EssentialSalad	2 cups	20	0%
Balsamic Vinaigrette	2 tablespoons	10	0%
Mango-Apricot Bread Pudding	1 serving	194	17%
DINNER			
Wonderful Russian Borscht	1 serving	99	20%
Wild Rice and Asparagus Salad	1 serving	126	5%
Total:		1,166	
Day Twenty			
BREAKFAST			
Manoa Sunrise Smoothie	8 oz	122	2%
Yamcakes	2 servings	220	9%
Fresh Fruit Syrup	¼ cup	24	0%
LUNCH			
Roasted Vegetable Pizzas	1 serving	122	7%
EssentialSalad	2 cups	20	0%
Thousand Island Dressing	2 tablespoons	40	21%
Fruit Cake	1 serving	280	13%
Dinner			
Healthy Caesar Salad	1 serving	157	19%
VeggiePack	2 cups	80	5%
Whole-Grain Rolls	1 roll	70	13%
Total:		1,135	

CALORIES FROM FAT	SERVING SIZE MEN	CALORIES	% FROM FAT	CALORIES FROM FAT	AVERAGE DAILY % FROM FAT	
					MEN	WOMEN
27.60	1 serving	276	10%	27.60		
0.00	3 tablespoons	36	0%	0.00		
5.76	3 tablespoons	27	32%	8.64		
14.00	1 serving	187	10%	18.70		
129.53		1,766		197.90	11.21%	11.21%
23.43	16 oz	426	11%	46.86		
70.08	1 cup	438	32%	140.16		
0.00	½ cup	43	0%	0.00		
0.64	1 orange	64	1%	0.64		
24.92	2 servings	356	14%	49.84		
0.00	3 cups	30	0%	0.00		
0.00	3 tablespoons	15	0%	0.00		
32.98	1 serving	194	17%	32.98		
19.80	1 serving	99	20%	19.80		
6.30	1 serving	126	5%	6.30		
178.15		1,791		296.58	16.56%	15.28%
2.44	16 oz	244	2%	4.88		
19.80	3 servings	330	9%	29.70		
0.00	⅓ cup	32	0%	0.00		
8.54	2 servings	244	7%	17.08		
0.00	3 cups	30	0%	0.00		
8.40	3 tablespoons	60	21%	12.60		
36.40	1 serving	280	13%	36.40		
29.83	2 servings	314	19%	59.66		
4.00	3 cups	120	5%	6.00		
9.10	2 rolls	140	13%	18.20		
118.51		1,794		184.52	10.28%	10.44%

	SERVING SIZE WOMEN	CALORIES	% FROM FAT
Day Twenty-One			
BREAKFAST			
Very Strawberry Smoothie	8 oz	126	2%
Hot and Hearty Five-Grain Cereal	1 cup	227	17%
Almond, Rice, or Skim Milk (43 calories or more)	½ cup	43	0%
LUNCH			
Middle Eastern Pita Sandwich	1 sandwich	269	17%
Whole-Grain Satay Salad	1 serving	118	18%
Barley Succotash	1 serving	111	3%
DINNER			
Exotic Stir-fry (without cheese)	1 serving	188	36%
EssentialSalad	2 cups	20	0%
Raspberry Vinaigrette	2 tablespoons	8	0%
Total:		1,110	

CALORIES FROM FAT	SERVING SIZE MEN	CALORIES	% FROM FAT	CALORIES FROM FAT	AVERAGE DAILY % FROM FAT	
					MEN	WOMEN
2.52	16 oz	252	2%	5.04		
38.59	2 cups	454	17%	77.18		
0.00	1 cup	86	0%	0.00		
45.73	1 sandwich	269	17%	45.73		
21.24	1 serving	118	18%	21.24		
3.33	2 servings	222	3%	6.66		
67.68	1 serving	188	36%	67.68		
0.00	3 cups	30	0%	0.00		
0.00	3 tablespoons	12	0%	0.00		
179.09		1,631		223.53	13.71%	16.13%

CHAPTER 12

Taking the Garden on the Road

Staying True to the Garden When You're Not at Home

If you're worried about falling off—or out of—the garden while traveling, while at business meetings or conventions, while visiting friends or on vacation, this chapter contains a number of tips of dietary damage control when you're out on the road. I've spent about half of the last eleven years on the road myself and have learned how to take a piece of the garden with me, no matter where I'm going or how I go about getting there.

Let's look at a number of situations, one by one, that often leave many who want to eat "right" at a loss.

Airlines and Other Transport

More of us are traveling on airlines these days—and airline food often conflicts with our style of eating. Things used to be much worse than they are today, however, and it is easier now than ever before to get something you really want to eat on an airline.

Whether you are traveling first class, business class, or coach, almost all airlines allow you to order special meals at the same time that you or your travel agent makes your reservation. Vegetarian fare is almost always available, including dairyless vegan meals. In fact, to make sure they are covering all bases, many airline caterers now make all of their vegetarian meals vegan.

Note that vegetarian meals are not the only special orders airlines will fill. There are special meals for diabetics, for example, and many airlines offer low-fat/low-cholesterol meals that are not strictly vegetarian. When all else fails, most airlines offer "fruit plates."

If you make your reservation fewer than 24 hours prior to departure, your special order may not be filled. And even when you are promised a special meal, there might be a glitch. So go prepared. If you think you won't get what you want, or just as a precaution, do what I do and pack a few snacks, such as fresh, cut-up fruit in a plastic container (apples need a little lime or lemon squeezed on them so they don't turn brown), organic (and sulfur-dioxide-free) dried fruits (such as papaya, pineapple, raisins, currants, figs, cranberries, cherries), and/or a pack of bite-size vegetables.

If you have to take a regular meal, you can sometimes still "modify" it to make at least parts of it acceptable. Eat the roll if it's whole-grain, but leave the margarine; skip the meat, eat the salad or other vegetables, or ask for two or more extra side salads or veggies.

I am never afraid to ask if there's a Gardenburger on board. Many airlines serve them—and other meatless burgers—these days.

Both airlines and airports can seem like nutritional deserts at times. They are definitely not all equal when it comes to providing healthier alternatives. The nonprofit Physicians Committee for Responsible Medicine studied both airline and airport food and came up with some interesting findings you might find helpful in making your own travel plans.

Among seven of the biggest airlines studied, the group ranked United number one, finding that it provided a good range of low-fat fare, including low-fat vegetarian fare. It observed that a number of other nutritional experts had also given United top ranking.

Next in the lineup was TWA, followed, in order of ranking, by Continental, USAir, American, and Northwest. Delta was contacted but declined to offer information necessary to make a determination of rank.

The group also analyzed the food in nineteen of the biggest airports in the country. Many airline employees are so turned off that they pack their own food. Nonetheless, some airports do offer good choices. You're most likely to find something you can eat in good conscience at airports in Los Angeles, Pittsburgh, Vancouver, B.C., Seattle, or Albuquerque (in that order). You're much less likely to find good low-fat, vegetarian fare at airports in St. Louis, Phoenix, Memphis, Dallas, or Atlanta (which came in at the bottom of the list).

Many are not aware of the growing number of menu options on airlines; fewer still know that you can also get vegetarian food on most long-haul Amtrak dining cars—without advance order. Most of these vegetarian dishes, however, contain some dairy products—so if you're a strict vegan, you may have to order side dishes of fruits and salads or pack some of your own foods. Many Canadian and European trains will provide special meals with adequate advance notice—usually at least forty-eight hours.

Cruise ships increasingly offer vegetarian fare, as well as low-fat fare. You generally can't find out what a vegetarian meal will consist of on a plane, but you can sometimes get complete menus from cruise lines, if you request them well in advance of your departure date. Many of the cruise lines will make some effort to provide for special dietary needs and desires. But, again, they need lots of advance notice—thirty days and often more.

Restaurants, Hotels, Room Service

Just because you are in a restaurant is no reason to abandon your nutritional principles. A great many restaurants now have salad bars, low-fat and even vegetarian choices. In addition, most restaurants really don't mind modifying many of the items on their menus to suit your needs. Obviously, if the modifications are extensive, you will want to check in advance—but there's nothing wrong with asking right at the table whether some changes can be made. A recent Restaurant Association survey revealed that 90 percent of all sit-down restaurants will make some menu modifications on request.

Meatless and vegetarian entrées are becoming commonplace in restaurants and hotels. Gardenburgers, and other meatless burgers, are now on more than forty thousand menus. Whenever possible, check over the menu before you sit down; otherwise, see what's on the menu and whether there are items you can work with.

I usually quickly scan menus for whole foods, such as baked potatoes, brown rice, whole-grain breads. You can ask for combinations that aren't specifically on the menu—and often you'll get them with a smile. If I don't see anything that appeals to me, for example, I often ask for a baked potato or two served with a red marinara sauce and some steamed veggies on top.

There are usually vegetable side dishes you can order—but be wary of added fats; many of these dishes are afloat in them. Don't be afraid to ask how things are prepared. Ask for fats such as vegetable oils—if you want them at all—to be served on the side. That way you control how much fat is added. Sometimes you can use appetizers and tasty side dishes to garnish your rice, potatoes, or pasta. Maintain a friendly, inquisitive but cooperative tone, and before long you'll feel as if you're in your own kitchen—except that here you'll have some "assistant chefs" and you won't have to do the dishes!

If you decide to go with the salad bar, don't smother your veggies in salad dressings. Try a little lemon or vinegar.

If you're calling down to room service and all you're seeing on the menu are meat entrées, ask what vegetables come with them. Believe it or not, many hotels will be glad to serve you just the vegetable side dishes. I've combined as many as four or five or these side dishes and come up with a delicious, healthy meal. And even if there is no fruit plate listed on the room sevice menu, ask for one; you'll almost always get it.

Finally, here's a checklist of things *not* to say to yourself when you're eating out: (1) This is a special occasion; (2) It can't hurt to eat junk foods once in a while; (3) I don't eat out that often; (4) This food isn't very healthy, but I don't want to waste any of it. It is through just such "justifications" that we heap one nutritional insult after another on our bodies.

Business Meals

One of the commonest justifications for eating poorly is "My job requires it." Maybe it isn't said quite that way, but that's what this lame excuse boils down to in the end. Those who use this excuse argue that if they don't eat the way others eat at a business luncheon, breakfast, banquet, or convention, they will seem "odd" or "out of step." Or they say they have to eat what's available and "not make a fuss."

Well, I have news: In my many years in business, I have never heard of anyone being fired, demoted, or held back because of healthy eating habits. Most employers respect those who have sound principles, in life as well as in business, including diet. And a healthy employee is far more valuable than a sick one or one who dies prematurely of heart disease or cancer.

If you are going to a company banquet or convention, find out who is handling the food and call them. Just like airlines, railways, and hotels, most of these caterers are happy to accommodate special needs.

If you are going to a restaurant with business associates, don't hesitate to ask for modifications, or simply stick to the salad bar and fruit plates. If you are taking clients to lunch or dinner, choose a restaurant where you know you can get good vegetarian food for yourself and a wide selection for your guests.

Family and Friends

One of the biggest challenges you will face comes when you are invited to the homes of family or friends who are not aware of or appreciative of your eating style. That's why I always advise people not to hide their vegetarianism under a bushel basket (or anything else). That way when people invite you over, they will know what to expect—and so will you.

The best policy when you are invited to dinner at someone else's home is to say, "I'd love to come, but you should know that I'm a vegetarian for health, environmental, and other reasons; it's important to me and I stick to it. At the same time, I don't want to make life difficult for you and I don't want you to be offended if I come to your home and don't eat what you serve. So if you think it's going to be a problem, don't hesitate to say so." Let the other party know what you *do* eat. Chances are many of these things will be on the menu as side dishes. Most people are quite understanding—and often you will discover that you are talking to another vegetarian or near-vegetarian anyway—or else someone who is curious to learn more.

If you find yourself in a really unpleasant situation at a "culinarily hostile" table, you can always fall back on this: "Oh, I should have warned you; I'm on a strict dietary regimen of zero-cholesterol, zero-fat." That will rescue you from all the meat and dairy products.

If you're comfortable with the people who are inviting you to a meal at their home, you might even suggest bringing your own food and say: "You're a great cook, but you know I'm a vegetarian; anyway, it's the company that counts and I don't want to miss this occasion."

What do you do when it's your turn to invite people to your home and you know they aren't vegetarian? If you stick to my GardenCuisine recipes, you'll have no problem. These dishes have satisfied the palates of everyone from vegan to traditional meat eater. People like food that *tastes good*. Enough said.

Holidays can be particularly difficult since so many of them seem to revolve not only around food but also around the *wrong* foods. The best advice for holidays is to try to reorient them away from food toward some enjoyable activity. If you go skiing over Christmas, for example, that in itself serves as a reward for both you and family members and makes it easier to resist the temptation of eating high-fat foods. Even going to a movie on a major holiday—or to an ethnic restaurant with good vegetarian choices—can suffice.

Last year, I took my whole extended family to a Middle East/Indian restaurant for Christmas. Most of them had never tasted these foods. They found it exciting to eat such delicious and eye-appealing foods—and no one even noticed the absence of meat!

In general, it all becomes easier with time and practice. The more you've got the garden within you, the easier it is to take it on the road and have it with you always.

PART FOUR

GardenCuisine

Recipes for a Clean Planet, Good Health, Lean Body, High Energy

gardencuisinegardencuisinegardencuisine
gardencuisinegardencuisinegardencuisine
gardencuisinegardencuisinegardencuisine
gardencuisinegardencuisinegardencuisine
gardencuisinegardencuisinegardencuisine
gardencuisinegardencuisinegardencuisine

CHAPTER 13

Bringing the Garden into the Kitchen

Making the Transition

To make the transition to GardenCuisine easy and enjoyable, I'm going to help you clear your kitchen of foods that do little or nothing to nourish you and replace them with the healthful staples you'll need to make GardenCuisine a daily success in your home. I'll also give you tips on getting the right tools in place to help you make the recipes you'll soon be sampling.

Apart from helping you restock your pantry and retool your kitchen in a few easy steps, I'll also be giving you tips on how to shop for fresh, whole foods, how to store and prepare basic foods, and how to modify other foods and recipes to conform with GardenCuisine principles and goals.

I'm providing you with a master shopping list that covers the ingredients of every recipe in this book. Those items you will need for your basic pantry are identified as well.

I recognize that many of you don't really like to cook all that much or don't have the time for it. For those of you who fall into this large category, I've selected what I call my "Super Sixteen"—sixteen life-enhancing recipes that can sustain you and your family, if desired, *for life.* Just sixteen recipes, easily mastered, can give you a broad range of tasty, whole foods that will keep your nutritional act in balance.

As you begin to make the transition toward vegetarian fare, remember that any movement in this direction is progress. And if you backslide from time to time, don't become discouraged or think that you've "blown it."

To help ensure success over the long haul, take some time to plan your transition and to maintain it. An hour a week to plan your shopping lists and menu selections is time particularly well spent. Start studying labels for fat content, in particular, but also for sugars and sodium.

As you begin to adapt to this new way of eating, you will, I am confident, note benefits quickly—in the form of clearer skin, heightened energy and awareness, slimmer profile. Success, I have found, really does breed success. As you successfully transit from higher-fat foods to lower-fat foods, you will find it increasingly easier to take the next steps.

All of you, no doubt, have personal goals. Use those to monitor your progress, as well as to gauge the success of GardenCuisine. Perhaps you've been told your cholesterol is too high; try GardenCuisine for a few months and then get retested. The results, I predict, will cause you to embrace GardenCuisine with even greater enthusiasm. Or if your goal is to lose weight, follow the Lean Green program and see what happens.

I firmly believe that almost all physical conditions, and many "mental" ones, can be significantly improved with better nutrition—and so, whether your goal is to lower your blood pressure or overcome depression, I think you'll find the results you get with GardenCuisine ample motivation to keep on cultivating the garden.

Whenever possible, share cooking ideas with others who are exploring vegetarianism. There may even be vegetarian groups in your area with whom you can share meals and potlucks. The feedback you get from others can be very reinforcing.

And when you achieve your goals, at each step, reward yourself. Note your success in a diary or on a chart you may choose to keep or do something special—a trip, a play, a movie, anything you enjoy doing. For those of you who are losing weight, the reward is obvious—buy a size-smaller dress or pair of pants!

But, ultimately, the real reward is a better inner environment and good health, a better outer environment and improved conditions for millions of animals.

Reorganizing and Stocking Your Kitchen

Take a close look at your kitchen. Examine the foods you keep on hand. For most of you, some nutritional housekeeping is in order. Remember, what you keep on hand is what you and your family will eat. When we're hungry, we "go with what we've got." So make sure that what you've got is both healthy and tasty.

So let's roll up our sleeves and start cleaning up the kitchen. Start at one end and go to the other, asking yourself, "Does this item fit into my new eating style?" Your objective is to rid your kitchen of high-fat, junk-food items—which you can either toss out or contribute to a food bank or soup kitchen.

Don't let any of the following come in under your radar:

- Fats that are solid at room temperature (such as Crisco).

- High-fat snack foods (more than 3 grams of fat per serving).

- Any product containing more than 20 milligrams of cholesterol per serving.

- Anything made with white flour.

- White sugar or brown sugar.

- Oils that have been on the shelf for more than a couple of months. (Always refrigerate your oils to help retard free-radical activity and rancidity.)

Don't stop at food items. Reevaluate the tools you have been using in the kitchen. Since you're going to be working with a lot of fruits and vegetables, check your cutting board and your knives and make sure they are clean and sharp and situated where they are convenient to use—generally, close to the sink, where you will be washing those vegetables.

By the way, when it comes to cutting boards, studies have shown that *wood* is better than plastic. The wood contains natural antibiotics that help fend off bacteria better than plastic. Of course, you should still clean your wood cutting boards with warm water and mild organic detergent after each use.

For knives, I recommend a good-quality paring knife, an eight- to ten-inch French chef knife, and a long slicing knife.

The following are also important (if someone asks what you want for a birthday or anniversary or Christmas gift, you might suggest one of these):

- Blender (the higher quality the better).

- Rice cooker (buy the size that fits the needs of your family).

- Measuring cups (I like stainless steel and glass).

- Kitchen shears (great for snipping off the ends of pea pods, green beans, etc.).

- Salad spinner (designed to remove excess water from washed greens).

- Waffle iron (I prefer the type that makes thick "Belgian"-style waffles so that you can add pieces of fresh or dried fruit, grains, and, occasionally, a few nuts).

- Steamer basket (or a separate vegetable steamer).

- Food processor (see Resources section).

- Air popcorn popper.

- Juicer (buy a better-quality machine, because the cheap ones don't last).

- Sprout machine (automatically waters the seeds).

Okay, now that you've cleaned out the old, let's start thinking about bringing in the new. First, you need to reevaluate where you stock things. Can you rearrange your pantry so that it's more user-friendly? If you have the space, buying some staples in larger quantities—by the case, even—can often save you money and can certainly save you time, cutting down on trips to the market.

Before we proceed to your new shopping list, let's take a little time to review some shopping tips.

Shopping Tips

WHERE TO SHOP

Increasingly, even major supermarket chains carry a lot of "natural-food" items and organic produce—so don't hesitate to start there. Then try natural-food stores, specialty markets, and farmers' markets. Roadside stands are sometimes not the bargains or the fresh-from-the-field outlets they may seem to be; they may actually be selling grocery-store produce at higher prices!

If you are anywhere near organic farms, make inquiries to see whether you can buy in bulk direct from these farmers. Also look into "co-ops" where you can trade your time for reduced prices. This is ideal for those who have extra time to spend in the production or sale of food through the co-op. This is a great way to learn about foods and the food business, especially the organic-food business.

Don't assume that because you are buying produce at a farmers' market that it is organic. You need to ask. Of course, not all produce has to be organic to be good (more on this below), and you can usually save a lot by buying at a farmers' market. Another advantage is that the produce is usually very fresh. Close your eyes and smell the quality!

Specialty shops can also be fertile shopping grounds. Check in your area for Chinese, Japanese, Greek, and other ethnic groceries. Many of these carry fresh, whole foods you will have trouble finding elsewhere.

HOW TO SHOP

The first thing I tell my students is to shop on a full stomach! (Eat an apple before you go shopping—nourishing and filling.) This helps reduce the temptation to buy those high-fat snacks and other junk foods. When your shopping basket or cart is full, take a last look at what you've purchased before proceeding to the checkout. You may find a few items you want to put back on the shelf.

The best approach is to take a copy of our shopping list with you, or one that selects from that list and has been carefully thought out, based on what recipes you plan to prepare in the next week. Stick to the list as much as possible rather than making impromptu impulse selections.

Again, remember, what you have on hand is what you are going to end up eating. So select carefully. And to help ensure that you will not get a "fat attack," purchase a variety of healthy snack foods to have on hand at all times. A lot of fresh vegetables and fruits that are immediately prepped for easy eating at home will top your shopping list. I'll tell you a little later how to make "VeggiePacks" and dressings, which make great snack material at any time of day or night.

Other good snack items are whole-grain rice cakes, whole-grain pretzels and bagels (go for the low-salt, low-fat variety), air-popped popcorn; Gardenburgers; Garden-Sausage; toasted pita wedges with instant bean dip; low-fat, low-sodium baked chips with salsa; vegetarian chili; vegetarian burritos.

Be aware that in most stores, the most highly refined and highly processed foods are found in the center aisles; the freshest foods are stocked at the perimeters of these stores. So learn to hug the outside edges of your supermarket and tread cautiously through the interior aisles.

Whenever possible, buy organic. It really does make a difference. Organic-food production is based on a system of farming that maintains and replenishes the fertility of the soil while avoiding toxic additives such as pesticides. If you can't get organic produce, however, it is still better to eat what produce you can find, rather than avoid it altogether. Just wash it thoroughly. And even if the produce is nonorganic, I don't recommend peeling because you lose so many protective nutrients.

Some supermarkets and other groceries provide produce with a stamp that says "Nutriclean." This isn't the same as "organic," but it means that some significant measures have been taken to ensure that the produce you are buying has only very low residues of pesticides. So finding this stamp on produce is a definite plus. Look for it, and if you don't find it, ask the grocer if they can provide produce that qualities for the "Nutriclean" label. An independent testing company awards the label.

Here are some tips for selecting produce:

- Generally pick produce that is firm and heavy for its size; it will usually be tastier and more nutrient-filled.

- Don't pick produce by looks alone; smell is also very important. Practice shutting your eyes and sampling the aroma of the produce. If a tomato, for example, really smells like a tomato, it will also taste like one.

- Cantaloupe and similar melons are ripe when they "give" a little when you push in on them at the stem end (the "belly button").

- Pineapples are ripe when you can easily pull out a center leaf.

- Avocados and bananas ripen quickly when placed in a paper bag with any citrus fruits.

- Smaller ears of light yellow corn are likely to be sweeter.

- When it comes to cucumbers and celery, the smaller they are, the more flavorful they are likely to be.

- Baby vegetables, although more expensive, are a real treat once in a while; they often have intense, exceptional flavor.

- Buy prewashed greens in a bag (saves a lot of preparation), but be sure they are not brown or sticky-looking. Check dates.

- Try unusual veggies and fruits. Be adventuresome.

- Dried-out or limp veggies can sometimes be revived somewhat by dipping them in ice water.

- When you buy mushrooms, put them in a brown paper bag, not in a plastic container; they will keep better. The mushrooms should be firm and dry and closed up tight.

READ LABELS!

Always look at the label on prepared foods. Ask yourself: Is this made of whole foods? How many grams of fat per serving? What percent of total calories comes from fat? Does the product have any cholesterol? Are there artificial additives? Are the flavorings natural or synthetic?

Be aware that gelatin, which is added to many foods, comes from animal parts; whey comes from cow's milk. On the other hand, lecithin is of plant origin; carrageenin comes from seaweed.

Also be aware that ingredients on labels are listed in order of proportion. If you're buying a cereal and some form of sugar is listed even before the grain itself, you know you're being taken—offered empty calories instead of nutritional substance. And note that if "wheat flour" is listed as an ingredient, this is not the same as "whole-wheat flour." It is flour devoid of both the wheat germ and the bran. Always check the labels on your breads and baked goods.

As for food additives, according to the Center for Science in the Public Interest, the ten worst (all of which you definitely want to avoid) are:

- Acefulfame-K
- Artificial colorings of any kind
- Aspartame
- BHA and BHT
- Caffeine

- Monosodium glutamate (MSG)
- Propyl gallate
- Saccharin
- Sodium nitrite
- Sulfites

If you select from the shopping list that follows, you will avoid all or nearly all food additives. Also, avoid Olestra.

One final shopping tip: If you can arrange things so that you shop just once a week, you will save time, money, and energy. It just takes a little extra planning.

Shopping List

(Whenever you can, buy organic!)

HOW TO USE:

❑ *Check or place the number of items you want in this box.*

❦ *Buy all of these items and you will be ready to make the "Super Sixteen" menu items.*

NFG *Natural-food grocery or natural foods section of the supermarket.*

R *Refrigerated section.*

✳ *Reduced-fat or nonfat.*

Some help for ethnic dishes: A *Asian* IN *Indian* I *Italian* M *Mexican* ME *Middle Eastern*

Baked Goods *(bakery fresh)*

❑ corn tortillas

❑ multigrain whole-grain bread

❑ whole-grain bagels ❦

❑ whole-grain bread cubes

❑ whole-grain burger buns ❦

❑ whole-grain English muffins ❦

❑ whole-grain rye bread (with caraway seeds) ✳

❑ whole-wheat bread crumbs

❑ whole-wheat pita bread ❦

❑ whole-wheat sweet baguette

❑ whole-wheat tortillas ❦

Baking Supplies

- ❑ arrowroot powder
- ❑ almond extract
- ❑ baking powder (aluminum-free) NFG
- ❑ baking soda
- ❑ cocoa powder NFG
- ❑ coconut extract
- ❑ cornstarch
- ❑ cream of tartar
- ❑ egg substitute (dry)
- ❑ whole-grain baking mix NFG
- ❑ whole-wheat flour
- ❑ whole-wheat pastry flour

Beans, Peas, and Legumes (dried)

- ❑ baby lima beans
- ❑ black-eyed peas
- ❑ cannellini beans
- ❑ chickpeas (garbanzos)
- ❑ dried black beans
- ❑ fava beans
- ❑ instant bean dips (very handy)
- ❑ kidney beans
- ❑ lentils
- ❑ lima beans
- ❑ pinto beans
- ❑ soybeans
- ❑ yellow split peas

Beverages

- ❑ green tea
- ❑ herbal teas (hundreds of varieties)
- ❑ orange spice tea bags
- ❑ Republic of Tea (cardamom cinnamon)
- ❑ sparkling water
- ❑ water (distilled or filtered) ❧

Cans and Jars

- ❑ artichoke hearts (water-packed)
- ❑ black beans NFG ❧
- ❑ black-eyed peas NFG ❧
- ❑ Bush's Vegetarian Baked Beans NFG
- ❑ cannellini beans NFG
- ❑ chili (vegetarian) NFG ❧
- ❑ cream-style corn
- ❑ crushed pineapple (unsweetened)
- ❑ crushed tomatoes ❧
- ❑ diced chilies (like Ortega)
- ❑ fruit chutney
- ❑ chickpeas (garbanzos) NFG
- ❑ garlic salsa NFG
- ❑ green chilies
- ❑ kidney beans ❧
- ❑ mandarin oranges
- ❑ olives NFG ❧
- ❑ pineapple chunks (unsweetened)

- ❏ pineapple slices (unsweetened)
- ❏ pinto beans
- ❏ pizza sauce NFG
- ❏ pumpkin filling
- ❏ spaghetti sauce (fat free)
- ❏ Swanson's Vegetable Broth ❦
- ❏ tomato paste

- ❏ tomato salsa NFG ❦
- ❏ tomato sauce ❦
- ❏ unsweetened applesauce (variety of flavors) NFG ❦
- ❏ water chestnuts

Cereal

- ❏ Barbara's High 5
- ❏ Erewhon Fruit 'N Wheat
- ❏ Erewhon Raisin Bran
- ❏ Erewhon Wheat Flakes
- ❏ Familia No Added Sugar Swiss Müesli
- ❏ General Mills Multi-Grain Cheerios ❦
- ❏ Golden Temple Low Fat Muesli
- ❏ Health Valley Fat-Free Granola
- ❏ Health Valley 100% Natural Bran with Apples and Cinnamon
- ❏ Health Valley Real Oat Bran
- ❏ Kellogg's All-Bran
- ❏ Kellogg's Almond Raisin Nutri-Grain ❦

- ❏ Kellogg's Golden Wheat Nutri-Grain ❦
- ❏ Kellogg's Low Fat Granola ❦
- ❏ Kellogg's Raisin Squares ❦
- ❏ LifeStream Fruit and Nut Muesli
- ❏ Nabisco Shredded Wheat 'N Bran
- ❏ New Morning Bran Flakes
- ❏ New Morning Honey-and-Almond Oatios
- ❏ New Morning Raisin Bran
- ❏ Post Bran Flakes
- ❏ Shredded Wheat
- ❏ U.S. Mills Skinner's Raisin Bran

Condiments

- ❏ capers
- ❏ cocktail sauce
- ❏ dressings: Italian, ranch (low- or no-fat) ❦
- ❏ ketchup NFG ❦
- ❏ mustards: stone-ground, jalapeño, or Dijon ❦

- ❏ nonfat mayonnaise (far from a perfect food, but better than pure fat)
- ❏ olives: black, Greek, or green
- ❏ oyster sauce (vegetarian) NFG
- ❏ pickles (dill) NFG ❦
- ❏ pickled ginger
- ❏ red pepper sauce (like Tabasco)

Condiments (cont.)

- red sauce (fat-free) NFG
- salsa: regular, roasted garlic NFG ❦
- sauerkraut
- sesame seeds or gomashio (sesame salt) NFG ❦
- soy sauce
- sweet pickle relish NFG

- tamari soy sauce NFG ❦
- teriyaki sauce NFG
- vegetarian hoisin sauce NFG
- vinegars: apple cider, balsamic, distilled white, raspberry, rice, and seasoned rice ❦
- wasabe

Dairy/Dairy Substitutes

WHEN YOU READ THE LABELS ON ALTERNATIVE CHEESES, YOU WILL FIND THAT THEY CONTAIN DAIRY CASEIN BUT USE VEGETABLE OIL IN PLACE OF THE ANIMAL FATS, WHICH CONTAIN CHOLESTEROL.

- almond milk NFG ❦
- buttermilk R
- cheddar cheese NFG/R * ❦
- coconut milk (low-fat) ❦
- egg substitute R ❦
- egg whites R
- feta cheese NFG
- jack cheese NFG/R *

- jalapeño cheese NFG/R *
- low-fat cheddar cheese NFG/R *
- milk, nonfat dairy R ❦
- nonfat cream cheese NFG/R ❦
- oat milk NFG
- Parmesan cheese NFG/R * ❦
- plain nonfat yogurt (Nancy's is my favorite brand) NFG/R * ❦
- rice milk NFG ❦
- soy milk NFG ❦
- Swiss cheese NFG/R *
- tofu sour cream NFG/R
- white cheddar cheese NFG/R * ❦

Dried Fruits and Vegetables (organic and sulfur-free)

- apricots ❦
- banana pieces
- cranberries ❦
- currants ❦
- dates ❦
- figs: golden figs ❦

- mangoes
- papayas ❦
- peaches
- pineapples
- raisins: golden, sultana ❦
- sun-dried tomatoes

Flavor Bases

- ❑ Bragg's Liquid Aminos NFG
- ❑ cubed vegetable broth NFG
- ❑ yellow miso, or others NFG
- ❑ vegetarian chicken-style seasoning (powder) NFG

Fresh Fruits

(Remember to get a variety of colors.)
- ❑ apples: green, red, and yellow ❧
- ❑ apricots ❧
- ❑ avocados ❧
- ❑ bananas: regular, red, finger ❧
- ❑ bell peppers: green, red, and yellow ❧
- ❑ berries: black, blue, boysen, logan, marion, and raspberries ❧
- ❑ cherries ❧
- ❑ cherry tomatoes
- ❑ chili peppers
- ❑ cucumbers
- ❑ eggplant: Japanese or globe
- ❑ figs ❧
- ❑ grapefruit ❧
- ❑ grapes, any varieties ❧
- ❑ guava ❧
- ❑ kiwi ❧
- ❑ lemons ❧
- ❑ limes ❧
- ❑ mangoes ❧
- ❑ melons: musk, cantaloupe, and honeydew ❧
- ❑ nectarines ❧
- ❑ oranges ❧
- ❑ papayas ❧
- ❑ passion fruit ❧
- ❑ peaches ❧
- ❑ pears
- ❑ pineapple ❧
- ❑ plums ❧
- ❑ pumpkin
- ❑ squash: butternut, kabocha, yellow, winter, summer, spaghetti, and zucchini ❧
- ❑ star fruit ❧
- ❑ strawberries ❧
- ❑ tangelos ❧
- ❑ tangerines ❧
- ❑ tomatoes ❧
- ❑ watermelon ❧

Fresh Herbs

- ❑ basil I ❧
- ❑ cilantro IN M ❧
- ❑ dill
- ❑ kaffir lime leaves I
- ❑ lemongrass A
- ❑ mint sprigs ME ❧
- ❑ oregano ❧
- ❑ rosemary
- ❑ sage
- ❑ tarragon
- ❑ thyme ❧

Fresh (Unopened) Vegetable Flowers

- ❏ artichokes
- ❏ asparagus
- ❏ broccoli ❦
- ❏ Brussels sprouts
- ❏ cabbage: red, green, and Chinese
- ❏ cauliflower ❦
- ❏ edible decorative flowers (unsprayed)

Fresh Vegetable Greens

- ❏ baby
- ❏ bok choy
- ❏ butter lettuce
- ❏ celery
- ❏ collard
- ❏ endive
- ❏ fennel
- ❏ field
- ❏ green onions ❦
- ❏ kale
- ❏ lettuce: green, red, and romaine ❦
- ❏ mustard greens
- ❏ parsley I ❦
- ❏ radicchio
- ❏ red cabbage
- ❏ scallions
- ❏ spinach
- ❏ Swiss chard
- ❏ watercress

Fresh Vegetable Roots

- ❏ beets
- ❏ carrots ❦
- ❏ cassava
- ❏ daikon
- ❏ garlic ❦
- ❏ ginger ❦
- ❏ horseradish
- ❏ jicama
- ❏ leeks
- ❏ onions: red, white, or yellow ❦
- ❏ potatoes: red, white, yellow, russet, sweet ❦
- ❏ radishes
- ❏ turnips
- ❏ yams, jewel

Fresh Vegetable Sprouts and Mushrooms

- ❏ alfalfa
- ❏ bean sprouts: Azuki, mung
- ❏ buckwheat sprouts
- ❏ mushrooms: standard, button, portobello, shiitake ❦
- ❏ pea sprouts
- ❏ sunflower shoots

Fresh Vegetables—Grains and Legumes

- ❏ beans: Chinese, long, green, and string
- ❏ corn ❧
- ❏ peas: green, snow ❧

Frozen Foods

- ❏ apple juice concentrate
- ❏ chopped spinach
- ❏ corn NFG ❧
- ❏ cranberry juice concentrate
- ❏ GardenBeef
- ❏ Gardenburger ❧
- ❏ GardenChick'n
- ❏ GardenSausage ❧
- ❏ lima beans ❧
- ❏ mixed vegetables (for emergency backup) ❧
- ❏ orange juice concentrate
- ❏ peas ❧
- ❏ strawberries (when fresh is out of season)
- ❏ vanilla nondairy, low-fat, or nonfat dessert
- ❏ vanilla yogurt (nonfat)
- ❏ white grape juice concentrate

Grains / Grain Products

- ❏ barley ❧
- ❏ brown basmati rice ❧
- ❏ brown rice ❧
- ❏ buckwheat
- ❏ bulgar wheat
- ❏ corn ❧
- ❏ corn chips ❧
- ❏ cornmeal
- ❏ five-grain cereal (rolled) ❧
- ❏ millet ❧
- ❏ oat groats
- ❏ pearl barley
- ❏ popcorn
- ❏ rolled oats
- ❏ rye berries ❧
- ❏ sorghum
- ❏ tortilla chips (baked)
- ❏ wheat berries ❧
- ❏ wheat germ
- ❏ whole-wheat couscous
- ❏ whole-grain pasta ❧
- ❏ wild rice
- ❏ whole-grain rice cakes
- ❏ whole-grain popcorn cakes
- ❏ whole-grain crackers

Herbs / Spices / Flavor Extracts

- ❏ allspice
- ❏ basil I ❧
- ❏ bay leaves I IN
- ❏ black mustard seeds I ME
- ❏ black peppercorns ❧
- ❏ caraway seeds

Herbs / Spices / Flavor Extracts (cont.)

- ☐ cardamom I
- ☐ cayenne pepper powder I ❦
- ☐ celery seeds
- ☐ chili powder M ❦
- ☐ chives
- ☐ cinnamon IN ❦
- ☐ cinnamon sticks
- ☐ cloves IN ❦
- ☐ coconut extract
- ☐ coriander IN A ❦
- ☐ crystallized ginger IN
- ☐ cumin M IN ❦
- ☐ cumin seeds M IN ❦
- ☐ curry powder (or garam masala is better) IN
- ☐ dill seed
- ☐ dill weed
- ☐ dried basil I
- ☐ dry mustard A
- ☐ fennel seeds
- ☐ fresh-ground black pepper
- ☐ garlic granules A I ❦
- ☐ garlic powder A I ❦
- ☐ ginger powder A IN ❦
- ☐ ground white pepper
- ☐ Italian mixed herbs
- ☐ marjoram
- ☐ mint
- ☐ multiherb blend
- ☐ mustard seeds (black)
- ☐ nutmeg
- ☐ oregano I ❦
- ☐ paprika
- ☐ poultry seasoning
- ☐ red pepper flakes
- ☐ rosemary
- ☐ sage
- ☐ sea salt ❦
- ☐ tarragon
- ☐ thyme ❦
- ☐ turmeric IN ❦
- ☐ vanilla (pure)
- ☐ white peppercorns ❦

Juices

(Homemade, fresh is ideal)
- ☐ apple juice, unfiltered NFG/R
- ☐ apricot nectar NFG
- ☐ grapefruit juice NFG
- ☐ lemon juice NFG
- ☐ orange juice NFG/R
- ☐ pineapple juice NFG/R

Meat Substitutes (see also Frozen Foods)

- ☐ falafel
- ☐ firm silken tofu NFG/R
- ☐ firm tofu NFG/R ❦
- ☐ seitan NFG/R
- ☐ tempeh

Miscellaneous

- ❑ agar flakes
- ❑ ice (cracked) ❦
- ❑ nori seaweed

Nuts/Nut Butters/Seeds

- ❑ almonds (whole, sliced, or slivered)
- ❑ almond butter
- ❑ cashews (raw)
- ❑ hazelnuts (raw)
- ❑ peanut butter
- ❑ peanuts (raw)
- ❑ pecans (raw)
- ❑ roasted peanuts
- ❑ sesame seeds (unhulled)
- ❑ sunflower seeds (toasted or raw) ❦
- ❑ tahini (sesame seed butter)
- ❑ walnuts

Oils

- ❑ canola oil NFG
- ❑ extra-virgin olive oil NFG ❦
- ❑ flaxseed oil (refrigerated)
- ❑ olive oil spray ❦
- ❑ sesame oil (toasted) NFG ❦

Pasta

- ❑ soba noodles
- ❑ whole-grain pasta of choice (rainbow rotini, bows, etc.)
- ❑ whole-grain ramen soup
- ❑ udon
- ❑ whole-wheat fettuccine
- ❑ whole-wheat lasagna noodles
- ❑ whole-wheat linguine
- ❑ whole-wheat spaghetti ❦

Sweeteners

- ❑ brown rice syrup
- ❑ fruit juice concentrate, dry or liquid
- ❑ jaggery sugar (East Indian, delicious but hard to find)
- ❑ pure maple syrup ❦
- ❑ molasses (unsulfured)
- ❑ Sucanat (sun-dried whole cane)

Wine

- ❑ dry white wine ❦
- ❑ red wine
- ❑ sherry
- ❑ sweet white wine, like Sauternes

Food Storage and Preparation

PREPARING VEGGIEPACKS AND ESSENTIALSALAD

As soon as you return home from shopping, prepare your vegetables so that they will be ready to eat—either in cooked form or raw (as snacks and for salads). VeggiePacks will soon become your everyday lifesavers. Each pack should contain a variety of green, yellow, orange, and leafy vegetables. If you are preparing the pack for cooking purposes, note that those veggies that take longer to cook must be cut smaller and thinner, so that all of those in the pack will cook in about the same amount of time.

The VeggiePack, along with the EssentialSalad, are the foundation of GardenCuisine and are used in many of the recipes that follow. If you include one of each of these food components in your menu each day, every week, every month, all year long, you will travel far down the garden path to optimal health.

Let me walk you through the steps that will get you to your destination.

Making VeggiePacks. When you are out shopping, envision in your mind the empty space inside a gallon jar. Now imagine filling that jar with a wide variety of colorful veggies, each cut up into appetizing bite sizes. Purchase enough vegetables so that each adult in your family will have enough to fill a gallon jar. You can modify the amount for children. Remember that your goal is to get as large a variety as possible; so buy smaller amounts of lots of different kinds of vegetables.

Select from the categories of roots, leaf, and flower vegetables (see Shopping List). Each category has different nutrients. Feel free to experiment with any vegetables that appeal to you.

I find that after you wash your vegetables (I use a tiny bit of mild organic soap such as Dr. Bronner's and a bristled scrub brush), it is best to dry them so that they have longer shelf lives. Now you're ready to start cutting them up. Here are some tips for prepping your veggies for use in the Packs:

- Peel broccoli stems: break apart bite-size flowerets. The stalks should be cut diagonally about a quarter inch thick.

- Do not peel or scrape carrots; cut julienne-style about ⅛ inch long; if carrot tops are fresh, cut into bite-size pieces and use in the EssentialSalad.

- Always pack beets separately or they will color everything else.

- Leave the skin on the potato and cut into ½-inch cubes.

- Slice fresh corn in 1-inch circles. (Be careful.)

- Cut leafy greens, kale, cabbage, into ½ × 2-inch pieces.

- Cut onions in quarters and break sections apart.

- Break off woody ends of asparagus and slice the stalks into ½-inch pieces; leave the tips about 1½ to 2 inches long.

- Do not peel zucchini or yellow squash; cut diagonally into ¾-inch slices.

- Break cauliflower into 1 × 1-inch pieces.

- Core bell peppers (these are actually fruit) and cut into 1-inch pieces.

- Trim the ends of pea pods and green beans.

- Trim both ends off radishes and slice in half.

- Cut off the roots of scallions and quarter.

- Discard the outer leaves of all nonorganic leafy vegetables to reduce pesticide contamination.

Okay, now your veggies are chopped up. How do you store them? Place two cups of prepared veggies in each quart-size ziplock bag. (You can also use the new "green bags" that are designed to allow produce to "breathe" and thus last longer in storage, if you can find them.) Make seven to eight bags each week for each person in the family. Then refrigerate.

The key to all this is to do the prep work just as soon as you get back from shopping. You want to act while both the veggies and your resolve are fresh. And once you put in the time to prepare these fresh foods, I guarantee you will eat them!

Besides the many recipes (such as Tostada Grande, Vegetable Stroganoff, and Exotic Stir-fry) that call for VeggiePacks, they can be used in a variety of other ways:

- As is, raw.

- Dip in flavored vinegars (balsamic, seasoned rice, and herb vinegars; add, if desired, tamari soy sauce and/or lemon and lime juice).

- Use with any of the dips in the recipe section.

- Steam plain or shake flavored seasonings over them (gomashio, toasted ground sesame seeds, sea vegetable flakes [the Sea Seasonings brand], garlic, etc.).

- Squeeze lemon or lime juice on them or add to a red marinara or other sauce from the recipe section.

- Steam and use as a topping on baked potatoes or over brown rice (pilaf), bulgur wheat, or whole-grain pasta.

- Serve steamed over whole-grain waffles made with onions and garlic for a nice savory treat.

- Use commercial low-fat or fat-free instant whole-food soups as a base, throw in a VeggiePack, heat—and in a few minutes, you'll have an instant veggie stew.

- Make a cup or two of broth with Bragg Liquid Aminos, available in natural food stores, then add a generous helping of chopped scallions and a VeggiePack. This makes a great energizing and warming soup.

- When a recipe calls for finely chopped veggies (such as cabbage for a slaw, carrots for a carrot salad, parsley for tabouli salad, potatoes for hash brown potato pancakes, or mixed veggies for a marinated salad), fill your blender about halfway with your single veggie or VeggiePack pieces and add cold filtered water to the top of the blender. Then pulse or turn the blender on and off very quickly, all the while keeping an eye on the size of the pieces you want to end up with for your recipe. When ready, pour through a strainer and use. You can retain the liquid (it makes a nutrition-packed drink!) or add as a soup base or turn it into a hot broth.

Making EssentialSalad. This is another vital component of GardenCuisine. As before, picture the space inside an empty gallon jar. As you shop, start filling that space with a variety of fresh greens. And, remember, "greens" actually come in different shades and colors. Try for a colorful mix (see Shopping List for different types).

The EssentialSalad is made with about 80 percent leaves and about 20 percent VeggiePack pieces (sliced into ¼-inch pieces). Once again, variety is very important. Combine many different kinds of leaves and always include finely chopped parsley, since it is so packed with nutrients—and, as a bonus, leaves you with pleasant breath.

When you return home with your "green gold," fill your sink full of cold water. Add ice cubes if the water is not cold. Tear off the stalks and soak all of your leaves for three to four minutes. Drain the sink, rinse the leaves, and tear or cut them into bite-size pieces about 2 × 2 inches or smaller. Then spin them dry in your salad spinner. If you don't have a spinner, roll them out on a clean towel to soak up the moisture.

Toss all of your mixed greens into a clean plastic trash bag, shake, and mix. Next get out your ziplock bags, "green bags," or recycled plastic produce bags and store the greens in individual salad portions.

In addition to the VeggiePacks, you can also add extra shredded cabbage or carrots to your mix. Be creative! With the EssentialSalad already prepared for a whole week, there will be no more reasons to skip the greens. For those of you who can't find the time to prepare the EssentialSalad, there are some great precleaned and mixed bags of greens on sale in many produce departments. Bring them home and use as is or enhance them with VeggiePacks.

Tips for Basics, Modifications, and Enhancements

- Cook and prepare foods, when practical, in double or triple batches and store appropriately. Even a single person can prepare a good-sized portion of soup and enjoy it three or four times in a week. This tip applies to potatoes (bake and refrigerate), all grains (make up a big batch in a rice cooker), and pastas (I often buy whole-grain fresh pastas and then store them at home in the refrigerator or freezer, depending upon quantity; divide them up into individual serving sizes and put them in ziplock bags).

- Mix up a wide variety of cold cereals—making sure they are whole-grain—in a single airtight container and keep on hand for breakfasts and snacks.

• Applesauce is a great fat replacement in cakes, muffins, and other baked goods. So are fruit purees made from prunes, figs, or bananas. You can replace up to two-thirds of oils and fats with these nutritious whole foods.

• Use Sucanat cane or fruit juice sweetener in place of white sugar.

• Use fruit purees instead of sugary jams.

• Cook or sauté with lemon or lime juice, white wine, fresh vegetable juice, or vegetable broth stock instead of oil.

• Beware of store-brought bran muffins; they are seldom made with whole wheat and often contain eggs, butter, oil, lots of sugar, and fat. Ask what they are made from.

• Store all nuts in the refrigerator since they are high in fat and can become rancid quickly.

• Thicken a cream soup or sauce with blended, cooked potato in place of dairy.

• Use tofu in egg salad in place of the egg. Take about one-third of the tofu volume and sprinkle the spice turmeric on it to add a yellow color; then, when you make the recipe, you have a chopped-egg look.

• Use a thick, nonfat yogurt with a touch of fresh lemon in place of sour cream.

• If you drink cow's milk, you can spare yourself twenty thousand calories a year by switching to skim milk. Even better, switch to a milk substitute, but keep your eye on the fats.

• In place of butter or margarine, use mustard or other nonfat spreads in your sandwiches.

• Sauté in vegetable broth instead of oil or a cooking spray and use nonstick cookware to reduce the amount of oil needed to brown foods.

• If you feel that you have to have a meat substitute to add texture to a recipe, use ground beans, extra-firm crumbled tofu marinated in Bragg's Liquid Aminos, diced Gardenburgers, GardenChick'n, GardenBeef, or bulgur wheat.

• Some egg replacements: 1¼ cup tofu in place of one egg (blend tofu with liquid ingredients before adding to dry ingredients); two egg whites in place of one whole egg (thus eliminating all the cholesterol); one egg white plus two teaspoons of vegetable oil in place of one egg; commercial egg substitutes (refrigerated or in dry form).

• For toast spreads, try the following in place of butter or margarine: pure fruit jam, jelly, or spread, unsweetened applesauce with cinnamon, fresh or jarred salsa (nonfat variety), hummus (homemade or store-bought).

• For toppings on whole-grain pancakes or whole-grain waffles (if you have a thick waffle maker, you can throw some of these items right into the batter), try sliced ripe fresh fruits with an optional touch of pure maple syrup, some sweet spices such as cinnamon, nutmeg, allspice, pure vanilla; a great standby is unsweetened applesauce with cinnamon and a splash of pure maple syrup.

• For both cold and hot cereal toppings, try oat milk, almond milk, rice milk, soy milk, skim milk, fresh or unfiltered applejuice, fresh fruits, dried fruits, frozen fruits and berries, a few nuts or seeds such as almonds or sunflower seeds.

• For a sweet treat, try a Yam Cone. Place medium scrubbed, unpeeled yams in a foil-lined baking dish (first pierce yams with a sharp knife). Bake at 350° for two hours or until tender when pierced with a fork. Refrigerate and eat as a cold treat.

• To make healthy sandwiches, always use multigrain breads. For spreads, try bean purees, hummus, ketchup, various mustards such as jalapeño, garlic (microwave a whole bulb for three or four minutes), salsa (great cool spread). For fillings, try sautéed mushrooms, roasted veggies (such as bell peppers, eggplant, and onions), grilled tofu slices, tabouli. When you're making sandwiches to go, pack your wet ingredients separately and then toss together just before eating. This avoids the soggy sandwich syndrome and tastes a lot fresher.

• Last, but far from least, for the best source of the "omega-3 fatty acids" that help protect against heart disease, buy whole flaxseeds and grind them up in a good processor, blender, or coffee grinder; prepare a quantity you can use each week. Try on any salad, entrée, vegetable, or grain dish. Flaxseeds actually have more of the omega-3 fatty acids than fish!

A Level of Cooking for Everyone

WHAT'S YOUR LEVEL?

Are you the sort of person who buys a cookbook and immediately launches into an ambitious repertoire of new recipes? If so, you're someone who loves to cook and is willing to devote the time to it. Most of the recipes in this book are quick and easy, so the "break-in" learning process is minimized. Even then, however, I recognize that many people who love good food don't really like to cook—or don't have time for it.

There are a great many people who repeat the same few recipes over and over, and this works well for them, provided those recipes are well balanced. But that's usually the problem. As emphasized earlier in this book, a wide variety of whole, fresh foods is necessary. It's possible to limit the number of recipes you have to master and still get optimal nutrition that is always tasty and never bores.

In between these two groups or "levels" is a third category. Here's how I stratify the cooks out there:

Level I. These are the folks who have had little cooking experience or who have little time to cook. Over the years, I've discovered that a great many people master a few dishes and repeat them over and over again. As I said, there's nothing wrong with this *provided* care is taken to ensure that those few selections provide a good balance of nutrients.

For Level I people, I've created what I call my "Super Sixteen"—sixteen carefully selected, carefully balanced recipes that you can repeat in various combinations indefinitely. Master these sixteen quick-and-easy recipes and you'll change your style of eating for the better in short order. You'll also most likely bring a lot of new taste experiences into your life.

Level II.   These are the "in-between" folks. They want a basic repertoire to rely on most of the time but are open to experimentation. Level II people should master the Super Sixteen and then, when they are comfortable with those recipes, begin trying two or three new recipes each week.

Level III.   These are the "love-to-cook" folks. I don't have to tell them how to proceed. They've got more than 150 new recipes to play with.

The Super Sixteen

These sixteen recipes can be repeated over and over again and, in various combinations, will give you the optimal nutritional return for your money. They'll also keep your nutritional act in balance indefinitely.

All sixteen recipes are easy to prepare, most taking thirty minutes or less. Many can be prepared ahead of time and all can be eaten at any time of day or night, though many readers will prefer to have their smoothies and Fresh Fruit Toss in the morning.

Keys to making the Super Sixteen work are my VeggiePacks and the EssentialSalads that you use each day in combination with the Super Sixteen.

The Super Sixteen
1. Fresh Fruit Toss
2. Manoa Sunrise Smoothie
3. Surfers' Favorite Beverage
4. Hot and Hearty Five-Grain Cereal
5. Mighty Multigrain Cereal
6. Savory Breakfast Sandwich
7. Vegetable Pita Pizza
8. Border Town Burritos
9. Pasta Gone Wild
10. Exotic Stir-fry
11. Tostada Grande
12. All-American Gardenburger
13. Healthy Caesar Salad
14. World Grains
15. Power Baked Potato
16. Bountiful Bean Blend

Here's how the Super Sixteen work: Each morning, drink either a smoothie or have a Fresh Fruit Toss. Follow this, either right away or midmorning, with a grain combination (such as the Savory Breakfast Sandwich or the Hot and Hearty Five Grains).

For lunch and dinner, choose from any of the remaining entrées. Once again, the secret to getting the optimal variety of essential nutrients is always to include the

VeggiePack and the EssentialSalad—every day, all year long. You should consume at least five or six servings from these two components daily. One half cup of a VeggiePack equals one serving. One cup of the EssentialSalad equals one serving. You can get your daily quota in any of a wide variety of possible combinations. Here's one possible scenario, covering a sample week:

Day One	LUNCH	Vegetable Pita Pizza made with ½ cup VeggiePack and 2 cups EssentialSalad.
	DINNER	Border Town Burritos made with 1 cup VeggiePack and 1 cup EssentialSalad.
Day Two	LUNCH	All-American Gardenburger with ½ cup VeggiePack and 2 cups EssentialSalad.
	DINNER	Pasta Gone Wild with 1 cup VeggiePack and 1 cup Essential-Salad.
Day Three	LUNCH	Tostada Grande made with 1 cup VeggiePack and 1 cup EssentialSalad.
	DINNER	Power Baked Potato with 2 cups EssentialSalad and ½ cup VeggiePack.
Day Four	LUNCH	Savory Breakfast Sandwich with 2 cups EssentialSalad.
	DINNER	Exotic Stir-fry made with 2 cups VeggiePack.
Day Five	LUNCH	Healthy Caesar Salad made with 2 cups EssentialSalad.
	DINNER	Bountiful Bean Blend made with 1 cup VeggiePack and served with 1 cup EssentialSalad.
Day Six	LUNCH	Border Town Burritos made with 1 cup VeggiePack and 1 cup EssentialSalad.
	DINNER	World Grains served with 2 cups EssentialSalad.
Day Seven	LUNCH	All-American Gardenburger with 2 cups EssentialSalad.
	DINNER	Power Baked Potato with 1½ cups VeggiePack.

Remember: One half cup VeggiePack equals one serving. One cup EssentialSalad equals one serving.

Remember, too, that you can use the VeggiePacks as snacks at any time in addition to including them in a wide variety of recipes.

GardenChef Paul's
Recipe Book

Beverages

Banana Frappé

MAKES 4 SERVINGS

This frothy and refreshingly light beverage provides a wonderful opportunity to get the potassium your body needs.

PER 8-OUNCE SERVING • 213 CALORIES (11% FROM FAT) • 3 G FAT • 3 G PROTEIN
44 G CARBOHYDRATE • 0 MG CHOLESTEROL • 97 MG SODIUM • 5 G FIBER

6 bananas, peeled and broken into 1-inch pieces

2 cups milk: almond, soy, rice, or nonfat dairy

2 tablespoons chopped dates

¼ teaspoon nutmeg

3 cups crushed ice

Additional nutmeg, for sprinkling

Place the bananas, milk, dates, and nutmeg into a blender and process on high speed until smooth. Add the ice and blend another 1 to 2 minutes. Pour into 4 glasses and garnish with a sprinkle of nutmeg.

Chai with Almond Milk

MAKES 2 SERVINGS

"Chai" means "tea" in India. Now you can enjoy this traditional beverage wherever you are.

PER 12-OUNCE SERVING • 110 CALORIES (33% FROM FAT) • 4 G FAT • 2 G PROTEIN
16 G CARBOHYDRATE • 0 MG CHOLESTEROL • 190 MG SODIUM • 2 G FIBER

1 tablespoon Republic of Tea Cardamom Cinnamon Tea

4 teaspoons Sucanat

2 cups almond milk, heated

Grind the tea lightly in a spice mill or blender, then brew it with 1 cup of water (it will be very strong). Pour the tea through a strainer into 2 large cups. Stir 2 teaspoons of Sucanat into each cup. Pour the hot milk into the cups and stir to mix.

Fresh Almond Milk

MAKES 4 SERVINGS

t's a little more work than buying it, but well worth the effort!

PER SERVING WITH OIL • 83 CALORIES (62% FROM FAT) • 6 G FAT • 2 G PROTEIN
6 G CARBOHYDRATE • 0 MG CHOLESTEROL • 136 MG SODIUM • 1 G FIBER

WITHOUT OIL • 73 CALORIES (57% FROM FAT); 5 G FAT • 2 G PROTEIN
6 G CARBOHYDRATE • 0 MG CHOLESTEROL • 136 MG SODIUM • 1 G FIBER

3¾ cups distilled water

¼ cup blanched, slivered almonds

1 tablespoon Sucanat or rice syrup
(Sucanat will give milk a slightly
darker, tan color)

¼ teaspoon sea salt

¼ teaspoon vanilla

1 teaspoon canola oil (optional)

Place all ingredients in your blender. Turn on to high speed for 3 to 4 minutes, or until all particles have disappeared. If you don't mind the fiber, just use it as is. If you want the smoothness of milk, then pour it through a fine screen, retaining the almond fiber for a future recipe. Keep refrigerated in a covered container.

Frozen Mango Lassi

SERVES 3

In most places, mangoes are available only for a short time; try them every chance you get, including in this refreshing beverage.

PER SERVING • 106 CALORIES (3% FROM FAT) • 0.2 G FAT • 2 G PROTEIN
23 G CARBOHYDRATE • 1 MG CHOLESTEROL • 22 MG SODIUM • 3 G FIBER

1 orange, peeled
1 cup banana chunks
1 cup frozen mango chunks

½ cup milk: almond, soy, rice, or nonfat
dairy
1 cup crushed ice

Cut the orange in half and remove any seeds. Place the orange in blender with the remaining ingredients and process until thick and very smooth.

Fruity Sangria

MAKES 8 SERVINGS

Try to imagine all of the colors of a breathtaking sunset and you'll find them swirling in this drink.

PER 1-OUNCE SERVING • 195 CALORIES (0% FROM FAT) • 0 G FAT • 1 G PROTEIN
38 G CARBOHYDRATE • 0 MG CHOLESTEROL • 4 MG SODIUM • 1 G FIBER

1 12-ounce can cranberry juice
concentrate
1 6-ounce can orange juice concentrate
Juice of 1 lemon

2 cups red wine (nonalcoholic if desired)
1 quart sparkling water
1 orange, thinly sliced, for garnish

In a large pitcher, combine the cranberry juice concentrate, the orange juice concentrate, the lemon juice, and 2 cups of water. Stir to mix, then add the wine, if desired. Just before serving, stir in the sparkling water and garnish with orange slices.

Hot Almond Cocoa

MAKES 2 SERVINGS

This quick, hot beverage will warm you from head to toe.

PER 8-OUNCE SERVING • 117 CALORIES (33% FROM FAT) • 4 G FAT • 2 G PROTEIN
16 G CARBOHYDRATE • 0 MG CHOLESTEROL • 191 MG SODIUM • 3 G FIBER

2 cups almond milk

2 teaspoons cocoa powder

4 teaspoons Sucanat

⅛ teaspoon vanilla

Sprinkle of cinnamon

Combine the almond milk, cocoa, Sucanat, vanilla, and cinnamon in a saucepan. Stir constantly over medium heat until hot and steamy.

Mango Dango Cocktail

MAKES 4 SERVINGS

The refreshing nature of this beverage may move you to dance!

PER 8-OUNCE SERVING • 140 CALORIES (1% FROM FAT) • 0.2 G FAT • 1 G PROTEIN
33 G CARBOHYDRATE • 0 MG CHOLESTEROL • 4 MG SODIUM • 3 G FIBER

2 mangoes, peeled and sliced

2 cups orange juice

Juice of 1 lime

1 tablespoon Sucanat

1½ cups sparkling water

Ice, for serving

Place the mangoes, orange juice, lime juice, and Sucanat in a blender. Blend until smooth, then mix in the sparkling water. Serve over ice.

Manoa Sunrise Smoothie

MAKES 5 SERVINGS

*W*ake up to one of life's little miracles: fruit! I've had some of my best mornings while sipping on this absolute favorite of mine. Mmm! Good and refreshing, too. Aloha!

PER 8-OUNCE SERVING • 122 CALORIES (2% FROM FAT) • 0.3 G FAT • 1 G PROTEIN
28 G CARBOHYDRATE • 0 MG CHOLESTEROL • 3 MG SODIUM • 3 G FIBER

½ cup fresh strawberries (optional)
2 oranges, peeled, seeds removed
1 papaya, peeled, seeds removed
2 ripe bananas, peeled

2 cups chopped fresh pineapple
¾ cup crushed ice
5 wedges orange, for garnish
5 slices pineapple, for garnish

Combine the oranges, papaya, bananas, pineapple, strawberries, if desired, and ice in a blender. Blend on high speed until smooth. Pour into glasses and garnish with a wedge of orange and a slice of pineapple. Feel free also to experiment with your own combinations. It can be a lot of fun!

Orange Spice Juice Fizz

MAKES 6 SERVINGS

*T*his tangy combination makes a great festive, fizzy treat.

PER 8-OUNCE SERVING • 127 CALORIES (2% FROM FAT) • 0.2 G FAT • 0.5 G PROTEIN
31 G CARBOHYDRATE • 0 MG CHOLESTEROL • 18 MG SODIUM • 2 G FIBER

2 cups boiling water
3 orange spice tea bags
1 12-ounce can white grape juice
concentrate

Juice of 1 orange
1 quart sparkling water
Ice, for serving

Pour the boiling water over the tea bags and steep until the tea is cool. Remove the tea bags.

Pour the cooled tea into a pitcher and add the white grape juice concentrate, the orange juice, and the sparkling water. Stir to mix. Add ice and serve.

Surfers' Favorite Beverage

MAKES 4 SERVINGS

After experiencing this combination, you'll have an abundance of energy to ride the waves of life! Add a ripe, peeled mango for a tasty tropical variation. May your sunsets always be breathtaking!

PER 8-OUNCE SERVING • 149 CALORIES (20% FROM FAT) • 3 G FAT • 1 G PROTEIN
28 CARBOHYDRATE • 0 MG CHOLESTEROL • 49 MG SODIUM • 3 G FIBER

1 cup fresh pineapple chunks
½ cup low-fat coconut milk
1 cup milk: almond, soy, rice, or nonfat dairy
3 ripe bananas, peeled

1 tablespoon Sucanat
2 cups cracked ice
4 pineapple slices, for garnish
4 mint sprigs, for garnish

Combine the pineapple chunks, coconut milk, additional cup of milk, bananas, Sucanat, and ice in a blender. Blend at high speed until smooth. Garnish drink with a slice of pineapple and a sprig of mint.

Very Strawberry Smoothie

MAKES 5 SERVINGS

This is a "very berry" way to get a high level of nutrients!

PER 8-OUNCE SERVING • 126 CALORIES (2% FROM FAT) • 0.3 G FAT • 1 G PROTEIN
29 G CARBOHYDRATE • 0 MG CHOLESTEROL • 6 MG SODIUM • 3 G FIBER

2 cups banana chunks

2 cups frozen or fresh strawberries

1 cup unsweetened apple juice, or try

2 apples peeled and cored, in the blender

1 cup ice cubes, small or crushed

Peel and break the bananas into 1-inch lengths. Frozen strawberries may be purchased in your grocery store.

Place all the ingredients into a blender and process on high speed until thick and smooth. You will have to stop the blender occasionally to stir the unblended fruit toward the center.

NOTE: Fresh fruit may be substituted for frozen. In this case, you will want to double the amount of ice to obtain a cold, thick consistency.

Breakfast

Breakfast Barley Pudding

SERVES 4

This is a "pearl" of a recipe!

PER SERVING • 271 CALORIES (4% FROM FAT) • 1 G FAT • 4 G PROTEIN
60 G CARBOHYDRATE • 0 MG CHOLESTEROL • 195 MG SODIUM • 9 G FIBER

1 cup pearl barley

¼ teaspoon salt

1 cup chopped dried fruit, apricots, dates,
    pineapple, peaches, golden raisins, etc.

1 cup milk: almond, soy, rice, or nonfat
    dairy

2 tablespoons Sucanat

¼ teaspoon cinnamon

Pinch cardamom

Additional milk for serving

Rinse the barley and place it in a saucepan with 2 cups of water and the salt. Bring to a simmer, then cover and cook until tender, about 25 minutes. Add the dried fruit, milk, Sucanat, cinnamon, and cardamom. Cover and continue cooking 15 minutes. Serve hot with additional milk if desired.

Brunch Fruit Compote with Whole-Grain Dumplings

SERVES 12

This is a truly satisfying meal, best served on a cool morning, to warm you up.

PER SERVING • 145 CALORIES (7% FROM FAT) • 1 G FAT • 3 G PROTEIN
31 G CARBOHYDRATE • 0 MG CHOLESTEROL • 175 MG SODIUM • 5 G FIBER

Compote

3 bags caffeine-free orange spice tea bags

1 cup dried figs, stems removed

2 cups dried peaches, cut in half

2 green apples, sliced

½ cup golden raisins

¼ cup orange juice concentrate, frozen

2 cinnamon sticks

3 thin slices fresh gingerroot

¼ teaspoon orange zest

Dumplings

1 cup whole-grain baking mix

2 tablespoons slivered almonds

Nonfat frozen vanilla yogurt, or almond,
    soy, rice, or nonfat dairy milk, for
    serving

Bring 3 cups of water to a boil in a large pot. Turn off the heat and add the tea bags. Allow to steep 5 minutes, then remove the tea bags. Add the figs, peaches, apples, raisins, orange juice concentrate, cinnamon sticks, ginger, and orange zest. Refrigerate for 3 to 4 hours or overnight.

Place the pan over medium heat and simmer gently for 20 to 30 minutes.

At the end of this time, combine the baking mix and almonds with ½ cup of water. Mix completely, but do not overmix. Drop spoonfuls on top of the hot fruit mixture. Cover and simmer for 20 minutes. Serve immediately with frozen yogurt or milk.

Fresh Fruit Toss

MAKES 1 CUP

Start your picture-perfect morning with one of the building blocks of the Super Sixteen. They say that a journey of a thousand miles begins with one step, and what better first step than eating fresh fruit every morning! Fruit is a very powerful and healing food and a natural way to break your daily fast: breakfast. Enjoy and heal thyself cell by cell each day!

PER SERVING • 90 CALORIES (4% FROM FAT) • 5 G FAT • 1 G PROTEIN
23 G CARBOHYDRATE • 0 MG CHOLESTEROL • 0 MG SODIUM • 3 G FIBER

apricots	guava	plums
avocado, only small amounts	honeydew melon	raspberries
	kiwis	red apples
blackberries	mangoes	red grapes
blueberries	marionberries	star fruit
cantaloupe	muskmelon	strawberries
cherries	nectarines	tangelos
figs	oranges	tangerines
grapefruit	papayas	watermelon
green apples	passion fruit	whatever else you
grapes	peaches	can find

(continued)

Chop enough fruit to make at least a 1-cup serving per person. A minimum of 3 fruit combinations is recommended for healthy eating.

This is one of two key sources for getting fruits in your menu every day. The other is the sumptuous fruit smoothie. The more variety the better, since each fruit offers many nutrients and much-needed phyto (plant) chemicals in varying amounts. Choose your fruits from this list and don't be afraid to try a couple of new or seldom-eaten fruits on a regular basis.

Makes a great complement to the Savory Breakfast Sandwich (page 219)!

Golden Garden Sausage Waffles

MAKES 8 WAFFLES

A spicy breakfast GardenSausage accents the tart apple and mild red potato flavors of these thick and substantial whole-grain waffles. Try them for breakfast (or any meal) with a drizzle of pure maple syrup and a glass of fresh-squeezed orange juice.

PER WAFFLE • 42 CALORIES (20% FROM FAT) • 1 G FAT • 1 G PROTEIN
7 G CARBOHYDRATE • 0 MG CHOLESTEROL • 165 MG SODIUM • 7 G FIBER

1 small red potato, diced

1½ cups whole-wheat pastry flour

1½ teaspoons baking powder

½ teaspoon baking soda

¼ teaspoon sea salt

1¼ to 1½ cups milk: almond, soy, rice, or nonfat dairy

3 egg whites or egg substitute for 3, beaten

1 tablespoon olive or canola oil

1 apple, diced into ¼-inch cubes

Vegetable oil spray

4 patties GardenSausage, chopped into ½-inch pieces

Tart green apples, sliced, for topping

Applesauce, for topping

Maple syrup, for topping

Sprinkle of cinnamon

Steam the diced potato until it is tender when pierced with a fork, about 8 minutes.

Preheat the oven to 200°F. Preheat a waffle iron (Belgian-style is my favorite).

In a medium-size bowl, combine the flour, baking powder, baking soda, and salt.

In a separate bowl, whisk together the milk, egg white or egg substitute, and olive or canola oil. Pour into the flour mixture, stirring with a few quick strokes to form a lumpy batter. Stir in the cooked potatoes and the apple.

Spray the waffle iron with a vegetable oil spray, then pour in the batter, spreading it almost to the edges. Sprinkle with 1 ounce of the crumbled GardenSausage. Cook until the waffles are golden brown, their edges look dry, and they do not stick to the grid, about 2 to 3 minutes. Transfer the cooked waffles to the oven, placing them directly on the rack. When all the batter has been cooked, transfer the waffles to plates and top them with sliced apples, apple sauce, maple syrup, and a sprinkle of cinnamon.

Top these scrumptious waffles with our Fresh Fruit Syrup (page 334) and you're off to a delicious start to your day!

High-Fiber French Toast

MAKES 6 SERVINGS

Good morning! This healthier version of a breakfast classic is sure to please.

PER SERVING • 92 CALORIES (16% FROM FAT) • 2 G FAT • 5 G PROTEIN
14 G CARBOHYDRATE • 0 MG CHOLESTEROL • 227 MG SODIUM • 4 G FIBER

Canola oil spray
¼ cup milk, almond, soy, rice, or nonfat dairy
½ cup egg substitute or egg whites, refrigerated
¼ cup orange juice, fresh-squeezed

½ teaspoon cinnamon
¼ teaspoon pure vanilla extract
¼ teaspoon sea salt
9 slices multigrain whole-grain bread (slices should be ¾ inch thick and cut in half)

Spray griddle with nonstick spray and heat to medium. Whisk all ingredients together except the bread. Now dip half slices of the multi-grain whole-grain bread in the mixture and place on a griddle or nonstick pan. When golden brown on both sides, serve with unsweetened applesauce or one of my homemade Fresh Fruit Syrups (page 334).

Add a Banana Frappé (page 204) on the side and you're charged up with fiber and fruit energy to see you through your morning.

Home-Fried Potatoes

SERVES 8

What? Delicious home-fried potatoes with no added fat? Simple, just be sure to use a nonstick skillet.

PER SERVING • 164 CALORIES (8% FROM FAT) • 1 G FAT • 6 G PROTEIN
32 G CARBOHYDRATE • 0 MG CHOLESTEROL • 246 MG SODIUM • 5 G FIBER

3 russet potatoes	Black pepper
1 onion, thinly sliced	Pinch cayenne pepper powder
4 patties GardenSausage	5 to 6 cherry tomatoes, cut into halves
4 teaspoons soy sauce	2 green onions, thinly sliced

Scrub the potatoes, then bake or steam them until they are just tender. Cool. Cut into ½-inch cubes.

Heat ½ cup of water in a large nonstick skillet and add the onion. Cook until the water has evaporated and the onion pieces begin to stick to the pan. Add another ¼ cup of water, stirring to remove any stuck bits of onion. Cook until the water evaporates again. Repeat this process of adding water and cooking until it evaporates until the onions are very brown and sweet. This will take about 15 minutes.

Move the onions over to one side of the pan and place the GardenSausage patties in the pan. Cook both sides until golden brown, then use the spatula to cut into ¼-inch pieces.

Add the diced potatoes, then sprinkle with soy sauce, black pepper, and cayenne. Cook, turning gently with a spatula until the potatoes are golden brown. Garnish with cherry tomatoes and green onions.

Hot and Hearty
Five-Grain Cereal

MAKES 6 SERVINGS

This hot cereal turns an everyday breakfast into a celestial experience! It is one of the most popular food inventions I have ever come up with. It tastes so good and is so healthy. I've made it for many of my friends and always get a big "thumbs up"! Quality breakfasts make quality days, and quality days make a quality life!

PER 1-CUP SERVING • 227 CALORIES (17% FROM FAT) • 4 G FAT • 8 G PROTEIN
39 G CARBOHYDRATE • 0 MG CHOLESTEROL • 90 MG SODIUM • 6 G FIBER

5 cups filtered water

1 orange, peeled and diced

1 crisp green apple, diced

2⅔ cups five-grain cereal, not instant

⅓ cup raisins, currants, or any dried
   fruits, cut into ¼-inch pieces

1 teaspoon cinnamon

¼ teaspoon salt

2 tablespoons raw sunflower-seed
   kernels, chopped

2 tablespoons chopped dates (optional)

Milk: almond, soy, rice, or nonfat dairy

¼ cup maple syrup (2 teaspoons
   per serving)

Apple slices, for garnish

Additional raisins or currants, for garnish

Additional cinnamon, for sprinkling

The main ingredient is multigrain hot cereal, which you will find in natural-food stores and some supermarkets, or you can mix your own. One of my favorite combinations uses about ⅔ cup each rolled oats, rolled wheat, rolled rye, rolled barley, and ½ ounce of flaxseeds.

Bring 5 cups of water to a boil and stir in the diced orange, diced apple, five-grain cereal, raisins or currants, cinnamon, and salt. When the mixture returns to a boil, stir in the sunflower seeds and dates. Cover and turn off the heat (leave the pan on the burner). Allow to sit for 10 to 15 minutes. Spoon into bowls and serve with milk and maple syrup. Garnish with fresh apple slices, raisins or currants, and a sprinkling of cinnamon. Holds up well under refrigeration for up to 7 days. Just microwave and enjoy!

For a refreshing variation, try our Fresh Fruit Syrup (page 334) as a topping instead of maple syrup!

Mighty Multigrain Cereal

I love variety in my meals, both in terms of taste and texture; one type of cereal can become boring! Many years ago, I began this tradition of mixing whole-grain cereals and storing them in the freezer to keep fresh. Enjoy this recipe for a while and then branch off and try to make your own blend. Variety is the spice of life and the secret to this power-house medley.

PER 2-OUNCE SERVING • 202 CALORIES (10% FROM FAT) • 2 G FAT • 6 G PROTEIN
39 G CARBOHYDRATE • 0 MG CHOLESTEROL • 196 MG SODIUM • 4 G FIBER

1 10-ounce box New Morning Honey-and-Almond Oatios

1 11.25-ounce box General Mills Multi-Grain Cheerios

1 12.2-ounce box Kellogg's Golden Wheat Nutri-Grain

1 20.5-ounce box Kellogg's Low Fat Granola

1 17.2-ounce box Kellogg's Almond Raisin Nutri-Grain

1 16.5-ounce box Kellogg's Raisin Squares

Combine all the cereals in a very large bowl or large plastic bag and mix completely. Store in the refrigerator or freezer in airtight containers or ziplock bags. Serve as you would any breakfast cereal.

Here are some other quality dry cereals that can be substituted for any or all of the above:

Barbara's High 5
Erewhon Fruit 'N Wheat
Erewhon Raisin Bran
Erewhon Wheat Flakes
Familia No Added Sugar Swiss Müesli
Golden Temple Low Fat Muesli
Health Valley Fat-Free Granola
Health Valley 100% Natural Bran with Apples and Cinnamon

Health Valley Real Oat Bran
Kellogg's All-Bran
LifeStream Fruit and Nut Muesli
Nabisco Shredded Wheat
New Morning Bran Flakes
New Morning Raisin Bran
Post Bran Flakes
Post Grape-Nuts
U.S. Mills Skinner's Raisin Bran

Savory Breakfast Sandwich

SERVES 1

f I had to choose a favorite morning sandwich, this one would top the charts in a big way. The GardenSausage can become absolutely habit-forming. It's fast, easy, and it tastes sensational! Savoring life's pleasures and taking the time to enjoy those moments between waking and sleeping can be one of our greatest rewards.

PER SERVING (WITH CHEESE) • 450 CALORIES (16% FROM FAT) • 8 G FAT • 28 G PROTEIN
68 G CARBOHYDRATE • 5 MG CHOLESTEROL • 620 MG SODIUM • 15 G FIBER

1 2.5-ounce GardenSausage

Olive oil spray

1 ounce low-fat cheddar cheese
  (optional)

¼ cup egg substitute (optional)

1 slice tomato

1 whole-grain English muffin, toasted

Salt and pepper, to taste

Heat the GardenSausage in a hot skillet sprayed with olive oil spray. Approximately 3 minutes on each side will be needed. Place the cheese on top of the GardenSausage.

Heat an additional skillet; spray with olive oil spray. If using, pour the egg substitute into the bottom of the pan as if for a small omelette. Cook the thin layer of egg until set. Flip the egg over onto itself four times.

Place the egg, GardenSausage, cheese, and tomato on your toasted whole-grain muffin and enjoy. Salt and pepper to taste.

When you add our Fresh Fruit Toss (page 213) to this breakfast, you've got a powerful nutritional start to your day!

Spinach Omelette

SERVES 6

This nondairy omelette is filled with wonderful fresh vegetables and GardenSausage.

PER SERVING • 119 CALORIES (18% FROM FAT) • 2 G FAT • 8 G PROTEIN
16 G CARBOHYDRATE • 0 MG CHOLESTEROL • 401 MG SODIUM • 5 G FIBER

Omelette

1 10-ounce package frozen chopped
   spinach, thawed

1 10.5-ounce package firm silken tofu

¼ cup milk: almond, soy, rice, or nonfat
   dairy

1 teaspoon dried basil

½ teaspoon salt

¼ teaspoon black pepper

¼ teaspoon nutmeg

¼ teaspoon celery seeds

⅛ teaspoon turmeric

2 tablespoons couscous

Vegetable oil spray

Filling

1 onion, chopped

2 cloves garlic, minced

1½ cups sliced mushrooms

¼ teaspoon salt

¼ teaspoon basil

⅛ teaspoon black pepper

2 patties GardenSausage, crumbled

3 green onions, finely chopped

Preheat the oven to 350°F. Squeeze the spinach to remove excess water, then place it in a bowl.

To make the omelette, combine the tofu, milk, basil, salt, black pepper, nutmeg, celery seeds, and turmeric in a blender and process until completely smooth. Add to the spinach along with the couscous and stir to mix. Spray a 10-inch pie pan with vegetable oil spray, then spread the tofu-spinach mixture evenly across the bottom and up the sides of the dish. Bake for 30 minutes.

While the omelette bakes, prepare the filling. Heat ½ cup of water in a skillet and add the chopped onion and minced garlic. Cook 5 minutes, then add the mushrooms, salt, basil, and black pepper. Cook 3 minutes, then stir in the crumbled GardenSausage and cook another 3 minutes. Remove from the heat and stir in the green onions.

Use a spatula to loosen the omelette from the pie plate and carefully slide it onto a serving platter. Mound the filling evenly over half the omelette. Using a spatula, carefully fold the omelette over the filling. Serve immediately.

Tropical Granola

MAKES 5 CUPS

*Y*ou *can almost feel the warm island breeze when crunching on this magical cereal blend!*

PER 1/2-CUP SERVING • 219 CALORIES (32% FROM FAT) • 8 G FAT • 7 G PROTEIN
31 G CARBOHYDRATE • 0 MG CHOLESTEROL • 3 MG SODIUM • 4 G FIBER

3 cups rolled oats, or a combination of
    other rolled grains
⅓ cup raw sunflower-seed kernels
⅓ cup sliced almonds
⅓ cup cashews

¼ cup dried papaya
¼ cup dried pineapple
¼ cup golden (sultana) raisins
1 teaspoon coconut extract
⅓ cup maple syrup

Preheat the oven to 350°F. Mix the rolled oats or other grains, sunflower seeds, almonds, cashews, papaya, pineapple, and raisins together in a large bowl. Blend the coconut extract into the maple syrup and then mix all ingredients together. Spread in thin layers on two large baking sheets and bake until the edges begin to turn golden. Use a spatula to turn the granola and continue baking until it is dry and crispy, about 20 minutes total. Remove from the oven and allow to cool. Store in an airtight container.

Zucchini Waffles

SERVES 8

This recipe is a variation on the ever-popular zucchini bread, which is so abundant in the fall. Now you can enjoy that treat all year round.

PER 4½-INCH WAFFLE • 126 CALORIES (15% FROM FAT) • 2 G FAT • 4 G PROTEIN
22 G CARBOHYDRATE • 0 MG CHOLESTEROL • 197 MG SODIUM • 5 G FIBER

⅓ cup milk: almond, soy, rice, or nonfat dairy

Egg substitute, to equal 3 eggs

2 cups grated zucchini

1 tablespoon olive oil

¼ teaspoon salt

¼ cup Sucanat

1 tablespoon cinnamon

¼ teaspoon allspice

1½ cups whole-wheat flour

2 teaspoons baking powder

Vegetable oil spray

Mix all the wet ingredients together (milk, egg substitute, zucchini, and oil). In a separate bowl mix together the dry ingredients, then add this to the wet mixture. (For a shortcut, try whole-grain pancake and waffle mix and follow the directions on the package. Then simply add the zucchini and spices.)

Spray a waffle iron with nonstick spray. Heat, fill, and cook according to the directions for your waffle iron.

Serve with applesauce or a splash of pure maple syrup, or our Fresh Fruit Syrup (page 334).

Appetizers

Crisp Pita Chips

MAKES 36 CHIPS

Snack on these low-fat chips for a tasty treat.

PER CHIP • 25 CALORIES (8% FROM FAT) • 0.2 G FAT • 1 G PROTEIN
5 G CARBOHYDRATE • 0 MG CHOLESTEROL • 82 MG SODIUM • 1 G FIBER

6 pieces whole-wheat pita bread

1 to 2 teaspoons olive oil

Garlic granules, to taste

Chili powder, to taste

Paprika, to taste

Salt, to taste

Preheat the oven to 350°F. Brush the tops of the pita breads very lightly with olive oil, then sprinkle with garlic granules, chili powder, paprika, and salt. Cut each piece into 6 triangular wedges and spread in a single layer on 2 baking sheets. Bake until very crispy, 20 to 25 minutes.

Our Refreshing Cucumber Dip (page 326) and Energetic Eggplant Dip (page 324) are excellent toppers for these chips.

Island Salsa

MAKES 3 CUPS

Salsa can be used for a topping on many dishes or on separate foods like baked potatoes.

PER 2 TABLESPOONS • 19 CALORIES (3% FROM FAT) • 0.1 G FAT • 1 G PROTEIN
4 G CARBOHYDRATE • 0 MG CHOLESTEROL • 12 MG SODIUM • 0 G FIBER

½ 15-ounce can black beans, drained and rinsed

½ red bell pepper, finely diced

½ green bell pepper, finely diced

1 small red onion, finely diced

½ cup chopped fresh pineapple

2 small papayas, peeled, seeded, and diced

¼ cup chopped cilantro

1 to 3 red chili peppers (you choose the heat level!)

Juice of 1 lemon or lime

1 tablespoon cumin

⅛ teaspoon salt, or to taste

⅛ teaspoon fresh-ground black pepper, or to taste

Combine all the ingredients in a large bowl. Stir just enough to mix. Be careful not to over-mix! Cover and refrigerate a couple of hours or more for maximum flavor.

Alternate recipe: Tomato Salsa

Replace papayas with ripe tomatoes, leave out the pineapple, and add 6 to 8 cloves of roasted garlic.

Meditation Sushi

MAKES 4 ROLLS (24 PIECES)

This recipe was inspired by the tranquil beauty of Japanese Zen gardens.

PER ROLL • 123 CALORIES (16% FROM FAT) • 2 G FAT • 3 G PROTEIN
23 G CARBOHYDRATE • 0 MG CHOLESTEROL • 213 MG SODIUM • 3 G FIBER

½ cup sweet brown rice ("sticky" rice)

1 cup boiling water

1 teaspoon seasoned rice vinegar, or to taste

2 teaspoons tamari soy sauce, or to taste

1 carrot

¼ cucumber

¼ red bell pepper

¼ ripe medium avocado

8 to 10 small green leaves, such as spinach

4 sheets nori seaweed

1 teaspoon wasabe (horseradish paste), mixed with 1 tablespoon water

1 tablespoon pickled ginger, for garnish

Combine the rice and boiling water and cook until all the water is absorbed, about 50 minutes. Stir in the seasoned rice vinegar and tamari soy sauce; set aside to cool.

Cut the carrot, cucumber, bell pepper, avocado, and spinach into shoestring strips.

Lay a sheet of nori on a sushi mat and spread it with about ¾ cup of cooked sweet brown rice, leaving a ¾-inch strip uncovered on the top and bottom. Form a little trough from side to side in the middle of the rice bed and lay 4 or 5 strips of each of the vegetables into it, allowing some of them to stick out the ends. Brush the top and bottom edges of the nori with a small amount of the wasabe mixture, then roll the nori up as tightly as you can. Repeat with additional nori sheets until all the rice is used.

To serve, slice across the roll in whatever thickness you desire (about 1 inch gives you 6 per roll). Garnish with the pickled ginger.

Quick and Easy Brown Bread

MAKES 1 LOAF

Now you can have old-fashioned homemade bread without all the fuss.

PER SERVING • 180 CALORIES (0% FROM FAT) • 0.5 G FAT • 7 G PROTEIN
39 G CARBOHYDRATE • 0 MG CHOLESTEROL • 270 MG SODIUM • 4 G FIBER

2 cups whole-wheat flour

1 cup whole-wheat pastry flour

2 teaspoons baking soda

½ teaspoon salt

2 cups nonfat yogurt

½ cup molasses

½ cup raisins

Canola oil spray

Preheat the oven to 325°F. In a large mixing bowl, stir the dry ingredients together. Add the yogurt, molasses, and raisins. Stir the batter until completely mixed. The batter will be very stiff and sticky. Spoon the batter into a pan sprayed with canola oil spray. Bake at 325°F for 1 hour.

Shrimp-Free Tofu Cocktail

MAKES 6 APPETIZERS

A great start to a relaxing meal. These were a big hit at my gourmet restaurant.

PER SERVING • 106 CALORIES (37% FROM FAT) • 4 G FAT • 8 G PROTEIN
8 G CARBOHYDRATE • 0 MG CHOLESTEROL • 269 MG SODIUM • 1 G FIBER

1 pound firm tofu

⅓ cup sliced celery

12 pitted olives, cut into 3 or 4 pieces

2 teaspoons lime juice

1 teaspoon olive oil

1 teaspoon olive juice

1 pinch black pepper

½ teaspoon vegetarian oyster sauce (optional)

1 sprinkle cayenne pepper powder

1 small bottle cocktail sauce

6 sprigs parsley, for garnish

6 lime wedges, for garnish

Preheat the oven to 200°F. Slice the tofu into ½-inch cubes. Place on a nonstick baking sheet and bake 1½ hours, turning occasionally. The tofu will brown slightly and will shrink to about half its original size. Remove from the oven and cool completely.

Mix the celery, olives, lime juice, olive oil, olive juice, black pepper, vegetarian oyster sauce, and cayenne pepper in a bowl, then add the tofu. Stir gently to mix, then refrigerate and marinate for 1 to 2 hours.

To serve, divide the tofu mixture among 6 small serving cups and top with 2 to 3 teaspoons of cocktail sauce. Garnish with a sprig of parsley and a wedge of lime.

Spinach and Onion Turnovers

MAKES 12 TURNOVERS

It's easy to turn toward healthy eating after enjoying this savory treat!

PER TURNOVER • 59 CALORIES (24% FROM FAT) • 1.5 G FAT • 2 G PROTEIN
9 G CARBOHYDRATE • 0 MG CHOLESTEROL • 188 MG SODIUM • 3 G FIBER

3 10-ounce packages frozen chopped spinach, thawed	¾ teaspoon salt
1 onion	½ teaspoon black pepper
¼ cup chopped parsley	¼ cup lemon juice
1½ teaspoons dried dill	6 large whole-wheat flour tortillas
	1 tablespoon olive oil, for brushing

Squeeze as much water as possible from the thawed spinach and set aside. Heat ¼ cup of water in a large skillet and cook the onion until it is soft, about 5 minutes. Stir in the parsley, dill, salt, pepper, and chopped spinach. Cook over medium heat, stirring often, until the mixture is very dry. Stir in the lemon juice.

Preheat the oven to 375°F. To assemble the turnovers, cut a tortilla in half and wet all the edges of one half with water, using your fingers or a pastry brush. Place about 2 tablespoons of filling in the center of the tortilla half. Now, imagine the tortilla divided into thirds. Fold one edge over, matching the curves, and press the curved edge firmly to seal it. Fold the remaining edge over and press firmly to seal. Brush or spray lightly with olive oil. Repeat with the second tortilla half and the remaining tortillas.

Place the turnovers on a baking sheet and bake until lightly browned, about 25 minutes.

Sun-Dried Tomato Crostini

Crisp whole-grain baguette slices are topped with a flavorful blend of tomatoes and roasted red peppers in this fat-free version of crostini.

PER SLICE • 27 CALORIES (2% FROM FAT) • 0.1 G FAT • 1 G PROTEIN
6 G CARBOHYDRATE • 0 MG CHOLESTEROL • 59 MG SODIUM • 1 G FIBER

1 cup boiling water
6 sun-dried tomato halves
⅔ cup roasted red peppers (about
   2 peppers)
4 cloves roasted garlic, chopped or
   mashed

2 to 3 tablespoons finely chopped fresh
   basil or 2 teaspoons dried basil
⅛ teaspoon black pepper
⅛ teaspoon salt, to taste
1 baguette, whole-grain

Pour boiling water over the tomatoes and set aside until softened, about 30 minutes. Pour off the water (it can be used in other recipes in place of vegetable stock) and coarsely chop the tomatoes. Chop the roasted red peppers and add to the tomatoes, along with the garlic, basil, pepper, and salt. Let stand while you prepare the bread.

Preheat the oven to 350°F. Cut the whole-grain baguette into ½-inch-thick slices and arrange on a nonstick baking sheet. Bake until the outside is crisp, 10 to 15 minutes. Remove from the oven and cool slightly, then spread each piece with the tomato mixture.

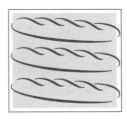

Main Courses

Lunch and Dinner

All-American Gardenburger

SERVES 1

Almost one quarter billion Gardenburgers have been served worldwide! Thousands of letters from all corners of the earth have found their way to our home office with the most uplifting, positive, and heartwarming messages of appreciation for providing this flavor-filled, meatless patty. I'd like to take this opportunity to say "Thank you" to all of you for your support over the years. May love always be your gift!

PER SERVING • 194 CALORIES (19% FROM FAT) • 4 G FAT • 12 G PROTEIN
43 G CARBOHYDRATE • 0 MG CHOLESTEROL • 499 MG SODIUM • 8 G FIBER

1 Gardenburger	3 slices red onion
Olive oil spray	3 leaves green leaf lettuce
1 whole-grain bun	2 slices tomato
1 tablespoon ketchup	Pickles
1 tablespoon mustard	

Heat the Gardenburger in a nonstick pan sprayed lightly with olive oil spray for 3 minutes on each side, or until golden brown. Place in the bun, and garnish with the above condiments. Serve with a generous portion of EssentialSalad (page 304). A very quick and easy meal.

Look for our other exciting renditions of the Gardenburger sandwich, like Gardenburger Maui (page 241) and Gardenburger Olé (page 242).

Have our Golden Potato Medley (page 274) on the side for an added nutritional bonus!

Artichoke Hearts and Fava Beans

SERVES 6

This combination forms a delightful balance among great tastes, great smells, and great textures.

PER SERVING • 227 CALORIES (14% FROM FAT) • 4 G FAT • 9 G PROTEIN
36 G CARBOHYDRATE • 0 MG CHOLESTEROL • 606 MG SODIUM • 8 G FIBER

2 15-ounce cans water-packed artichoke hearts

½ cup filtered water

1 cup chopped green onions

2 carrots, finely diced

4 tablespoons chopped fresh dill

½ cup dry white wine

1 15-ounce can fava beans, drained and rinsed

½ teaspoon salt

Fresh-ground black pepper

2 tablespoons lemon juice

1 tablespoon olive oil

2 tablespoons whole-wheat pastry flour

1 cup milk: almond, soy, rice, or nonfat dairy

2 teaspoons stone-ground mustard

8 ounces whole-wheat pasta, cooked according to package directions

Drain the artichoke hearts but save the liquid. Cut the hearts into quarters and set aside.

Heat the water in a large skillet and cook the onions, carrots, and 3 tablespoons of dill for 5 minutes, stirring often. Stir in another ½ cup of filtered water, the wine, artichoke hearts, fava beans, salt, and a generous grinding of black pepper. Simmer 5 minutes, then stir in the lemon juice. Remove from the heat.

Mix the oil and flour in a saucepan to form a thick, smooth paste. Heat 1 to 2 minutes, stirring constantly, then whisk in the milk. Cook over medium heat, stirring constantly, until thickened. Add to the artichoke mixture and cook over low heat for 3 minutes.

Serve over the cooked pasta and garnish with the rest of the chopped fresh dill. It can also be used to top my Power Baked Potato (page 249).

Black Bean Hash

SERVES 4

This hash is hearty brain food!

PER SERVING • 202 CALORIES (11% FROM FAT) • 3 G FAT • 8 G PROTEIN
37 G CARBOHYDRATE • 0 MG CHOLESTEROL • 145 MG SODIUM • 8 G FIBER

2 teaspoons olive oil

1 onion, chopped or sliced

3 cloves garlic, minced

1 large red potato, cut into ¼-inch dice

1 small green bell pepper, chopped

1 cup chopped tomatoes, fresh or canned

1 tablespoon chili powder

¼ teaspoon cumin

1 15-ounce can black beans, drained and rinsed

1 cup frozen corn, thawed

¼ to ½ teaspoon salt

Heat the oil in a large skillet or pot and add the onion, garlic, and potato. Cook over high heat, stirring frequently, for 3 minutes. Add the bell pepper, tomatoes, chili powder, cumin, and ¾ cup of water. Reduce the heat slightly, then cover and simmer until the potatoes are soft, about 10 minutes. Stir in the beans and corn and cook until heated through. Add salt to taste.

Black Beans and Tofu "Chicken" over Soba Noodles

SERVES 6

An Asian-influenced work of art!

PER SERVING • 291 CALORIES (27% FROM FAT) • 9 G FAT • 14 G PROTEIN
35 G CARBOHYDRATE • 0 MG CHOLESTEROL • 721 MG SODIUM • 5 G FIBER

8 ounces Tofu "Chicken" (page 285) or
GardenChick'n

1 tablespoon olive oil

8 ounces whole-grain soba noodles
(Chinese noodles, or thin whole-
wheat spaghetti)

⅓ cup seasoned rice vinegar

⅓ cup lime juice

2 tablespoons tamari soy sauce

1 tablespoon toasted sesame oil

2 teaspoons Sucanat

¼ teaspoon red pepper flakes

1 15-ounce can black beans, drained and
rinsed

5 green onions, sliced on the diagonal

4 cups EssentialSalad, rinsed and patted
dry (page 304)

2 tablespoons finely chopped dry-roasted
peanuts

¼ cup cilantro leaves

Pull the Tofu "Chicken" or GardenChick'n into bite-sized pieces, then cook it in the olive oil in a nonstick skillet until it begins to brown, about 5 minutes.

Cook the noodles in boiling water until just tender. Rinse, drain, and set aside.

Combine the vinegar, lime juice, soy sauce, sesame oil, Sucanat, and red pepper flakes in a large bowl. Stir to mix. Add the Tofu "Chicken" or GardenChick'n, the cooked noodles, the rinsed black beans, and the green onions. Toss to mix.

Divide the EssentialSalad among 6 plates, then top with the Tofu "Chicken" or GardenChick'n mixture. Garnish with finely chopped peanuts and fresh cilantro leaves.

Border Town Burritos

SERVES 6

This burrito is powered by black beans and our versatile VeggiePack. I selected this as one of the Super Sixteen because it packs a nutritional wallop in a compact hand-held "handwich"! All of life's journeys and adventures can be rolled into one simple philosophy: Live each day to its fullest and as if it were your last.

PER BURRITO • 331 CALORIES (12% FROM FAT) • 4 G FAT • 13 G PROTEIN
60 G CARBOHYDRATE • 0 MG CHOLESTEROL • 70 MG SODIUM • 10 G FIBER

1 15-ounce can black beans, drained and rinsed

1 carrot, finely diced

⅓ cup salsa (you pick the heat!)

½ teaspoon cumin

½ teaspoon garlic powder

2 cups VeggiePack, chopped small (page 284)

6 whole-wheat tortillas

2 cups cooked Brown Rice (page 268)

1 tomato, diced

3 green onions, sliced

½ avocado, sliced

Extra salsa, for topping

Combine the black beans, carrot, salsa, cumin, and garlic powder in a saucepan. Cover and simmer until the carrot is just tender, about 10 minutes. Add the VeggiePack, then cover the pan and cook over medium heat until tender, about 5 minutes. Stir occasionally.

Heat the tortillas, one at a time, in a dry skillet until soft, then place a spoonful of the black bean mixture down the center. Top with cooked Brown Rice, diced tomato, sliced green onions, and a slice of avocado. Add extra salsa if desired. Roll the tortilla up around the filling and enjoy.

While you have all the food out, make a few spares to have 2-minute meals on hand at a later date. You can freeze and reheat any time.

Cajun Tofu "Chicken"

SERVES 6

*T*ry this great dish with the Calcutta Cauliflower on page 269! A Louisiana heart-healthy favorite.

PER SERVING • 162 CALORIES (19% FROM FAT) • 4 G FAT • 6 G PROTEIN
25 G CARBOHYDRATE • 0 MG CHOLESTEROL • 105 MG SODIUM • 2 G FIBER

2 teaspoons olive oil
1 onion, chopped
4 cloves garlic, minced
2 celery stalks, thinly sliced
8 ounces Tofu "Chicken" (page 285), or
    GardenChick'n, bite-size pieces
1 cup crushed tomatoes

2 teaspoons apple juice concentrate
1 teaspoon dried coriander
½ teaspoon turmeric
¼ teaspoon black pepper
⅛ teaspoon cayenne pepper powder
¾ cup cooked Brown Rice
    (page 268)

Heat the olive oil in a large nonstick skillet and add the onion and garlic. Cook over medium heat for 3 minutes, then add the celery and either Tofu "Chicken" or GardenChick'n. Cook, stirring frequently until the Tofu "Chicken" or GardenChick'n begins to brown, about 5 minutes. Add the tomatoes, 1 cup of water, apple juice concentrate, coriander, turmeric, pepper, and cayenne. Simmer 10 minutes. Serve over cooked Brown Rice.

Exotic Stir-fry

SERVES 6

This stir-fry is delicious, quick, and tasty! Thousands of people raved about this "classic" at my gourmet restaurant over a four-year period. I hope it becomes a regular in your household. It is now your turn to become one with this time-honored dish!

WITH CHEESE: PER SERVING • 196 CALORIES (37% FROM FAT) • 8 G FAT • 14 G PROTEIN
16 G CARBOHYDRATE • 1 MG CHOLESTEROL • 403 MG SODIUM • 5 G FIBER

WITHOUT CHEESE: PER SERVING • 188 CALORIES (36% FROM FAT) • 7 G FAT • 13 G PROTEIN
16 G CARBOHYDRATE • 0 MG CHOLESTEROL • 372 MG SODIUM • 5 G FIBER

6 cups VeggiePack (page 284)

1 cup sliced red onion

5½ cups mushrooms, cut in thick slices

1 tablespoon minced garlic

2 teaspoons minced fresh ginger

1 teaspoon fresh thyme, or ¼ teaspoon dried thyme

1 teaspoon fresh oregano, or ¼ teaspoon dried oregano

1 tablespoon chopped fresh basil leaves, or ¾ teaspoon dried basil

1 pound very firm tofu, cut into ¾-inch cubes

1 to 2 teaspoons olive oil

2 tablespoons tamari soy sauce

1 tablespoon unhulled sesame seeds or gomashio for garnish

2 tablespoons chopped green onions for garnish

2 tablespoons grated Parmesan cheese (optional)

Steam the VeggiePack until tender but crisp. Be sure to keep an eye on the vegetables so they don't get too soft. While they are steaming, sauté the onion, mushrooms, and tofu cubes in olive oil until light brown. Add the garlic, ginger, thyme, oregano, and basil. Cook 2 additional minutes, then stir in the soy sauce.

To serve, place 1 cup of the steamed vegetables on a plate and top with the tofu mixture. Garnish with sesame seeds or gomashio, green onions, and, if desired, Parmesan cheese.

Crunchy Vegetable Burritos

SERVES 4

Munch on the crunch of this luscious combination!

PER SERVING • 253 CALORIES (33% FROM FAT) • 9 G FAT • 13 G PROTEIN
28 G CARBOHYDRATE • 20 MG CHOLESTEROL • 478 MG SODIUM • 9 G FIBER

½ cup shredded carrot
½ cup chopped broccoli
½ cup chopped cauliflower
2 green onions, thinly sliced
1 cup reduced-fat cheddar cheese
(4 ounces)

¼ cup nonfat ranch dressing
½ teaspoon chili powder
4 7-inch whole-wheat tortillas
1 cup shredded romaine lettuce

In a bowl, combine the carrot, broccoli, cauliflower, and onions, then mix in the cheese, dressing, and chili powder.

Spoon about ½ cup of the vegetable mixture toward one end of each tortilla. Top each with ¼ cup lettuce. Wrap each tortilla around the vegetable mixture and serve.

Chili Non Carne

SERVES 8

This low-fat chili is a treat on a wintry or rainy afternoon. It's a meat-free South of the Border specialty!

PER SERVING • 135 CALORIES (3% FROM FAT) • 0.4 G FAT • 5 G PROTEIN
27 G CARBOHYDRATE • 0 MG CHOLESTEROL • 733 MG SODIUM • 7 G FIBER

1 onion, chopped
4 cloves garlic, minced
1 green bell pepper, diced
1 15-ounce can tomato sauce
1 4-ounce can diced green chilies
1 15-ounce can pinto beans, drained and
rinsed

1 15-ounce can kidney beans, drained
and rinsed
2 teaspoons chili powder (add more
for hotter chili)
¾ teaspoon cumin
⅛ teaspoon black pepper
Pinch cinnamon
⅓ cup bulgur wheat   *(continued)*

Heat ½ cup of water in a large pot and cook the onion, garlic, and bell pepper until the water has evaporated and the vegetables begin to stick to the pan. Add ¼ cup of water, stirring to loosen the vegetables. Repeat this process until the onion is lightly browned, about 15 minutes. Stir in the tomato sauce, chilies, pinto beans, kidney beans, chili powder, cumin, black pepper, and cinnamon. Bring to a slow simmer, then cover and cook 20 minutes, stirring occasionally.

Sprinkle the bulgur over the top, then cover and continue cooking until the bulgur is soft, about 10 minutes.

Fettuccine Southwest

SERVES 10

A mouth-watering dish with a New Mexico flair.

PER SERVING • 165 CALORIES (6% FROM FAT) • 1 G FAT • 6 G PROTEIN
32 G CARBOHYDRATE • 0 MG CHOLESTEROL • 25 MG SODIUM • 5 G FIBER

1 15-ounce can cream-style corn
1 teaspoon cumin seeds
1 large onion, chopped
2 cloves garlic, minced
1 red bell pepper, cut into 1-inch strips
1 10-ounce package frozen corn, thawed

½ teaspoon red pepper flakes
12 ounces whole-wheat fettuccine,
   cooked, rinsed, and drained
¼ cup chopped cilantro
10 cherry tomatoes, cut in half
Garlic salsa, for seasoning

Puree the cream-style corn in a blender until it is completely smooth.

Toast the cumin seeds in a dry nonstick skillet until they are slightly browned and just beginning to smoke.

Heat ½ cup of water in a large skillet, and cook the onion, garlic, and bell pepper until the onion is soft, about 8 minutes. Stir in the thawed corn, the blended cream-style corn, the toasted cumin seeds, and the red pepper flakes. Reduce the heat and cook until the sauce just begins to bubble.

Arrange the cooked pasta on a platter, then spread the sauce over the top. Garnish with chopped cilantro and cherry tomatoes. Serve with salsa on the side.

Madras Tofu "Chicken" Curry

SERVES 8

A popular South Indian dish that's easy to prepare and well loved by those who like the spicy flavors of life.

PER SERVING • 276 CALORIES (29% FROM FAT) • 9 G FAT • 11 G PROTEIN
36 G CARBOHYDRATE • 0 MG CHOLESTEROL • 726 MG SODIUM • 4 G FIBER

2 tablespoons canola oil

2 cups diced Tofu "Chicken" (page 285) or GardenChick'n

1 onion, chopped

3 celery stalks, sliced

¾ cup mushrooms, sliced

¼ cup whole-wheat flour

2 tablespoons cornstarch

1 15-ounce can Swanson's Vegetable Broth

1 teaspoon tamari soy sauce

1 teaspoon salt

5½ teaspoons curry powder

¼ teaspoon cayenne pepper powder

½ cup golden raisins

1 carrot, grated

½ bell pepper, diced

3 cups cooked Brown Rice (page 268)

2 tablespoons chopped roasted peanuts

Heat 1 tablespoon of oil in a large nonstick skillet and sauté the diced Tofu "Chicken" or GardenChick'n until it is lightly browned. Remove the Tofu "Chicken" or GardenChick'n from the skillet and set aside.

Heat the remaining tablespoon of oil in the skillet and sauté the onion, celery, and mushrooms until the onion is soft and the mushrooms are brown, about 5 minutes.

Combine the whole-wheat flour, cornstarch, and vegetable broth and whisk smooth. Add to the vegetable mixture, along with the soy sauce, salt, curry powder, and cayenne. Cook, stirring constantly, until the sauce thickens. Stir in the Tofu "Chicken" or GardenChick'n, the raisins, grated carrot, and bell pepper. Serve over Brown Rice and garnish with chopped roasted peanuts.

Garden Lasagna

SERVES 10

What? I don't have to cook the noodles before baking? No, the noodles soften in the pan while baking. This recipe is a breeze. Delicious!

PER SERVING • 226 CALORIES (12% FROM FAT) • 3 G FAT • 13 G PROTEIN
36 G CARBOHYDRATE • 0 MG CARBOHYDRATE • 365 MG SODIUM • 10 G FIBER

Tomato Sauce

2 large onions, chopped

12 cloves garlic, minced

1 carrot, grated

2 cups mushrooms, sliced

2 15-ounce cans crushed tomatoes

2 15-ounce cans tomato sauce

2 teaspoon each: dried basil and oregano

1 teaspoon each: dried thyme, marjoram,
  and fennel seeds

½ teaspoon black pepper

White Sauce

1 onion, diced

1 potato, peeled and diced

½ pound very firm tofu

2 tablespoons tahini

1½ tablespoons lemon juice

¾ teaspoon salt

Filling

½ pound firm tofu (You could also substitute minced GardenChick'n.)

2 tablespoons soy sauce

1 teaspoon garlic powder

10 ounces whole-wheat lasagna noodles
  (about 10 noodles), uncooked

2 10-ounce packages frozen chopped
  spinach, thawed

½ cup chopped fresh fennel (optional)

For the tomato sauce, heat ½ cup of water in a large skillet or pot and add the onion, garlic, and carrot. Cook until the water has evaporated and the vegetables begin to stick. Add ¼ cup water, stirring to remove any stuck vegetable bits. Cook until the vegetables begin to stick again, then add another ¼ cup of water along with the mushrooms. Continue cooking until all the liquid has evaporated and the mushrooms are brown. Stir in the tomatoes, tomato sauce, basil, oregano, thyme, marjoram, fennel seeds, and black pepper. Cover and simmer 15 minutes.

To make the white sauce, combine the onion and potato in a small pan with 1¼ cups of water. Cover and simmer until the potato is tender, about 15 minutes, then pour the entire mixture into a blender. Add the tofu, tahini, lemon juice, and salt. Blend until completely smooth.

For the filling, crumble ½ pound of tofu and mix it with the soy sauce and garlic powder.

To assemble the lasagna, spread about 1 cup of the tomato sauce over the bottom of a large (at least 12 × 9-inch) baking dish. Cover with a layer of uncooked lasagna noodles, then with one of the packages of thawed spinach. Sprinkle with half the fennel, half the tofu mixture, a third of the evenly spread white sauce, and half the tomato sauce. Repeat the layers. Set aside the remaining white sauce.

Refrigerate the lasagna at least 4 hours (this allows the noodles to soften), then bake covered at 350°F until hot and bubbly, about 25 minutes, the last 5 minutes uncovered. Spoon the remaining white sauce over the top.

Gardenburger Maui

MAKES 4 BURGERS

Definitely one of my favorite ways to enjoy the "Mercedes" of meatless burgers. Aloha!

PER BURGER • 329 CALORIES (10% FROM FAT) • 4 G FAT • 13 G PROTEIN
60 G CARBOHYDRATE • 0 MG CHOLESTEROL • 851 MG SODIUM • 9 G FIBER

4 Gardenburger patties

4 pineapple slices, fresh

1 red bell pepper, cut into quarters

Teriyaki or sweet and sour sauce

4 whole-grain buns

4 romaine lettuce leaves

1 tomato, sliced

Brush the Gardenburger patties, pineapple slices, and bell pepper with teriyaki or sweet and sour sauce, then grill or broil until the patties are golden brown. Brush with additional sauce and turn the patties to brown on both sides.

Toast the whole-grain buns, then place lettuce leaves on each of the bottom buns. Add the Gardenburger patties, pineapple, and bell pepper. Top with a tomato slice, additional sauce, and the top of the bun.

Gardenburger Olé

MAKES 4 BURGERS

This spicy and meatless Gardenburger is sure to please your palate. Yes, my favorite burger with a South of the Border kick!

PER BURGER • 330 CALORIES (23% FROM FAT) • 9 G FAT • 15 G PROTEIN
47 G CARBOHYDRATE • 5 MG CHOLESTEROL • 470 MG SODIUM • 9 G FIBER

4 Gardenburger patties
¼ cup grated low-fat jalapeño jack
  cheese
4 whole-grain buns, toasted

½ yellow onion, thinly sliced
½ avocado, thinly sliced
Island Salsa or Tomato Salsa
  (page 224)

Broil or grill the Gardenburger until golden brown on both sides. Top with cheese and allow to melt slightly. Place a patty on the bottom half of each whole-grain bun. Top with onion, avocado, and salsa. Add the top of the bun. Serve hot!

Hungarian Goulash

SERVES 8

After enjoying the flavors of Budapest, I thought a low-fat version of this timeless favorite was in order!

PER SERVING • 222 CALORIES (9% FROM FAT) • 2 G FAT • 7 G PROTEIN
39 G CARBOHYDRATE • 0 MG CHOLESTEROL • 129 MG SODIUM • 7 G FIBER

2 teaspoons toasted sesame oil
2 large onions, thickly sliced
2 green bell peppers, diced
10 cloves garlic, minced
1 globe eggplant, diced
2 cups mushrooms, cut in half
1 28-ounce can chopped tomatoes
1 cup red wine
½ cup apple juice concentrate

2 bay leaves
2 teaspoons paprika
1 teaspoon dried basil
½ teaspoon black pepper
2 teaspoons tamari soy sauce
8 ounces whole-wheat fettuccine,
  cooked, rinsed, and drained
Healthful Homemade Sour Cream
  (page 334)

Heat the sesame oil in a large pot and sauté the onions, bell peppers, and garlic for 5 minutes. Add a small amount of water if needed to prevent the vegetables from sticking. Add the eggplant, mushrooms, tomatoes, wine, apple juice concentrate, bay leaves, paprika, basil, black pepper, and soy sauce. Bring to a simmer, then cover and cook until the flavors are well blended, about 1 hour. Remove the bay leaves and serve over cooked whole-wheat pasta with a generous spoonful of Healthful Homemade Sour Cream.

Linguine with Broccoli and Roasted Garlic

SERVES 6

Garlic adds a dimension of greatness to this dish!

PER SERVING • 154 CALORIES (32% FROM FAT) • 6 G FAT • 5 G PROTEIN
20 G CARBOHYDRATE • 0 MG CHOLESTEROL • 214 MG SODIUM • 4 G FIBER

1 garlic bulb

8 ounces whole-wheat linguine

1 bunch broccoli, about 1 pound

2 tablespoons minced garlic

¼ cup unhulled sesame seeds

1 tablespoon toasted sesame oil

1 tablespoon lemon juice

½ teaspoon salt

Place the whole unpeeled garlic bulb in a small ovenproof dish and roast it in a 375°F oven (or toaster oven) until it is fragrant and soft when squeezed, about 35 minutes. When cool enough to handle, separate and peel the cloves, and set aside.

Cook the linguine according to package directions. Drain and rinse, then set aside.

Remove the broccoli stems and cut or break the head into bite-sized florets. Steam until just tender, about 5 minutes.

While the broccoli is steaming, sauté the minced garlic and sesame seeds in the sesame oil for 3 minutes. Stir in the roasted garlic cloves, cooked pasta, steamed broccoli, lemon juice, and salt. Toss to mix and serve immediately.

Middle Eastern Pita Sandwich

MAKES 8 SANDWICHES

A spectacular lunch alternative! Place romaine lettuce leaves next to the whole-wheat pita so it won't get soggy.

PER SANDWICH • 269 CALORIES (17% FROM FAT) • 5 G FAT • 9 G PROTEIN
47 G CARBOHYDRATE • 0 MG CHOLESTEROL • 463 MG SODIUM • 7 G FIBER

Filling
½ cup lentils
½ cup Brown Rice
½ teaspoon salt

Salad
2 cups coarsely shredded romaine lettuce
1 carrot, grated
½ cup thinly sliced red or green onions
½ cucumber, peeled, seeded, and diced
10 cherry tomatoes, cut in half

½ avocado, diced

Dressing
Juice of 1 lemon (about 3 tablespoons)
1 tablespoon olive oil
1 teaspoon Sucanat
1 teaspoon dry mustard
½ teaspoon paprika
1 clove garlic, crushed or pressed
8 whole-wheat pitas
8 medium leaves romaine lettuce

Rinse the lentils and rice and place them in a saucepan with 3 cups of water and the salt. Bring to a simmer, then cover and cook until tender, about 45 minutes. Pour off any excess liquid.

Place the lettuce, carrot, onion, cucumber, tomatoes, and avocado in a salad bowl and toss to mix.

To prepare the dressing, mix the lemon juice, olive oil, Sucanat, dry mustard, paprika, garlic, and remaining ½ teaspoon of salt in a small bowl. Pour a small amount of dressing (about 2 teaspoons) over the lentil-rice mixture and toss to mix. Pour the remaining dressing over the salad and toss to mix.

To assemble the sandwiches, cut the pita bread open to make a pocket. Place romaine leaves to each side of the inside of the pita bread. Place a generous spoonful of the lentil-rice mixture in the pocket, then top with the salad. Serve immediately.

Mom's Tamale Pie

SERVES 10

This recipe has been in my family for years and I'd like to share it with everyone!
Thanks, Mom!

PER SERVING • 250 CALORIES (21% FROM FAT) • 6 G FAT • 14 G PROTEIN
34 G CARBOHYDRATE • 16 MG CHOLESTEROL • 493 MG SODIUM • 8 G FIBER

2 onions, chopped

3 cloves garlic, minced

1 bell pepper, diced

1 15-ounce can crushed tomatoes

1 15-ounce can kidney beans, drained
  and rinsed

1 10-ounce package frozen corn

2 tablespoons chili powder

⅛ teaspoon black pepper

1 10-ounce package Gardenburgers, pre-
  grilled, crispy, and diced into ¼-inch
  cubes

¾ cup yellow cornmeal

½ teaspoon salt

1 cup grated reduced-fat jack cheese,
  dairy or substitute

Heat ½ cup of water in a large nonstick skillet and add the onions, garlic, and bell pepper.
Cook until the onion is soft, about 5 minutes. Add the tomatoes, beans, corn, chili powder,
and black pepper. Simmer 20 minutes, then stir in the diced Gardenburger pieces. Spread in
a 13 × 9-inch baking dish.

Combine the cornmeal, salt, and 2 cups of water in a saucepan. Cook, stirring constantly,
until the mixture becomes very thick. Remove from the heat and stir in the grated cheese.

Preheat the oven to 350°F. Spread the cornmeal mixture evenly over the pie. Bake 40
minutes.

Pan-Roasted Portobello Mushrooms over Broiled Polenta

SERVES 6

Portobello mushrooms have a wonderful "meatiness" that is absolutely delicious when they are pan-roasted and served with grain or polenta. I usually make the polenta a day ahead so it can chill overnight.

PER SERVING • 208 CALORIES (8% FROM FAT) • 2 G FAT • 5 G PROTEIN
41 G CARBOHYDRATE • 0 MG CHOLESTEROL • 864 MG SODIUM • 5 G FIBER

½ cup yellow cornmeal

½ teaspoon salt

½ teaspoon dried rosemary, crushed

1 15-ounce can corn kernels

4 large portobello mushrooms

2 teaspoons olive oil

2 large onions, sliced

12 cloves garlic, minced

3 tablespoons tamari soy sauce

2 tablespoons balsamic vinegar

¼ cup chopped fresh basil

2 tablespoons red wine

2 teaspoons seasoned rice vinegar

2 tablespoons cornstarch

To make the polenta, combine the cornmeal with 1¾ cups of water in a saucepan. Add salt and rosemary, then simmer over medium heat, stirring often, until the cornmeal is very thick. Stir in the corn (including the liquid) and cook until the cornmeal has thickened again. Spread the cooked cornmeal into a large flat baking pan and refrigerate until it is completely cold.

Clean the mushrooms and cut into ½-inch-thick slices.

Heat the oil in a large nonstick skillet and sauté the onions and garlic until caramelized, about 10 to 12 minutes. Add 1 tablespoon of soy sauce, 1 tablespoon of balsamic vinegar, and 1 tablespoon of chopped basil. In the meantime, sauté the mushroom slices in a medium-hot nonstick pan and grill until tender.

In a small bowl, whisk the remaining soy sauce and balsamic vinegar together with the red wine, seasoned rice vinegar, cornstarch, and 1½ cups of water. Pour the mixture over the onions and cook, stirring constantly, until the sauce has the thickness of light gravy. Fold in the sautéed mushrooms and keep warm.

Preheat the broiler. Slice the polenta into ¼-inch-thick slices and broil on a nonstick or oil-sprayed baking sheet until crusty and golden brown, about 5 minutes. Turn and brown the other side. Top with the cooked mushroom sauce.

Parsley Pesto with Soba Noodles

SERVES 6

Here is a simple, delicious, and satisfying meal for those times when you just don't have the energy to put together a big supper. Italian gusto meets Japanese splendor in this recipe.

PER SERVING • 138 CALORIES (30% FROM FAT) • 5 G FAT • 5 G PROTEIN
19 G CARBOHYDRATE • 0 MG CHOLESTEROL • 183 MG SODIUM • 5 G FIBER

8 ounces soba noodles

½ cup chopped red onion

3 to 4 cloves garlic

2 bunches fresh parsley, stems removed

3 tablespoons fresh lemon juice

2 tablespoons olive oil

½ teaspoon salt

¼ teaspoon black pepper

Cook the pasta in boiling water until it is tender. Drain and rinse.

Process the onion and garlic in a food processor until finely chopped. Add the parsley, lemon juice, olive oil, salt, and black pepper. Process until smooth. Add to the pasta, toss to mix, and serve.

Pasta Gone Wild

SERVES 2

*M*any of us have a love affair with pasta—I know I do. The secret to "real" pasta is to search out a reliable source of fresh or dry whole-grain pasta. Buying enriched pasta instead of whole-grain is like paying for an item at the market and only getting 20 percent of your change back. Would that make you feel enriched? "High five" for whole grains! Eating food created by nature is more than a smart choice, it's the right choice!

PER SERVING • 200 CALORIES (9% FROM FAT) • 2 G FAT • 10 G PROTEIN
39 G CARBOHYDRATE • 0 MG CHOLESTEROL • 570 MG SODIUM • 8 G FIBER

1 Gardenburger or GardenSausage patty (optional)

Olive oil spray

¼ pound whole-wheat pasta

1 8-ounce jar fat-free tomato sauce or our Simple Marinara Sauce (page 336)

1 cup VeggiePack, ½-inch dice (page 284)

¼ cup sliced mushrooms

1 teaspoon grated Parmesan cheese

2 tablespoons minced parsley

Heat the Gardenburger or GardenSausage if you're using it, in a nonstick pan lightly sprayed with olive oil spray for about 3 minutes on each side, or until golden brown. Cut into ½-inch cubes. Set aside.

Prepare the whole-wheat pasta as suggested on the package. Heat the tomato sauce, then add the VeggiePack pieces and mushrooms. Simmer until the vegetables are crisp but tender (about 5 minutes).

Place the pasta in serving dishes, then cover with the sauce and vegetable mixture. Toss lightly. Sprinkle the diced Gardenburger or GardenSausage on top. Sprinkle with the Parmesan and minced parsley.

I could eat this pasta dish over and over and never get tired of it. However, if at some point you want to try another of our GardenCuisine pasta recipes, here are some suggestions: Fettuccine and Roasted Vegetables (page 272), Fettuccine Southwest (page 238), Parsley Pesto with Soba Noodles (page 247), Thai Peanut Noodles (page 283), Vegetable Stroganoff (page 259), Chinese Noodles and Cabbage (page 298), and Linguine with Broccoli and Roasted Garlic (page 243).

Power Baked Potato

One of the earliest foods in history, the baked potato is also one of the easiest fast foods on earth. Keep a big bowl of prebaked spuds in your refrigerator and you will definitely be in the winner's circle of low-fat eaters. Remember to top them with low-fat, high-fiber toppings. The potato is your canvas, and the toppings are your paints. Have fun creating a culinary masterpiece.

PER PLAIN POTATO • 220 CALORIES (<1% FAT) • 0.1 G FAT • 3 G PROTEIN
51 G CARBOHYDRATE • 0 MG CHOLESTEROL • 16 MG SODIUM • 5 G FIBER

8 large potatoes, russet, red, yellow, white, etc.   Olive oil spray

Preheat the oven to 400°F. Place the potatoes on baking tray and mist lightly with olive oil spray. Pierce them with a fork a couple of times and place in the oven. Baking time depends on the size of the potato. Start to check them at about 35 to 40 minutes. If you can easily push a fork into the center of the potato, it is done.

Now for the topping options that bring these humble potatoes to the *power level:* try a steamed VeggiePack (page 284) topped with Simple Marinara Sauce (page 336), Artichoke Hearts and Fava Beans (page 231), Vegetable Stroganoff (page 259), or Hungarian Goulash (page 242).

If you are in the mood for a smaller side dish, simply top the baked potato with Pea Guacamole (page 327), Guacabonzo (page 325), Energetic Eggplant Dip (page 324), or our Healthful Homemade Sour Cream (page 334) with chopped scallions.

Roasted Vegetable Enchiladas

MAKES 9 ENCHILADAS

Roasted vegetables make a perfectly delightful and delicious filling for enchiladas!

PER SERVING • 244 CALORIES (17% FROM FAT) • 5 G FAT • 11 G PROTEIN
39 G CARBOHYDRATE • 0 MG CHOLESTEROL • 370 MG SODIUM • 7 G FIBER

Vegetable Filling

1 red onion

1 red bell pepper

1 green bell pepper

1 large zucchini

2 cups small, firm mushrooms

1 teaspoon garlic powder

5½ teaspoons chili powder

½ teaspoon dried basil

½ teaspoon dried oregano

½ teaspoon salt

White Sauce

1 onion, diced

1 potato, peeled and diced

½ pound very firm tofu

2 tablespoons tahini

5½ tablespoons lemon juice

¾ teaspoon salt

Red Sauce

1 large onion, chopped

5 cloves garlic, minced

1 28-ounce can crushed tomatoes

1 6-ounce can tomato paste

1 tablespoon Sucanat

1 teaspoon tamari soy sauce

5½ teaspoons cumin

1 teaspoon chili powder

1 teaspoon cocoa powder

1 teaspoon dried oregano

¼ teaspoon black pepper

⅛ teaspoon cayenne pepper
powder

¼ cup chopped cilantro

9 corn tortillas

Preheat the oven to 500°F. Cut the onion, peppers, zucchini, and mushrooms into ½-inch pieces and place in a large bowl. Sprinkle with the garlic powder, chili powder, basil, oregano, and salt. Toss to mix. Spread the vegetables in a single layer (this will probably require two large baking pans) and bake in the preheated oven until just tender, about 10 minutes.

To make the white sauce, combine the onion and potato in a small pan with 1¼ cups of water. Cover and simmer until the potato is tender, about 15 minutes, then pour the entire mixture into a blender. Add the tofu, tahini, lemon juice, and ¾ teaspoon of salt. Blend until completely smooth.

To prepare the red sauce, heat ¼ cup of water in a large skillet, then add the onion and garlic. Cook until all the water has evaporated and the onion begins to stick to the pan.

Scrape it loose, then add another ¼ cup of water and repeat the browning and caramelization process several times until the onions are very brown and sweet. Add the tomatoes, tomato paste, 1½ cups of water, Sucanat, tamari, cumin, chili powder, cocoa powder, oregano, black pepper, and cayenne. Simmer 25 minutes. Stir in the cilantro, then puree the sauce in a blender or food processor.

Preheat the oven to 350°F. To assemble the enchiladas, spread a thin layer of the red sauce (about 1 cup) over the bottom of a large (at least 13 × 9-inch) baking dish. Place a generous portion (about ½ cup) of the roasted vegetables along the center of each tortilla, then top with 2 tablespoons of the white sauce. Roll the tortilla up around the filling and place it seam side down in the baking dish. Repeat with the remaining tortillas. When all the tortillas have been filled, spread the red sauce over them. Bake covered for 20 minutes, remove the cover, and bake 5 more minutes to brown.

Quick Black Bean Chili

SERVES 4 TO 6

This is a mild chili, delicious with brown rice and a green salad. If you like a hotter chili, add some cayenne or chopped jalapeño peppers.

PER SERVING • 161 CALORIES (3% FROM FAT) • 0.4 G FAT • 8 G PROTEIN
31 G CARBOHYDRATE • 0 MG CHOLESTEROL • 211 MG SODIUM • 8 G FIBER

1 tablespoon soy sauce
2 onions, chopped
4 cloves garlic, crushed
2 teaspoons dried oregano
½ teaspoon cumin
¼ teaspoon black pepper

1 4-ounce can diced chilies
1 15-ounce can crushed tomatoes
2 15-ounce cans black beans, drained and
  rinsed
¼ teaspoon salt
Chopped cilantro

Heat ½ cup water and the soy sauce in a large pan, then add the onions and garlic. Cook over medium heat until the onions are soft, about 5 minutes. Add the oregano, cumin, black pepper, and diced chilies. Cook 5 minutes over medium heat. Add the tomatoes, black beans, and salt. Cover and simmer 20 minutes or longer. Top with a sprinkling of chopped fresh cilantro.

Roasted Vegetable Pizzas

MAKES 6 PIZZAS

Let the roasted aromas of this recipe enhance this all-time American favorite.

PER PIZZA • 218 CALORIES (7% FROM FAT) • 2 G FAT • 8 G PROTEIN
42 G CARBOHYDRATE • 0 MG CHOLESTEROL • 482 MG SODIUM • 8 G FIBER

2 Japanese eggplants, cut into ¼-inch-
thick slices

2 yellow onions, cut in wedges

2 red bell peppers, diced

3 cups mushrooms, thickly sliced

4 teaspoons dried basil

½ teaspoon cinnamon

½ teaspoon coriander

½ teaspoon salt

1 cup roasted red peppers, chopped

1 cup chopped tomatoes, fresh or canned

4 cloves garlic, crushed

6 whole-wheat pitas

Preheat the oven to 450°F. Prepare the eggplants, onions, bell peppers, and mushrooms as directed. Place in a single layer in one or two large baking dishes. Toss with 3 teaspoons of the basil and the cinnamon, coriander, and salt. Bake in the preheated oven until the eggplant is fork-tender, about 30 minutes. Reduce the oven temperature to 350°F.

To make the sauce, combine the roasted red peppers with the tomatoes, garlic, and remaining teaspoon of basil.

To assemble the pizzas, spread a layer of the sauce on a whole-wheat pita. Top with a generous layer of the roasted vegetables. Place on a baking sheet. Repeat with the remaining pitas. Bake for 15 minutes.

Soft Tofu "Chicken" Tacos

MAKES 8 TACOS

ow! Cholesterol-free tacos! Yes, regular chicken is loaded with cholesterol!

PER TACO • 175 CALORIES (34% FROM FAT) • 7 G FAT • 7 G PROTEIN
21 G CARBOHYDRATE • 0 MG CHOLESTEROL • 192 MG SODIUM • 4 G FIBER

1 small white onion, chopped

3 cloves garlic, crushed

1 small bell pepper, finely diced

8 ounces Tofu "Chicken" (page 285) or GardenChick'n, shredded

½ cup tomato sauce

2 to 3 teaspoons chili powder

½ teaspoon cumin

½ teaspoon dried oregano

8 large corn tortillas

2 cups shredded romaine lettuce or green leaf lettuce

1 medium tomato, diced

4 green onions, sliced

½ cup salsa or taco sauce

1 avocado, cut into strips

Heat ½ cup of water in a large skillet and cook the onion, garlic, and bell pepper until the onion begins to brown and stick to the pan. Add another ¼ cup of water and continue cooking until it has evaporated. Stir in the Tofu "Chicken" or GardenChick'n, tomato sauce, ¼ cup water, chili powder, cumin, and oregano. Cook over low heat until the mixture is fairly dry.

Place a small amount of filling on a tortilla and lay it flat in a heavy, ungreased skillet. Heat until the tortilla is warm and pliable, then fold it in half. Cook each side for 30 to 60 seconds.

Garnish with lettuce, tomato, green onions, salsa, and avocado. *Olé!*

Stuffed Eggplant

SERVES 6

This recipe is a great choice for any holiday. Eggplant makes an amazingly delicious meal.

PER SERVING • 246 CALORIES (46% FROM FAT) • 13 G FAT • 6 G PROTEIN
25 G CARBOHYDRATE • 0 MG CHOLESTEROL • 227 MG SODIUM • 8 G FIBER

3 small globe eggplants
1 tablespoon olive oil
2 onions, chopped
2 cloves garlic, minced
2 bell peppers, diced
½ teaspoon salt

3 tablespoons finely chopped parsley
¼ teaspoon dried basil
1½ cups chopped fresh tomatoes
½ cup chopped walnuts
½ cup wheat germ
2 tablespoons olive oil

Slice each eggplant in half lengthwise and scoop out the insides, leaving a ¼-inch-thick shell. Place the shells on a baking sheet and bake them in a 350°F oven until they are just barely tender, about 20 minutes. Leave the oven on.

Coarsely chop the eggplant flesh. Heat the oil in a large skillet and add the chopped eggplant, the onions, garlic, and the bell peppers. Cook over medium heat, stirring often, until the eggplant begins to soften, about 10 minutes (add a small amount of water if necessary to prevent sticking). Add the salt, parsley, basil, and tomatoes. Simmer until the eggplant is tender when pierced with a fork. Divide the mixture among the six prebaked eggplant shells.

Combine the wheat germ, chopped nuts, and olive oil. Spread evenly over the six eggplant shells.

Place the shells in a large baking dish and bake at 350°F until the shells are completely tender, about 25 minutes.

Sweet and Sour Szechwan Tofu "Chicken"

SERVES 4

If you adore Chinese cuisine, you'll appreciate this meat-free favorite!

PER SERVING • 220 CALORIES (15% FROM FAT) • 4 G FAT • 20 G PROTEIN
27 G CARBOHYDRATE • 0 MG CHOLESTEROL • 731 MG SODIUM • 5 G FIBER

6 cloves garlic, minced

4 teaspoons soy sauce

¼ cup seasoned rice vinegar

2 cups vegetable broth

1 teaspoon chili powder

¼ cup cornstarch

1 tablespoon Sucanat

2 teaspoons toasted sesame oil

1 cup Tofu "Chicken" (page 285) or
  GardenChick'n

2 sweet (bell) or hot peppers, chopped

4 teaspoons minced fresh ginger

8 shiitake mushrooms, sliced

1 tablespoon sliced green onion

1 tablespoon chopped cilantro
  (optional)

In a mixing bowl, combine the garlic, soy sauce, vinegar, broth, chili powder, cornstarch, and Sucanat.

If using the GardenChick'n, separate and tear into small strips about 1 inch long. Set to one side.

Heat the oil in a wok or skillet, then add the peppers, ginger, and mushrooms. Cook for 3 to 5 minutes, until the mushrooms are tender. Reduce the heat to medium, add the liquid ingredients, and cook, stirring constantly, until thickened.

Add the Tofu "Chicken" or GardenChick'n, green onion, and cilantro if desired. Serve immediately.

Tofu "Chicken" Teriyaki Sandwich

MAKES 4 SANDWICHES

The exotic flavors of this recipe are sure to be a hit.

PER SANDWICH • 355 CALORIES (17% FROM FAT) • 7 G FAT • 27 G PROTEIN
46 G CARBOHYDRATE • 3 MG CHOLESTEROL • 791 MG SODIUM • 5 G FIBER

2 tablespoons reduced-calorie mayonnaise

2 teaspoons fruit chutney

6 tablespoons mashed fresh mango

4 whole-grain buns, split and toasted

1 teaspoon toasted sesame oil

10 ounces GardenChick'n, shredded

8 rings of thinly sliced bell peppers

2 to 3 tablespoons teriyaki sauce

8 slices tomato

8 slices mango

In a small bowl, mix the mayonnaise, chutney, and mango until smooth. Spread on the toasted buns.

Heat the sesame oil in a large nonstick skillet and sauté the shredded GardenChick'n and bell pepper rings until lightly browned. Brush the GardenChick'n generously with teriyaki sauce, then place it on a toasted bun. Add tomato and mango slices and sautéed bell pepper rings. Top with a bun and serve.

Tostada Grande

MAKES 4 SERVINGS

This dish lives up to its name; when you're ready for a filling "one-dish meal," this one's a front runner. It has all the right stuff, like crispy chips, flavorful chili and veggies, and cold refreshing greens. It's simple to throw together for one person or a big party. Thinking big is just right for this recipe. Muy buena!

PER SERVING • 276 CALORIES (10% FROM FAT) • 3 G FAT • 21 G PROTEIN
49 G CARBOHYDRATE • 0 MG CHOLESTEROL • 731 MG SODIUM • 21 G FIBER

4 cups baked corn chips

1 medium onion, chopped

4 cloves garlic, finely chopped

4 cups VeggiePack, chopped in ½-inch pieces (page 284)

2 15-ounce cans fat-free vegetarian bean chili (Add a touch of chili powder and cayenne pepper for a spicier taste.)

4 cups EssentialSalad cut into ½-inch pieces (page 304)

½ cup cilantro leaves

2 cups salsa, store-bought or Island Salsa (page 224)

Cilantro Vinaigrette

Juice of 1 large lemon or lime

2 tablespoons seasoned rice vinegar

1 tablespoon Sucanat

¼ teaspoon sea salt

1 tablespoon chopped cilantro

Place 1 cup of chips in four oven-safe serving bowls and put in a warm oven for a few minutes.

Place the chopped onion and garlic in a large nonstick pan and sauté for 3 to 4 minutes. Stir in the chopped veggies and sauté an additional 5 minutes. Fold in the canned bean chili until mixture is hot and blended.

Remove the bowls of chips from the oven and place equal amounts of the bean/veggie mixture on top of the chips.

Place the EssentialSalad, mixed with the cilantro, on top and serve with the salsa and vinaigrette dressing.

Vegetable Pita Pizza

SERVES 6

*W*ow! Here's an easy and nutritious way to enjoy the taste and textures of one of America's traditional favorite foods. Using simple whole-grain pita bread, you can transform a piece of pizze into a healthy fast food. Here we have a diverse group of vegetables and the round pita. These elements symbolize the circle of life, which reminds us that what goes around comes around.

PER PIZZA • 233 CALORIES (14% FROM FAT) • 4 G FAT • 10 G PROTEIN
40 G CARBOHYDRATE • 1 MG CHOLESTEROL • 437 MG SODIUM • 9 G FIBER

2 GardenSausage patties

Olive oil spray

1 15-ounce can crushed tomatoes or premade natural pizza sauce

1 teaspoon garlic powder

1 teaspoon dried basil

1 teaspoon dried oregano

½ teaspoon dried thyme

6 whole-wheat pitas

1½ cups VeggiePack, cut into ¼-inch pieces (page 284)

1 to 2 roasted red peppers, chopped

1 cup sliced green onions

6 black olives, pitted and chopped

¼ cup grated Parmesan cheese (optional)

Heat the GardenSausage in a hot skillet sprayed with olive oil spray. Approximately 3 minutes on each side will be needed. Dice into ¼-inch pieces and set aside.

Combine the crushed tomatoes, garlic powder, basil, oregano, and thyme in a saucepan. Bring to a simmer and cook 3 minutes. (Or use premade natural pizza sauce.)

Preheat the oven to 375°F. Spread each of the pitas with tomato sauce, then top with VeggiePack, pieces of red peppers, green onions, and olives. Sprinkle with the diced GardenSausage. Place on a baking sheet and bake until the edges just begin to brown, about 10 minutes. Sprinkle with Parmesan cheese if using and serve.

Vegetable Stroganoff

SERVES 8

M iso, lemon juice, and sherry give this unique stroganoff an unforgettable flavor.

PER SERVING • 263 CALORIES (16% FROM FAT) • 5 G FAT • 16 G PROTEIN
36 G CARBOHYDRATE • 0 MG CHOLESTEROL • 255 MG SODIUM • 9 G FIBER

3 large onions, thinly sliced

4 cloves garlic, minced

4 cups mushrooms, sliced

6 cups VeggiePack (page 284) or fresh
  green beans, cut into 1-inch pieces

½ cup white wine

2 10.5-ounce packages firm silken tofu

3 tablespoons white or yellow miso

¼ cup lemon juice

¼ cup cream sherry or white wine

¼ teaspoon black pepper

3 tablespoons chopped almonds, toasted

2 pounds fresh whole-wheat fettuccine,
  cooked and drained

Heat ½ cup of water in a large nonstick skillet and add the onions and garlic. Cook over medium-high heat until all the liquid has evaporated and the onions begin to stick to the pan. Add another ¼ cup of water, stirring the pan to remove any stuck bits of onion. Cook until the water evaporates, add another ¼ cup of water and repeat the process until the onions are very brown, about 15 minutes.

Stir in the mushrooms, vegetables or VeggiePack or green beans, and white wine. Cover and cook, stirring occasionally, until the beans are tender, about 10 minutes.

While the veggies or beans cook, combine the tofu, miso, lemon juice, sherry or wine, and pepper in a blender. Process on high speed until completely smooth. Pour the sauce over the veggies or cooked green beans and stir to mix. Sprinkle with the chopped almonds and serve over the cooked pasta.

Zucchini Pocket Pizzas

MAKES 6 PIZZAS

Try serving these healthy pizzas to your kids. They'll love them!

PER PIZZA • 107 CALORIES (19% FROM FAT) • 2 G FAT • 5 G PROTEIN
17 G CARBOHYDRATE • 2 MG CHOLESTEROL • 309 MG SODIUM • 3 G FIBER

1 teaspoon olive oil

2 medium zucchini, thinly sliced

½ teaspoon each: dried basil, dried
oregano, and garlic powder

1 tomato, diced

2 teaspoons soy sauce

3 whole-wheat pitas

3 tablespoons grated Parmesan cheese

Heat the oil in a large nonstick skillet, then add the sliced zucchini. Sprinkle with the basil, oregano, and garlic powder. Sauté until the zucchini begins to soften, about 4 minutes. Add the diced tomato and soy sauce and stir to mix. Remove from the heat.

Warm the pitas in a toaster oven or a steamer, then cut them in half and stuff with a generous serving of the zucchini mixture. Sprinkle with Parmesan cheese and serve immediately.

Wendy's Best "Baked" Beans

SERVES 8

Try these wonderful, easy-to-prepare beans with Brown Rice (page 268) and Whole-Grain Satay Salad (page 310).

PER SERVING • 167 CALORIES (6% FROM FAT) • 1 G FAT • 8 G PROTEIN
31 G CARBOHYDRATE • 0 MG CHOLESTEROL • 495 MG SODIUM • 8 G FIBER

1 16-ounce can Bush's Vegetarian Baked
Beans

1 15-ounce can kidney beans, drained and
rinsed

1 10-ounce package frozen baby lima beans

1 cup finely chopped red onion

2 tablespoons tomato paste

1 tablespoon cider vinegar

1 tablespoon molasses

2 teaspoons Dijon mustard

2 to 3 drops hot red pepper sauce

Stir all of the ingredients together in a saucepan. Cook at a very slow simmer for 25 to 30 minutes.

Zucchini Onion Pie

SERVES 8

Try this recipe and say good-bye to the old boring pot pies!

PER SERVING • 204 CALORIES (20% FROM FAT) • 4 G FAT • 9 G PROTEIN
32 G CARBOHYDRATE • 0 MG CHOLESTEROL • 444 MG SODIUM • 5 G FIBER

½ cup bulgur wheat

¼ teaspoon salt

¾ cup boiling water

1 tablespoon olive oil

3 large onions, thinly sliced

¾ cup firm tofu

1½ cups milk: almond, soy, rice, or nonfat
    dairy

3 tablespoons whole-wheat pastry flour

1 teaspoon salt

⅓ teaspoon nutmeg

¼ teaspoon black pepper

1½ tablespoons whole-wheat couscous

1 large zucchini, thinly sliced, about
    2½ cups

Sprinkle of paprika

Mix the bulgur and ¼ teaspoon salt in a bowl, then stir in the boiling water. Cover and let stand until all the water is absorbed, about 20 minutes.

Heat the olive oil in a large nonstick skillet and sauté the onions until browned, about 15 minutes. Stir frequently to prevent sticking. Remove from the heat.

Combine the tofu, milk, flour, 1 teaspoon salt, nutmeg, and black pepper in a blender. Blend until smooth. Add to the onions, along with the couscous, and stir to mix.

Preheat the oven to 350°F. Spread the bulgur in a 10-inch pie pan, then cover it with the sliced zucchini. Spread the onion mixture evenly over the top, sprinkle with paprika, and bake until set, about 45 minutes.

Vegetarian Reuben Sandwich

MAKES 6 SANDWICHES

This tangy recipe will really liven up your taste buds.

PER SANDWICH • 257 CALORIES (14% FROM FAT) • 4 G FAT • 18 G PROTEIN
36 G CARBOHYDRATE • 0 MG CHOLESTEROL • 904 MG SODIUM • 6 G FIBER

2 teaspoons toasted sesame oil
1 onion, chopped
2 cloves garlic, minced
1½ cups sauerkraut
1 teaspoon paprika
1 teaspoon caraway seeds
½ teaspoon dried thyme

¼ teaspoon black pepper
12 slices dark whole-grain rye bread
  with caraway
3 tablespoons Dijon mustard
1 8-ounce package seitan (beef-flavored)
  or GardenBeef, thinly sliced
2 tomatoes, sliced

Heat the oil in a large nonstick skillet and sauté the onion and garlic until the onion is soft, about 5 minutes. Stir in the sauerkraut, paprika, caraway seeds, thyme, and black pepper. Cook another 5 minutes.

To assemble the sandwiches, spread each slice of bread liberally with Dijon mustard. Top 6 of the slices with a generous spoonful of the onion mixture, slices of seitan or GardenBeef, and tomato slices. Top with the remaining bread.

Side Dishes

Barley Succotash

SERVES 8

This brave new barley recipe has both delightful flavor and color.

PER SERVING • 111 CALORIES (3% FROM FAT) • 0.4 G FAT • 4 G PROTEIN
23 G CARBOHYDRATE • 0 MG CHOLESTEROL • 234 MG SODIUM • 5 G FIBER

1 15-ounce can Swanson's Vegetable
    Broth
½ cup pearl barley, rinsed
2 cups corn kernels, fresh or frozen
1 red bell pepper, seeded and cut in
    julienne strips
2 tablespoons thinly sliced fresh fennel

½ cup finely sliced green onions,
    including tops
¼ teaspoon dried rosemary, crushed
¼ teaspoon fennel seeds, crushed
1 10-ounce package frozen baby lima
    beans
2 tablespoons balsamic vinegar

Add enough water to the vegetable broth to make 2 cups and pour it into a saucepan. Add the barley and simmer, uncovered, until tender, about 25 minutes.

Transfer the cooked barley and any remaining liquid to a large skillet and add all the remaining ingredients. Cook uncovered until all the liquid has evaporated. Serve with a simple cooked grain, like Brown Rice (page 268).

Basmati and Wheat Berry Pilaf

SERVES 6

A lovely dish made with fragrant rice and nutrient-packed wheat berries.

PER SERVING • 166 CALORIES (13% FROM FAT) • 2 G FAT • 3 G PROTEIN
33 G CARBOHYDRATE • 0 MG CHOLESTEROL • 298 MG SODIUM • 3 G FIBER

¼ cup wheat berries
1 cup brown basmati rice
1 15-ounce can Swanson's Vegetable
    Broth
2 teaspoons olive oil
1 onion, finely chopped
2 cloves garlic, minced

2 cups mushrooms, thinly sliced
2 stalks celery, thinly sliced
½ teaspoon black pepper
½ teaspoon dried thyme
½ teaspoon dried marjoram
¼ teaspoon dried sage
⅓ cup finely chopped fresh parsley

Soak the wheat berries in 2 cups of water overnight. Rinse and drain. Place in a saucepan with the rice and vegetable broth. Stir to mix, then cover and cook over low heat until the rice is tender, about 1 hour.

Heat the oil in a large pot or skillet and sauté the onion and garlic, about 3 minutes. Add the mushrooms and celery. Cook, stirring frequently, for 5 minutes. Stir in the cooked wheat-rice mixture, black pepper, thyme, marjoram, sage, and parsley. Cook over low heat, stirring frequently, until very hot. Add a little water (1 to 2 tablespoons) if the mixture begins to stick.

Bombay Potatoes, Tomatoes, and Chickpeas

SERVES 6

No need to worry with this curry. It tastes delicious!

PER SERVING • 236 CALORIES (8% FROM FAT) • 2 G FAT • 6 G PROTEIN
48 G CARBOHYDRATE • 0 MG CHOLESTEROL • 374 MG SODIUM • 7 G FIBER

2 teaspoons olive oil
2 large onions, chopped
3 cloves garlic, minced
2 teaspoons whole cumin seed
1 teaspoon coriander
½ teaspoon turmeric
½ teaspoon ginger

⅛ teaspoon cinnamon
3 russet potatoes
1 15-ounce can crushed tomatoes
1 15-ounce can garbanzo beans, drained
  and rinsed
½ teaspoon salt, or to taste

Heat the oil in a large pot or skillet and sauté the onions and garlic until soft, about 5 minutes. Add the cumin seed, coriander, turmeric, ginger, and cinnamon. Cook 2 to 3 minutes, stirring frequently.

Scrub the potatoes, then slice them in half lengthwise. Cut into ½-inch-thick slices. Add to the onions and cook 5 minutes. Stir in the tomatoes, garbanzo beans, and 1½ cups of water. Lower the heat, then cover and simmer until the potatoes are tender, about 25 minutes. Add salt to taste.

Baked Potato Skins

MAKES 8 POTATO HALVES

*H*earty, filling, and easy to prepare, these potato skins are delicious as a snack on the run, or could even fill in for a main course in a pinch!

PER ½ POTATO • 198 CALORIES (19% FROM FAT) • 4.5 G FAT • 9 G PROTEIN
30 G CARBOHYDRATE • 15 MG CHOLESTEROL • 164 MG SODIUM • 8 G FIBER

4 russet potatoes
Olive oil spray
4 cups mushrooms, sliced
2 roasted red bell peppers,
    julienned

1 cup low-fat white cheddar cheese,
    shredded
2 green onions, chopped
½ cup Island Salsa (page 224) or low-fat
    ranch dressing

Wash the potatoes and bake them for 1 hour at 350°F. Set aside until cool enough to handle, then cut in half lengthwise and scoop out the insides, leaving a ¼-inch-thick shell.

Increase the oven temperature to 400°F. Spray the potato skins with olive oil and place them skin side up on a rack in the oven until they are crispy and brown, 10 to 12 minutes.

Fill the potato skins with the mushrooms and julienned peppers. Top with the shredded cheese and return to the oven until the cheese melts. Remove from the oven and sprinkle with the green onions. Serve with Island Salsa or low-fat ranch dressing.

Greek Salad Pita

SERVES 1

*T*his salad in a sandwich with Yogurt Dill Dipping Sauce is fun and flavorful.

PER SERVING • 110 CALORIES (36% FROM FAT) • 4.5 G FAT • 5 G PROTEIN
15 G CARBOHYDRATE • 15 MG CHOLESTEROL • 340 MG SODIUM • 2 G FIBER

1 whole-wheat pita
Several leaves red lettuce
¼ green bell pepper, thinly sliced
3 Greek olives, pitted and sliced

2 ounces feta cheese, drained and
    crumbled
½ cup Yogurt Dill Dipping Sauce
    (page 325)

Toast or grill the pita. Cut in half to form pockets. Fill each pocket with lettuce, bell pepper, olives, and feta cheese. Drizzle 1 tablespoon Yogurt Dill Dipping Sauce inside each pocket. Serve an additional tablespoon of sauce on the side for dipping.

Broiled Polenta Squares and Tomato Chutney

SERVES 4

This is a perfect "make-ahead" dish: the chutney becomes more flavorful with time, and the polenta is best if it can chill overnight.

PER SERVING • 178 CALORIES (14% FROM FAT) • 3 G FAT • 4 G PROTEIN
33 G CARBOHYDRATE • 0 MG CHOLESTEROL • 325 MG SODIUM • 8 G FIBER

½ cup yellow cornmeal
½ teaspoon salt
½ teaspoon dried rosemary, crushed
1 15-ounce can corn
½ cup sun-dried tomatoes
½ cup roasted red peppers
3 cloves garlic

1 tablespoon capers, drained and rinsed
1 tablespoon finely chopped fresh basil
1 tablespoon red wine
2 teaspoons Sucanat
1 teaspoon olive oil
1 teaspoon Dijon mustard

To make the polenta, combine the cornmeal, 2 cups of water, salt, and rosemary in a saucepan and bring to a simmer. Cook, uncovered, over medium heat, stirring often, until the polenta is very thick. Stir in the corn (including the liquid) and cook until the polenta is thickened again. Spread the cooked polenta into a large bread pan and refrigerate until it is completely cold.

To prepare the chutney, pour about 1 cup of boiling water over the tomatoes and let them stand and soften at least 30 minutes. Drain and place in a food processor with the peppers, garlic, capers, basil, wine, Sucanat, oil, and mustard. Process in short bursts until well mixed (there should still be some chunks).

When the polenta is chilled, preheat the broiler. Using a very sharp knife, cut the polenta into ¼-inch-thick slices. Arrange the slices about 1 inch apart on a nonstick or oil-sprayed baking sheet and broil until the top is crusty and golden brown, 5 to 10 minutes. Turn and brown the other side.

To serve, arrange the polenta slices on a platter and top with generous spoonfuls of chutney.

Broiled Tofu in Sweet Ginger Marinade

MAKES 8 SLICES

These tasty slices of tofu can also be made into a knockout sandwich. (On whole-grain bread, of course!)

PER SERVING • 114 CALORIES (40% FROM FAT) • 5 G FAT • 9 G PROTEIN
8 G CARBOHYDRATE • 0 MG CHOLESTEROL • 511 MG SODIUM • 0 G FIBER

1 pound firm tofu

2 tablespoons minced fresh ginger

4 cloves garlic, crushed

½ cup tamari soy sauce

⅓ cup Sucanat

1 tablespoon toasted sesame oil

½ teaspoon dry mustard

Begin by pressing the tofu. Place it on a plate and cover it with a baking sheet or similar flat object. Place a book or other heavy object on top of the baking sheet and let stand at least 20 minutes.

Stir together the ginger, garlic, soy sauce, ¾ cup of water, Sucanat, sesame oil, and mustard.

Cut the pressed tofu into ¼-inch-thick slices and arrange it in a single layer in a 13 × 9-inch baking dish. Pour the marinade over it. Marinate 30 minutes or longer.

Preheat the broiler. Place the pan of marinated tofu directly under the broiler and broil until bubbly and brown, about 5 minutes on each side.

Brown Rice

MAKES 3 CUPS (SERVES 3)

PER SERVING • 115 CALORIES (4% FROM FAT) • 0.5 G FAT • 2.5 G PROTEIN
50 G CARBOHYDRATE • 0 MG CHOLESTEROL • 88 MG SODIUM • 1 G FIBER

1 cup short-grain brown rice

4 cups water

¼ teaspoon salt

Rinse and drain the rice. In a saucepan, bring the water to a boil, then add the rice (and salt, if desired). Once the water returns to a boil, lower the heat slightly. Cover and simmer about 40 minutes, until the rice is soft but still retains a hint of crunchiness. Pour off any excess water.

Calcutta Cauliflower

SERVES 6

he rich spices of the East make this a gem of a dish!

PER SERVING • 52 CALORIES (25% FROM FAT) • 1 G FAT • 2 G PROTEIN
8 G CARBOHYDRATE • 0 MG CHOLESTEROL • 109 MG SODIUM • 4 G FIBER

2 teaspoons olive oil

2 tablespoons minced fresh ginger

1 hot chili pepper, seeded and minced

1 teaspoon black mustard seeds

1 teaspoon cumin seeds

1 large cauliflower, broken or cut into
   bite-size pieces

1½ teaspoons coriander

½ teaspoon turmeric

½ cup distilled water

1 15-ounce can diced tomatoes

¼ teaspoon salt, or to taste

Cinnamon, for sprinkling

Chopped cilantro, for garnish

Heat the oil in a large skillet and cook the ginger, chili pepper, mustard seeds, and cumin seeds until the seeds begin to pop, about 2 minutes.

Stir in the cauliflower, coriander, turmeric, and the water. Cook 2 to 3 minutes, stirring frequently.

Add the tomatoes with their liquid, then reduce the heat, cover, and cook until the cauliflower is tender, about 5 minutes. Add salt to taste, sprinkle with cinnamon, and garnish with chopped cilantro.

Couscous-Filled Squash

SERVES 4

For something new, try kabocha—a delicious squash that has deep, wonderful flavor. Feel free to explore using other varieties of squash.

PER SERVING • 360 CALORIES (5% FROM FAT) • 2 G FAT • 7 G PROTEIN
78 G CARBOHYDRATE • 0 MG CHOLESTEROL • 155 MG SODIUM • 18 G FIBER

2 small kabocha squash, or your favorite
  squash
¾ cup whole-wheat couscous
¼ teaspoon salt
¾ cup boiling water
1 apple, cored and diced
1 pear, cored and diced

2 tablespoons chopped walnuts
2 tablespoons maple syrup
½ teaspoon cinnamon
¼ teaspoon ginger
¼ teaspoon allspice
⅛ teaspoon nutmeg
⅛ teaspoon cardamom

Preheat the oven to 350°F. Cut the squashes in half and remove the seeds. Place on a baking sheet with the cut sides down and bake 30 minutes.

Combine the whole-wheat couscous and salt in a mixing bowl. Pour the boiling water over and stir to mix. Cover and let stand until all the water is absorbed, 15 minutes, then fluff the couscous with a fork. Stir in the apple, pear, walnuts, maple syrup, cinnamon, ginger, allspice, nutmeg, and cardamom. Mix well.

Spoon the couscous mixture into the partially baked kabocha shells and place in a large baking dish. Cover and bake until the shells are tender when pierced with a fork, about 45 minutes.

Grilled Veggie Holiday Stuffing

SERVES 12

A festive, colorful, meatless rendition that's great any time of year!

PER SERVING • 281 CALORIES (33% FROM FAT) • 10 G FAT • 10 G PROTEIN
36 G CARBOHYDRATE • 0 MG CHOLESTEROL • 634 MG SODIUM • 8 G FIBER

3 vegetable broth cubes

3 cups boiling water

¾ cup dried cranberries

3 tablespoons poultry seasoning

1½ teaspoons salt

½ teaspoon black pepper

2 medium onions, chopped in ½- to 1-inch chunks

2 stalks celery, chopped in ½- to 1-inch chunks

1 medium globe eggplant, chopped in ½- to 1-inch chunks

1 yellow or red bell pepper, chopped in ½- to 1-inch chunks

2 tablespoons extra-virgin olive oil

¾ cup whole, shelled hazelnuts

1 green apple (Granny Smith or pippin)

5 cups dried bread cubes

10 GardenSausage patties

Parsley, for garnish

Dissolve the vegetable broth cubes in the boiling water. Mix in the dried cranberries, poultry seasoning, salt, and pepper.

Preheat the oven to 350°F. Place the onions, celery, eggplant, and bell pepper in a 13 × 9-inch baking pan and toss them with 1 tablespoon of the olive oil. Bake for 10 minutes, then add the hazelnuts and continue baking until the vegetables begin to brown around the edges and the skin of the hazelnuts cracks, about 15 minutes. Remove and transfer to a large bowl.

Core and dice the apple into ¾-inch cubes. Add it to the roasted vegetables, along with the bread cubes. Stir in the broth, then place the mixture into a lightly oiled 13 × 9-inch baking dish. Cover with foil and bake for 30 minutes. Remove the foil and bake an additional 10 to 15 minutes.

While the dressing is baking, sauté the GardenSausage patties in the remaining tablespoon of olive oil over medium heat until they are nicely browned. Cut into quarters and fold into the baked dressing. Garnish with fresh parsley.

Fat-Free Oven Fries

SERVES 6

Deliciously seasoned French fries without all the fat!

PER SERVING • 147 CALORIES (0.5% FROM FAT) • 0.1 G FAT • 2 G PROTEIN
34 G CARBOHYDRATE • 0 MG CHOLESTEROL • 100 MG SODIUM • 3 G FIBER

4 large russet potatoes

Vegetable oil spray

1 teaspoon garlic powder

1 teaspoon mixed Italian herbs

½ teaspoon paprika

¼ teaspoon salt

Fresh-ground black pepper

Preheat the oven to 500°F. Scrub the potatoes and cut them into long, thin strips. Lightly spray a 13 × 9-inch baking dish with nonstick spray and spread the potatoes in it. Sprinkle with the garlic powder, Italian herbs, paprika, salt, and black pepper. Toss to mix. Bake in the preheated oven until tender when pierced with a fork, about 30 minutes.

Fettuccine and Roasted Vegetables

SERVES 8

Power up your body with whole-wheat pasta!

PER SERVING • 91 CALORIES (20% FROM FAT) • 2 G FAT • 4 G PROTEIN
14 G CARBOHYDRATE • 1 MG CHOLESTEROL • 167 MG SODIUM • 3 G FIBER

1 red onion

1 large red bell pepper

1 pound fresh asparagus, with tough ends
   removed

2 cups small, closed mushrooms

1 teaspoon garlic powder

1 teaspoon chili powder

½ teaspoon dried marjoram

½ teaspoon dried thyme

½ teaspoon dried oregano

½ teaspoon dried basil

½ teaspoon salt

¼ teaspoon black pepper

8 ounces whole-wheat fettuccine or
   other pasta

2 teaspoons olive oil

2 tablespoons grated Parmesan cheese

Chopped parsley, for garnish

Preheat the oven to 500°F. Cut the onion, pepper, and asparagus into bite-sized pieces and place in a large bowl with the mushrooms. Toss with the garlic powder, chili powder, marjoram, thyme, oregano, basil, salt, and black pepper. Spread in a single layer in 1 or 2 large baking dishes, and bake until just tender, 10 to 12 minutes.

Meanwhile, cook the pasta in boiling water until it is just tender. Drain and rinse it briefly, then arrange it on a large platter. Sprinkle with the olive oil and Parmesan cheese and toss to mix. Spread the cooked vegetables over the pasta and sprinkle with chopped parsley.

Garlic-Infused Green Beans

SERVES 6

I first made this recipe using Chinese long beans, and everybody loved it. Since then, I've made it with string beans with equally tasty results. If you want to try the original version, look for long beans in Asian markets.

PER SERVING • 46 CALORIES (14% FROM FAT) • 1 G FAT • 2 G PROTEIN
8 G CARBOHYDRATE • 0 MG CHOLESTEROL • 440 MG SODIUM • 2 G FIBER

4 cups string beans, or Chinese long
  beans
1 teaspoon toasted sesame oil
8 cloves garlic, minced

1 red chili pepper, seeded and minced
2 tablespoons seasoned rice vinegar
2 tablespoons tamari soy sauce

Wash and trim the beans and break them into 1½-inch pieces. Steam over boiling water until just tender, about 7 minutes. Chill in ice water, then drain and set aside.

Heat the oil in a nonstick skillet and sauté the garlic and chili for 3 to 4 minutes. Stir in the vinegar and tamari, along with the cooked beans. Continue cooking, stirring constantly, until very hot, about 1 minute. Transfer to a serving dish. And don't forget to add a touch of garnish.

Green Beans with Toasted Almonds

SERVES 6

You'll go nuts over this recipe!

PER SERVING • 70 CALORIES (33% FROM FAT) • 3 G FAT • 2 G PROTEIN
9 G CARBOHYDRATE • 0 MG CHOLESTEROL • 106 MG SODIUM • 3 G FIBER

1 pound fresh green beans

1 teaspoon toasted sesame oil

1 onion, chopped

¼ cup slivered almonds

1 tablespoon seasoned rice vinegar

1 tablespoon soy sauce

Trim the beans and break them into bite-size pieces. Steam until just tender.

Heat the oil in a large nonstick skillet and sauté the onion and almonds for 5 minutes. Lower the heat, add the vinegar, and continue cooking, stirring often, until the onions are caramelized and the almonds browned, about 10 minutes. Stir in the soy sauce and the steamed green beans. Cook 1 to 2 minutes before serving.

Golden Potato Medley

SERVES 6

This dish will invite your eaters to sing praises!

PER SERVING • 186 CALORIES (1% FROM FAT) • 0.1 G FAT • 4 G PROTEIN
42 G CARBOHYDRATE • 0 MG CHOLESTEROL • 479 MG SODIUM • 5 G FIBER

1 tablespoon soy sauce

1 onion, thinly sliced

3 cloves garlic, minced

2 carrots, thinly sliced

4 russet potatoes, scrubbed and diced

1 cup mushrooms, sliced

1 red bell pepper, diced

1 zucchini, diced

¼ cup chopped parsley

1 teaspoon salt

1 teaspoon turmeric

½ teaspoon black pepper

½ teaspoon dried thyme

Heat ½ cup of water in a large skillet. Add the soy sauce, onion, and garlic. Cook until the onion is soft, about 5 minutes.

Add the carrots, potatoes, and another ½ cup of water. Cover and cook until the potatoes are just tender, about 15 minutes. Stir occasionally, and add a small amount of extra water if the mixture begins to stick.

Add the mushrooms, bell pepper, zucchini, parsley, salt, turmeric, black pepper, and thyme. Cover and cook another 5 minutes.

Garlicky Garbanzos and Kale

SERVES 6

If you love garlic the way I do, this is a match made in food heaven!

PER SERVING • 140 CALORIES (10% FROM FAT) • 2 G FAT • 5 G PROTEIN
25 G CARBOHYDRATE • 0 MG CHOLESTEROL • 313 MG SODIUM • 8 G FIBER

1 bunch kale

1 teaspoon olive oil

4 cloves garlic

1 tablespoon minced fresh ginger

1 small red chili pepper, seeded and finely chopped

2 tomatoes, coarsely chopped

1 15-ounce can garbanzo beans, including liquid

1 teaspoon soy sauce

1 teaspoon hoisin sauce

Brown Rice (page 268), or other favorite whole grain

Wash the kale, remove the stems, and chop the leaves.

Heat the oil in a large skillet and sauté the garlic, ginger, and 1 teaspoon of the chopped chili pepper for 2 minutes (use more chopped chili if you like a spicier dish).

Stir in the tomatoes and garbanzo beans with their liquid. Bring to a simmer and cook for 5 minutes.

Add the soy sauce, hoisin sauce, and stir to mix. Spread the kale evenly over the top, then cover the pan and cook over medium heat, stirring occasionally, until the kale is tender, 5 to 7 minutes. Do not overcook. Serve with Brown Rice, or a similar whole grain.

Kale with Winter Squash

SERVES 6

A terrific dish for all seasons. Kale has been my all-time favorite green since I was a kid! It also contains some powerful antioxidants.

PER SERVING • 81 CALORIES (13% FROM FAT) • 1 G FAT • 3 G PROTEIN
14 G CARBOHYDRATE • 0 MG CHOLESTEROL • 201 MG SODIUM • 6 G FIBER

2 cups diced winter squash

1 bunch kale

1 teaspoon olive oil

½ cup thinly sliced red onion

2 cloves garlic, minced

1 teaspoon toasted sesame seeds

1 tablespoon tamari soy sauce

Steam the winter squash until it is just tender.

Wash the kale, remove the stems, and tear or cut the leaves into small pieces.

Heat the oil in a large nonstick skillet and sauté the onion and garlic for 5 minutes. Add the kale and cook, stirring frequently, until tender, about 5 minutes. Add the cooked winter squash, sesame seeds, and the soy sauce, and stir gently for 3 to 4 minutes.

Mediterranean Vegetables

SERVES 6

Serve these flavorful vegetables with brown rice or with whole-grain pasta.

PER SERVING • 51 CALORIES (14% FROM FAT) • 1 G FAT • 1 G PROTEIN
10 G CARBOHYDRATE • 0 MG CHOLESTEROL • 197 MG SODIUM • 3 G FIBER

1 large onion, chopped

2 cloves garlic, minced

1 teaspoon olive oil

2 Japanese eggplants, cut into 1-inch cubes (optional: use 4 cups of VeggiePack pieces; page 284)

2 large tomatoes, cut into wedges

½ green bell pepper, cut into 1-inch pieces

2 stalks celery, sliced

½ teaspoon fresh basil

¼ teaspoon coriander

¼ teaspoon cinnamon

½ teaspoon salt

¼ teaspoon black pepper

1 tablespoon lemon juice

Cooked Brown Rice (page 268) or pasta, for serving

Sauté the onion and garlic in the olive oil in a large nonstick skillet for 3 minutes. Add the eggplant cubes and 2 tablespoons of water, then cover and cook until the eggplant is tender, about 15 minutes. Stir occasionally.

Add the tomatoes, bell pepper, celery, basil, coriander, cinnamon, salt, and pepper. Cover and cook over medium-low heat until the vegetables are just tender, about 10 minutes. Stir in the lemon juice.

Home-Style Spuds and GardenSausage

SERVES 8

There are some serious good-tasting home-fried potatoes that not only deliver on flavor but are low-fat as well.

PER SERVING • 279 CALORIES (5% FROM FAT) • 1 G FAT • 7 G PROTEIN
59 G CARBOHYDRATE • 0 MG CHOLESTEROL • 112 MG SODIUM • 8 G FIBER

7 red potatoes
4 GardenSausage patties
1 onion, chopped
3 cloves garlic, minced
1 cup VeggiePack (page 284)

⅓ cup chopped green onions
1 tomato, diced, for garnish
2 tablespoons chopped parsley, for garnish
Salt
Fresh-ground black pepper

Scrub the potatoes but do not peel them. Cut into ½-inch cubes. Steam over boiling water until just tender when pierced with a fork, 10 to 15 minutes. Remove from the pan and set aside.

Heat a large nonstick skillet to medium heat and fry the GardenSausage patties on both sides until golden brown. This will take 3 to 5 minutes per side. Dice and set aside.

Heat ½ cup of water in the same skillet and add the onion and garlic. Cook until the onion is soft and golden, about 5 minutes, then add the cooked potatoes and mixed vegetables. Cook, stirring gently, until the mixed vegetables are tender, about 5 minutes. Just before serving, fold in the GardenSausage and chopped green onions. Garnish with diced tomato and chopped parsley.

Sprinkle with salt and pepper.

Pilaf with Dried Fruits

SERVES 8

A lovely rainbow display of fruits and rice.

PER SERVING • 201 CALORIES (10% FROM FAT) • 2 G FAT • 5 G PROTEIN
40 G CARBOHYDRATE • 0 MG CHOLESTEROL • 221 MG SODIUM • 4 G FIBER

1 teaspoon olive oil

1 cup brown basmati rice

1 15-ounce can Swanson's Vegetable
Broth

2 cups apricot nectar

¼ teaspoon coriander

¾ cup yellow split peas, rinsed

½ cup chopped dried apricots

¼ cup golden raisins

¼ cup thinly sliced green onions

2 tablespoons coarsely chopped roasted
peanuts

Heat the oil in a large pot and sauté the rice until it becomes opaque, about 3 minutes. Add the vegetable broth and 2 tablespoons of water, then cover and cook until the rice is tender, about 50 minutes.

In the meantime, heat the apricot nectar and coriander in a saucepan. Add the split peas and chopped apricots, then cover and simmer until the peas are just tender, about 40 minutes.

Combine the rice and peas, then stir in the golden raisins. Transfer to a platter and top with chopped green onions and peanuts.

Pineapple-Glazed Butternut Squash

SERVES 8

This sweet dish is a swashbuckler of a squash recipe!

PER SERVING • 155 CALORIES (1% FROM FAT) • 0.2 G FAT • 2 G PROTEIN
36 G CARBOHYDRATE • 0 MG CHOLESTEROL • 129 MG SODIUM • 7 G FIBER

1 medium butternut squash
¼ cup orange juice concentrate
¼ cup white grape juice concentrate
2 teaspoons cornstarch

1 teaspoon minced fresh ginger
1½ tablespoons white or yellow miso
2 cups chopped fresh pineapple
Sucanat, for garnish

Cut the squash in half from stem to base and scoop out the seeds. Place in a vegetable steamer and cook until tender when pierced with a fork, about 30 minutes.

While the squash cooks, combine the orange juice concentrate, white grape juice concentrate, cornstarch, ginger, miso, and ½ cup water in a saucepan. Stir to mix, then cook over medium heat, stirring constantly, until clear and slightly thickened. Stir in the pineapple.

When the squash is tender, arrange both halves, cut side up, on an ovenproof platter.

Preheat the oven to 350°F. Using a spoon, gently loosen some of the squash flesh from the skin and spread it evenly within the shell, filling in the seed cavity (leave enough flesh attached to the shell so that it maintains its shape). Spread the pineapple mixture evenly over the top, then sprinkle lightly with Sucanat. Bake in the preheated oven for 10 minutes.

Red Potatoes with Kale

SERVES 8

A fabulous dish that gives you your "dark green" vegetables.

PER SERVING • 104 CALORIES (7% FROM FAT) • 1 G FAT • 4 G PROTEIN
20 G CARBOHYDRATE • 0 MG CHOLESTEROL • 242 MG SODIUM • 5 G FIBER

4 red potatoes

1 bunch kale

1 teaspoon toasted sesame oil

1 onion, thinly sliced

2 cloves garlic, minced

½ teaspoon black pepper

¼ teaspoon paprika

5 teaspoons tamari soy sauce

Scrub the potatoes and cut into ½-inch cubes. Steam over boiling water until just tender when pierced with a fork. Rinse with cold water, then drain and set aside.

Rinse the kale, then remove the tough stems. Cut or tear the leaves into small pieces.

Heat the oil in a large nonstick skillet and sauté the onion and garlic for 5 minutes. Add the cooked potatoes, pepper, and paprika, and continue cooking until the potatoes begin to brown, about 5 minutes. Use a spatula to turn the mixture gently as it cooks.

Spread the kale leaves over the top of the potato mixture. Sprinkle with 2 tablespoons of water and the soy sauce. Cover and cook, turning occasionally, until the kale is tender, about 7 minutes.

Savory Spinach Bread Pudding

SERVES 8

Savor the flavor of the new twist on this time-honored tradition.

PER SERVING • 155 CALORIES (26% FROM FAT) • 4 G FAT • 6 G PROTEIN
21 G CARBOHYDRATE • 0 MG CHOLESTEROL • 316 MG SODIUM • 5 G FIBER

1 ounce dried shiitake mushrooms

2 teaspoons olive oil

1 onion, chopped

4 cloves garlic, minced

2 stalks celery, sliced

2 cups fresh button mushrooms, sliced

1 teaspoon each: dried thyme and
  marjoram

½ teaspoon each: dried sage, salt, and
  black pepper

6 cups fresh whole-wheat bread cubes

1 10.5-ounce package firm silken tofu

2 cups milk: almond, rice, soy, or nonfat dairy

2 tablespoons seasoned rice vinegar

1 tablespoon cornstarch

Vegetable oil spray

1 pound fresh spinach

1 teaspoon toasted sesame oil

1 teaspoon tamari soy sauce

1 teaspoon balsamic vinegar

Soak the dried mushrooms in 1 cup of boiling water until soft, about 20 minutes. Drain, re-serving the soaking liquid. Remove the stems with a sharp knife and cut the mushrooms into thin strips.

Heat the olive oil in a large skillet and sauté the onion, garlic, and celery for 5 minutes. Add the button mushrooms and ¼ cup of the reserved soaking liquid along with the thyme, marjoram, sage, salt, and pepper. Cook, stirring frequently, until the mushrooms are browned. Transfer to a large bowl and add the whole-wheat bread cubes and sliced shiitake mushrooms.

Preheat the oven to 350°F. Combine the tofu, milk, vinegar, and cornstarch in a blender and process until smooth. Stir into the bread mixture and let stand 5 minutes. Spread in an oil-sprayed 9 × 9-inch baking dish, cover with foil, and bake for 40 minutes. Remove the foil and bake an additional 20 minutes.

Clean the spinach thoroughly and remove the stems. Heat the toasted sesame oil in a large skillet and add the spinach leaves. Cook, stirring frequently, until the spinach is uni-formly wilted, about 5 minutes. Sprinkle with the soy sauce and balsamic vinegar and toss to mix. Spread the spinach over the top of the baked pudding just before serving.

String Beans with Ginger

SERVES 4

This tangy rhizome really livens up this dish!

PER SERVING • 52 CALORIES (53% FROM FAT) • 3 G FAT • 1 G PROTEIN
5 G CARBOHYDRATE • 0 MG CHOLESTEROL • 137 MG SODIUM • 3 G FIBER

½ pound fresh green beans

1 teaspoon toasted sesame oil

1 tablespoon finely chopped fresh
ginger

1 stalk fresh lemongrass, finely chopped

1 red chili pepper, seeded and minced

½ cup reduced-fat coconut milk

¼ teaspoon salt

Trim the ends off the green beans and cut into 2-inch pieces. Heat the oil in a large skillet and add the ginger, lemongrass, and chili pepper. Cook for 2 to 3 minutes. Add the green beans, coconut milk, ½ cup of water, and salt. Cover and cook over medium heat until the green beans are tender, about 10 minutes.

Sweet and Sour Thai Vegetables

SERVES 4

Sweet and sour succulent nutrition! This is a wonderful recipe with a variety of spicy flavors.

PER SERVING • 103 CALORIES (20% FROM FAT) • 2 G FAT • 1 G PROTEIN
19 G CARBOHYDRATE • 0 MG CHOLESTEROL • 425 MG SODIUM • 3 G FIBER

2 teaspoons toasted sesame oil

5 cloves garlic, minced

1 Japanese eggplant, cut into ½-inch-
thick slices

1 red bell pepper, cut into 1-inch strips

1 green bell pepper, cut into 1-inch strips

2 cups mushrooms, thickly sliced

1 red chili pepper, finely chopped

¼ cup tomato sauce

2 tablespoon seasoned rice vinegar

¼ cup Swanson's Vegetable Broth

2 tablespoons Sucanat

½ teaspoon salt

2 tablespoons cornstarch

Chopped cilantro, for garnish

3 cups cooked Brown Rice (page 268)
for serving

Heat the oil in a large skillet and sauté the garlic for 2 to 3 minutes. Add the eggplant, peppers, and mushrooms, along with the red chili pepper, tomato sauce, vinegar, vegetable broth, Sucanat, and salt. Cook until the eggplant is just tender, 5 to 8 minutes.

In a small bowl, whisk the cornstarch and ½ cup of water together until smooth. Add to the vegetable mixture and cook until the sauce is thickened. Sprinkle with chopped cilantro. Serve with cooked Brown Rice.

Thai Peanut Noodles

SERVES 6

This flavor-packed dish is a potluck favorite!

PER SERVING • 181 CALORIES (32% FROM FAT) • 6 G FAT • 8 G PROTEIN
23 G CARBOHYDRATE • 0 MG CHOLESTEROL • 243 MG SODIUM • 3 G FIBER

8 ounces whole-grain udon, soba, or
   spaghetti
3 tablespoons peanut butter
2 tablespoons seasoned rice vinegar
2 tablespoons ketchup
1 tablespoon Sucanat
2 teaspoons soy sauce
1 teaspoon toasted sesame oil

1 red chili pepper, seeded and finely
   chopped
2 teaspoons finely chopped fresh ginger
2 cloves garlic, minced
2 cups fresh bean sprouts
¼ cup chopped cilantro
2 tablespoons dry-roasted peanuts,
   coarsely chopped

Cook the pasta in boiling water until tender. Rinse and drain, then set aside.

Whisk together the peanut butter, 3 tablespoons of water, vinegar, ketchup, Sucanat, and soy sauce.

Heat the oil in a nonstick skillet and sauté the chili, ginger, and garlic for 2 to 3 minutes. Stir in the sauce, then add the cooked pasta, bean sprouts, chopped cilantro, and chopped peanuts. Toss to mix. Serve immediately.

VeggiePack

This name either has or will pop up quite a bit as you discover my GardenCuisine Plan. If you can get into the habit of making these cut-up "VeggiePacks" along with the softer, leafy-greens-based EssentialSalad every week and eating them every day, you will reap some powerful nutritional rewards—I guarantee it! See pages 191 to 194 for more detailed information on how to shop for, prep, and store VeggiePacks and EssentialSalads.

PER 1 CUP • 40 CALORIES (5% FROM FAT) • 0.2 G FAT • 4 G PROTEIN
7 G CARBOHYDRATE • 0 MG CHOLESTEROL • 14 MG SODIUM • 3 G FIBER

6 cups fresh vegetable greens (any combination): bok choy, celery, collard greens, fennel, kale, spinach, Swiss chard

4 cups fresh vegetable roots (any combination): carrots, cassava, daikon, leeks, onions, radishes, sweet potatoes, turnip, yams

½ cup uncooked snow peas

½ cup uncooked red bell peppers

4 cups fresh vegetable flowers (any combination): broccoli, Brussels sprouts, red, green, or Chinese cabbage, cauliflower

2 cups fresh vegetable grains or legumes (any combination): beans (all kinds), corn on the cob, snow pea

Wash each vegetable and cut to appropriate size. Each needs to be cut so that they all cook about the same time. (Remember, these can also be eaten raw.) This may take a little experimenting the first time or two. Now toss all of the cut-up ingredients in a large mixing bowl or plastic bag. Place 2 cups of this mixture in a 1-quart ziplock or "green" bag. Place in the refrigerator for later use.

Tofu "Chicken"

MAKES 16 OUNCES (SERVES 8)

ou will find that this savory tofu can replace chicken in many recipes.

PER 2-OZ SERVING • 87 CALORIES (41% FROM FAT) • 4 G FAT • 8 G PROTEIN
3 G CARBOHYDRATE • 0 MG CHOLESTEROL • 179 MG SODIUM • 0.4 G FIBER

1 pound firm tofu
3 tablespoons chicken-style seasoning (vegetarian)

Dice the tofu into ½-by-1-inch-long pieces. In a medium bowl, combine 3 tablespoons water and the chicken-style seasoning. Add the tofu to the mixture and marinate for 15 to 20 minutes. After marinating, place the cubes on a nonstick baking sheet and bake 1½ hours in a 200°F oven, turning occasionally. The tofu will brown slightly and will shrink to about half its original size. Remove from the oven and use in recipes or store in the refrigerator.

World Grains

A variety of cooked whole grains is an essential part of a balanced diet. There are so many wonderful grains with great flavors and textures to choose from. Here is a classic pilaf-style mixed grain dish. Using this recipe two to three times a week provides a high-fiber foundation for your diet, which is necessary to promote a healthy, well-balanced body. When you decide to make healthier food choices, you also help make the world a better place to live. Everything is connected; we are all one.

PER SERVING • 103 CALORIES (11% FROM FAT) • 1 G FAT • 3 G PROTEIN
19 G CARBOHYDRATE • 0 MG CHOLESTEROL • 204 MG SODIUM • 3 G FIBER

2 teaspoons olive oil

1 onion, finely chopped

2 cloves garlic, minced

2 cups mushrooms, thinly sliced
   (optional)

1 cup chopped green onions

½ red bell pepper, finely diced (optional)

1 cup brown rice, wheat berries, brown basmati rice, barley, rye, or millet (use any combination of the grains)

½ teaspoon black pepper

¼ teaspoon dried thyme

1 15-ounce can Swanson's Vegetable Broth

3 tablespoons dry white wine (optional)

In a large pot or skillet, heat the oil and sauté the onion and garlic about 3 minutes. Add the mushrooms if desired, green onions, bell pepper, choice of grains, black pepper, and thyme. Cook, stirring frequently, for 5 minutes. Stir in the vegetable broth and wine if using, then cover the pan and cook, without stirring, over medium-low heat until the grain is tender and all the liquid is absorbed, about 45 to 50 minutes. If the grains are not quite cooked at this point, just add a touch more filtered or distilled water (½ to 1 cup) and continue cooking on simmer (keep the pan covered).

After perfecting this recipe over a period of time, you may want to venture out and try some of our other great grain recipes, such as Wild Rice and Asparagus Salad (page 312), Whole-Grain Satay Salad (page 310), Basmati and Wheat Berry Pilaf (page 264), Couscous Veggie Salad (page 303), and Bulgur Salad and Garbanzos (page 298).

Soups

Barley, Tomato, and Bean Soup

SERVES 8

This is a perfect, hearty, cold-day soup.

PER SERVING • 146 CALORIES (5% FROM FAT) • 1 G FAT • 6 G PROTEIN
29 G CARBOHYDRATE • 0 MG CHOLESTEROL • 461 MG SODIUM • 5 G FIBER

¼ cup pearl barley
2 15-ounce cans Swanson's Vegetable
   Broth
1 onion, chopped
1 stalk celery, thinly sliced, including top
1 carrot, diced
1 bay leaf

2 15-ounce cans cannellini beans, drained
   and rinsed
2 tomatoes, chopped
1 teaspoon dried thyme (use 2 teaspoons
   if fresh)
½ teaspoon salt
½ teaspoon black pepper

Combine the barley, vegetable broth, onion, celery, carrot, and bay leaf in a large pot. Simmer until the barley is tender, about 25 minutes. Add the remaining ingredients and simmer an additional 20 minutes.

Carrot Ginger Soup

SERVES 8

A bountiful soup chock-full of beta carotene and with a hint of fresh ginger.

PER SERVING • 107 CALORIES (14% FROM FAT) • 2 G FAT • 2 G PROTEIN
21 G CARBOHYDRATE • 0 MG CHOLESTEROL • 482 MG SODIUM • 4 G FIBER

3 cups sliced carrots
1 onion, coarsely chopped
1 potato, scrubbed and diced
2 cloves garlic, peeled
2 teaspoons minced fresh ginger
2 to 3 cups milk: almond, soy, rice, or
   nonfat dairy

1 15-ounce can corn, drained
¼ teaspoon paprika
¼ teaspoon cumin
¼ teaspoon coriander
¼ teaspoon chili powder
⅛ teaspoon black pepper
½ to 1 teaspoon salt

Combine the carrots, onion, potato, garlic, and ginger with 2 cups of water in a large pot. Bring to a simmer, then cover and cook until the carrots are tender, about 20 minutes. Transfer to a blender, add 2 cups of milk, and blend until completely smooth. Blend in the corn, paprika, cumin, coriander, chili powder, and black pepper. Add salt to taste and additional milk if a thinner soup is desired. Pour back into the pan and heat gently, without boiling, until very hot.

This makes a great side dish for the Couscous Veggie Salad (page 303)!

Creamy Cauliflower Soup

SERVES 8

This soup blossoms with great flavor.

PER SERVING • 150 CALORIES (7% FROM FAT) • 1 G FAT • 5 G PROTEIN
29 G CARBOHYDRATE • 0 MG CHOLESTEROL • 290 MG SODIUM • 4 G FIBER

1 onion, chopped	2 bay leaves
2 large carrots, diced	1 15-ounce can Swanson's Vegetable Broth
3 stalks celery, sliced	
4 cloves garlic, minced	1½ cups milk: almond, soy, rice, or nonfat dairy
¼ cup distilled water	
1 medium head cauliflower, chopped into bite-size pieces	1 15-ounce can cannellini beans, drained and rinsed
1 potato, scrubbed and diced	Fresh parsley, for garnish

Sauté the onion, carrots, celery, and garlic in water until brown.

Add the cauliflower, potato, bay leaves, and vegetable broth. Stir to mix, then cover and simmer over medium heat for 20 minutes.

Remove the bay leaves, then transfer 3 cups of the soup to a blender. Blend until smooth, then return to the pot along with the milk and cannellini beans. Heat gently (do not boil) until very hot. Garnish with parsley to serve.

This tasty soup goes well with Wild Rice and Asparagus Salad (page 312).

Creamy Tomato Potato Soup

SERVES 8

You say "potato" and I say "tomato"! Either way, this recipe delivers.

PER SERVING • 143 CALORIES (19% FROM FAT) • 3 G FAT • 3 G PROTEIN
26 G CARBOHYDRATE • 0 MG CHOLESTEROL • 444 MG SODIUM • 4 G FIBER

2 onions, chopped

2 stalks celery, chopped

1 russet potato, scrubbed and diced

2 15-ounce cans crushed tomatoes

1 cup distilled water

1 tablespoon olive oil

3 tablespoons whole-wheat pastry flour

2½ cups milk: almond, soy, rice, or nonfat dairy

1 tablespoon Sucanat

1½ teaspoons dried basil

1 teaspoon dried thyme

¼ teaspoon black pepper

3 to 4 drops red pepper sauce

Combine the onions, celery, potato, and tomatoes in a large pot. Add the water, then bring to a simmer. Cover and cook for 15 minutes.

Heat the oil in a saucepan, then whisk in the flour to form a thick paste. Stir constantly over low heat for 3 minutes, then whisk in the milk. Cook over medium heat, stirring constantly, for 5 minutes, then add to the tomato mixture. Add the Sucanat, basil, thyme, black pepper, and red pepper sauce. Heat over a low flame until very hot and steamy.

French Onion Soup

SERVES 6

*B*on appétit, *it's time to eat! A little high in fat, but can be eaten once in a while for a treat.*

WITH CHEESE: PER SERVING • 177 CALORIES (48% FROM FAT) • 7 G FAT • 5 G PROTEIN
15 G CARBOHYDRATE • 9 MG CHOLESTEROL • 343 MG SODIUM • 2 G FIBER

WITHOUT CHEESE: PER SERVING • 140 CALORIES (45% FROM FAT) • 7 G FAT • 2 G PROTEIN
15 G CARBOHYDRATE • 0 MG CHOLESTEROL • 340 MG SODIUM • 2 G FIBER

3 tablespoons olive oil

3 large onions, thinly sliced

1 clove garlic, minced

1½ tablespoons whole-wheat pastry flour

1 15-ounce can Swanson's Vegetable Broth

2 tablespoons dry white wine

½ teaspoon dried thyme

Pinch black pepper

2 cups dried whole-wheat bread cubes, for serving

¼ cup grated Swiss cheese (optional)

Heat 1 tablespoon of olive oil in a large nonstick skillet and sauté the onions over medium-high heat, stirring frequently, until they are shriveled and very brown. This is essential to develop a deep flavor for the base of this soup, and will take about 30 minutes.

Add the garlic, whole-wheat pastry flour, and remaining oil. Cook on medium-high heat, stirring constantly, for 5 to 6 minutes.

Add the vegetable broth, wine, thyme, and black pepper. Stir to blend, then simmer for 20 to 30 minutes. Serve with whole-wheat bread cubes and grated Swiss cheese if desired.

Green Green Asparagus Soup

SERVES 6

I suspect this beautiful and delicious soup is chock full of undiscovered nutrients.

PER SERVING • 112 CALORIES (16% FROM FAT) • 2 G FAT • 4 G PROTEIN
19 G CARBOHYDRATE • 0 MG CHOLESTEROL • 460 MG SODIUM • 4 G FIBER

1 teaspoon olive oil

1 onion, chopped

1 zucchini, diced

1 pound asparagus (separate tips from
   tender stalks)

1 russet potato, scrubbed and diced

1 15-ounce can Swanson's Vegetable
   Broth

2 cups fresh spinach leaves

⅓ cup minced parsley

1 cup milk: almond, soy, rice, or nonfat
   dairy

2 teaspoons white or yellow miso

1 teaspoon dried thyme

¼ teaspoon black pepper

3 drops red pepper sauce

Heat the oil in a large pot and sauté the onion until it begins to soften, about 3 minutes. Add the zucchini and continue cooking, stirring frequently, for 3 minutes. Add the asparagus stalks (keep tips in reserve), potato, and vegetable broth. Cover and simmer until the potato is tender, about 15 minutes.

Add the spinach and parsley and cook 5 minutes, then transfer to a blender. Add the milk, miso, thyme, black pepper, and red pepper sauce. Blend until completely smooth. Return to the pot and add the reserved asparagus tips. Heat very gently (do not boil) until the asparagus tips are tender, about 5 minutes.

Gypsy Soup

SERVES 6

omad or not, you'll love this soup! The combinations of flavors are sensational!

PER SERVING • 187 CALORIES (10% FROM FAT) • 2 G FAT • 6 G PROTEIN
36 G CARBOHYDRATE • 0 MG CHOLESTEROL • 647 MG SODIUM • 8 G FIBER

1 onion, chopped

2 cloves garlic, minced

1 cup canned pumpkin

1 15-ounce can Swanson's Vegetable
Broth

2 tablespoons tomato paste

1 15-ounce can kidney beans, drained
and rinsed

1 15-ounce can corn, including liquid

1 roasted red pepper, chopped

½ teaspoon cinnamon

½ teaspoon paprika

¼ teaspoon ginger

¼ teaspoon coriander

¼ teaspoon black pepper

2 cups milk: almond, soy, rice, or nonfat
dairy

3 tablespoons maple syrup

Fresh cilantro leaves or flowers, for
garnish

Heat ½ cup of water in a large pot and add the onion and garlic. Cook over medium-high heat until the water has evaporated and the onion begins to stick to the pan. Add another ¼ cup of water, stirring to remove any stuck bits of onion. Continue cooking until the onion begins to stick again, then add more water and repeat the process until the onion is browned and sweet.

Stir in the pumpkin, vegetable broth, tomato paste, kidney beans, corn, red pepper, cinnamon, paprika, ginger, coriander, and black pepper. Cover and simmer 10 to 15 minutes.

Add the milk and maple syrup, then heat gently until the soup is very hot and steamy. Garnish with fresh cilantro.

Lentil and Barley Soup

SERVES 8

A hearty dish you can serve in a hurry! Spruce this up with our Confetti Cole Slaw (page 302) for a fun meal.

PER SERVING • 92 CALORIES (6% FROM FAT) • 0.6 G FAT • 3 G PROTEIN
20 G CARBOHYDRATE • 0 MG CHOLESTEROL • 456 MG SODIUM • 3 G FIBER

⅓ cup lentils
½ cup pearl barley
2 15-ounce cans Swanson's Vegetable
  Broth
1 bay leaf
1 russet potato, scrubbed and diced
1 cup shredded green cabbage

1 stalk celery, thinly sliced
1 clove garlic, minced
¾ teaspoon dried sage
¾ teaspoon crushed dried rosemary
¾ teaspoon dried thyme
¼ teaspoon black pepper

Combine the lentils, barley, vegetable broth, and bay leaf in a large pot. Add 2 cups of water and simmer until the lentils and barley are tender, about 1 hour. Add all the remaining ingredients and simmer until the potato is tender, about 25 minutes.

Wonderful Russian Borscht

SERVES 10

A borscht is a borscht of course, of course, but this is my favorite borscht, of course.

PER SERVING • 99 CALORIES (20% FROM FAT) • 2 G FAT • 2 G PROTEIN
18 G CARBOHYDRATE • 0 MG CHOLESTEROL • 381 MG SODIUM • 3 G FIBER

2 beets, peeled and diced

1 medium onion, chopped

2 medium red potatoes, scrubbed and cut in ½-inch cubes

2 carrots, sliced or diced

2 stalks celery, sliced

2 cups finely shredded green cabbage

1 15-ounce can Swanson's Vegetable Broth

1 teaspoon dill weed

½ teaspoon caraway seeds

½ teaspoon black pepper

¾ teaspoon salt

1 tablespoon olive oil

2 tablespoons whole-wheat pastry flour

2 cups milk: almond, soy, rice, or nonfat dairy

Healthful Homemade Sour Cream (page 334)

Combine the beets, onion, potatoes, carrots, celery, cabbage, and vegetable broth in a large pot and bring to a simmer. Cover and cook until the beets and potatoes are tender, about 15 minutes.

Transfer 3 cups of the soup to a blender and add the dill, caraway, black pepper, and salt. Blend until completely smooth and return to the pot.

Combine the oil and flour in a small saucepan and whisk smooth (it will be very thick). Heat, stirring constantly for 2 minutes, then whisk in the milk and continue heating until the mixture is smooth and slightly thickened. Add to the soup and stir to mix. Heat gently without boiling until the soup is steamy.

Ladle into bowls and top with Healthful Homemade Sour Cream if desired.

Yammin' Ginger Soup

SERVES 8

A soup with a lot of spunk!

PER SERVING • 170 CALORIES (14% FROM FAT) • 3 G FAT • 2 G PROTEIN
34 G CARBOHYDRATE • 0 MG CHOLESTEROL • 281 MG SODIUM • 4 G FIBER

2 medium yams

2 teaspoons olive oil

1 onion, chopped

2 cloves garlic, minced

1 tablespoon minced ginger

1 teaspoon whole mustard seed

½ teaspoon cumin

¼ teaspoon turmeric

¼ teaspoon cinnamon

⅛ teaspoon cayenne pepper powder

2 to 3 cups milk: almond, soy, rice, or
   nonfat dairy

¾ teaspoon salt

Cook the yams in a vegetable steamer or microwave until tender when pierced with a fork. Peel and cut into ½-inch cubes.

Heat the oil in a large pot and sauté the onion for 3 minutes. Add the garlic, ginger, mustard seed, cumin, turmeric, cinnamon, and cayenne. Cook another 2 minutes, stirring constantly. Stir in 1 cup of water and the cooked yams. Cover and cook over low heat for 10 minutes. Stir frequently and add a bit of extra water if the mixture begins to stick.

Use the back of a spoon or a potato masher to mash some of the yam pieces, then stir in 2 cups of milk. Add salt to taste, and additional milk if a thinner soup is desired.

Salads

Bulgur Salad and Garbanzos

SERVES 8

This recipe also makes a wonderful whole-wheat pita bread stuffing mix.

PER SERVING • 148 CALORIES (13% FROM FAT) • 2 G FAT • 5 G PROTEIN
27 G CARBOHYDRATE • 0 MG CHOLESTEROL • 401 MG SODIUM • 5 G FIBER

1 cup bulgur wheat

½ teaspoon salt

2 cups boiling water

1 15-ounce can garbanzo beans, drained
  and rinsed

1 cup sliced green onions

1 carrot, grated

½ cucumber, peeled and diced

½ cup finely chopped parsley

1 clove garlic, crushed

¼ cup lemon juice

1 tablespoon olive oil

½ teaspoon salt

¼ teaspoon black pepper

Mix the bulgur and salt together in a bowl, then stir in the boiling water. Cover and let stand until the bulgur is tender, about 20 minutes. Pour off any excess water. Add the garbanzo beans, green onions, carrot, cucumber, parsley, and garlic. Stir to mix. Add the lemon juice, olive oil, salt, and pepper. Toss to mix. Chill before serving.

Chinese Noodles and Cabbage

SERVES 10

"Orient" yourself to the East with this terrific salad.

PER SERVING • 156 CALORIES (23% FROM FAT) • 4 G FAT • 4 G PROTEIN
26 G CARBOHYDRATE • 0 MG CHOLESTEROL • 614 MG SODIUM • 2 G FIBER

¼ cup cashew pieces

2 tablespoons unhulled sesame seeds

3 cups finely shredded green cabbage

2 cups finely shredded red cabbage

3 green onions, thinly sliced

1 package whole-grain ramen soup

1 teaspoon toasted sesame oil

⅓ cup seasoned rice vinegar

2 tablespoons raw sugar, or other
  sweetener

¼ teaspoon black pepper

Fresh cilantro, for garnish

Toast the cashews and sesame seeds in a 375°F oven (or toaster oven) until slightly browned and fragrant, about 10 minutes. Set aside to cool.

Place the shredded cabbage in a salad bowl and add the green onions and cooled nuts. Coarsely crush the ramen noodles and add them to the salad.

Pour the contents of the ramen seasoning packet into a small bowl and stir in the sesame oil, vinegar, sugar, and pepper. Pour the dressing over the salad and toss to mix.

For crunchy noodles, eat the salad immediately. For soft noodles, let the salad stand 30 minutes or more before serving.

Garnish with fresh cilantro just before serving, if desired.

Citrus Salad with Lime Dressing

SERVES 8

This salad is great on a summer evening.

PER SERVING • 69 CALORIES (42% FROM FAT) • 3 G FAT • 1 G PROTEIN
8 G CARBOHYDRATE • 0 MG CHOLESTEROL • 100 MG SODIUM • 3 G FIBER

⅓ head red leaf lettuce

4 leaves romaine lettuce

2 cups fresh spinach leaves

½ cucumber, half-peeled lengthwise and
thinly sliced on a diagonal

½ cup thinly sliced red onion

1 cup thin, long, and narrow julienne
strips jicama

2 oranges, peeled and cut into wedges

Juice of 1 lime

2 tablespoons olive oil

1 tablespoon balsamic vinegar

1 tablespoon seasoned rice vinegar

½ teaspoon celery seed

⅓ teaspoon salt

Wash the lettuce and spinach and pat or spin dry. Tear into bite-size pieces and place in a large salad bowl, along with the cucumber, onion, jicama, and oranges.

In a small bowl, mix the lime juice, olive oil, vinegars, celery seed, and salt. Pour over the salad just before serving. Toss to mix.

Bountiful Bean Blend

SERVES 10

eans and other legumes stimulate the brain to produce epinephrine and dopamine. They keep you alert and are truly the "cream of the crop" when it comes to brain food. Stock up on a few cases of a wide variety of canned beans. They are inexpensive, convenient, and can be used so many ways. Empower your gray matter with the abundant, magic bean.

PER SERVING • 165 CALORIES (2% FROM FAT) • 0.4 G FAT • 8 G PROTEIN
32 G CARBOHYDRATE • 0 MG CHOLESTEROL • 131 MG SODIUM • 9 G FIBER

1 15-ounce can kidney beans, drained and rinsed

1 15-ounce can black-eyed peas, drained and rinsed

1 15-ounce can black beans, drained and rinsed

1 10-ounce package frozen lima beans, thawed

1 red bell pepper, diced

½ cup finely chopped onion

2 cups corn, fresh or frozen

¼ cup seasoned rice vinegar

2 tablespoons apple cider vinegar

2 tablespoons lemon juice

2 teaspoons cumin

1 teaspoon coriander

⅛ teaspoon cayenne pepper powder

In a large bowl, combine the kidney beans, black-eyed peas, black beans, lima beans, bell pepper, onion, and corn.

Whisk the vinegars, lemon juice, cumin, coriander, and cayenne together and pour over the salad. Toss gently to mix. Chill at least 1 hour before serving.

This recipe can also be made with any combination of canned beans, such as pinto, Great Northern, garbanzo, cannelli, fava, kidney, soy, etc. Here are some of my favorite bean-based recipes from GardenCuisine: Black Bean Hash (page 232), Artichoke Hearts and Fava Beans (page 231), Chili Non Carne (page 237), Wendy's Best "Baked" Beans (page 260), and Garlicky Garbanzos and Kale (page 275).

Healthy Caesar Salad

SERVES 2

The traditional Caesar is one of my lifetime favorite eats, but, alas, it's high in fat and cholesterol. This low-fat version with nutritional superiority just came to me a few years ago. It will truly delight your taste buds! Once a week is not nearly often enough to sit down to this great salad. I think I'll go make one right now!

PER SERVING • 157 CALORIES (19% FROM FAT) • 3 G FAT • 12 G PROTEIN
19 G CARBOHYDRATE • 6 MG CHOLESTEROL • 271 MG SODIUM • 4 G FIBER

1 Gardenburger patty

Olive oil spray

2 tablespoons nonfat Yogurt Cheese (page 335) or nonfat cream cheese, chilled

1½ teaspoons grated Parmesan cheese, chilled

1½ teaspoons lemon juice, chilled

¼ teaspoon Dijon mustard, chilled

2 cloves garlic, minced, chilled

¼ teaspoon Sucanat, chilled

¼ cup nonfat yogurt

Salt and black pepper

4 cups torn romaine lettuce or EssentialSalad (page 304)

2 tablespoons shredded (not grated) Parmesan cheese

½ lemon, cut into 4 wedges

Grill the Gardenburger or fry it in a nonstick pan sprayed lightly with olive oil spray. Cool, then cut into ¼-inch pieces.

In a mixing bowl, combine the yogurt cheese or nonfat cream cheese, Parmesan cheese, lemon juice, mustard, garlic, and Sucanat. Whisk to blend completely. Mix in the yogurt, then add salt and black pepper to taste. Chill for 15 minutes more.

Toss the lettuce with the dressing and most of the shredded Parmesan cheese. When the leaves are well coated, turn out onto a serving platter. Garnish with lemon wedges, the rest of the shredded Parmesan cheese, and the crumbled Gardenburger. Serve with freshly ground black pepper.

Confetti Cole Slaw

SERVES 8

This colorful salad is like a work of art!

PER SERVING • 67 CALORIES (14% FROM FAT) • 1 G FAT • 3 G PROTEIN
11 G CARBOHYDRATE • 0 MG CHOLESTEROL • 285 MG SODIUM • 3 G FIBER

3 cups shredded green cabbage

1½ cups shredded red cabbage

2 carrots, grated

4 green onions, sliced, including tops

2 stalks celery, thinly sliced

1 apple, cored and diced

1 10.5-ounce package firm silken tofu

3 tablespoons seasoned rice vinegar

2 tablespoons apple cider vinegar

2 tablespoons lemon juice

2 tablespoons apple juice concentrate

½ teaspoon salt

¼ teaspoon black pepper

Mix the cabbage, carrots, onions, celery, and apple in a large bowl.

Combine the tofu, vinegars, lemon juice, apple juice concentrate, salt, and pepper in a blender and process until completely smooth.

Pour the dressing over the salad and toss to mix.

Cool Sesame Asparagus

SERVES 4

You've heard of "cool as a cucumber," well, try this recipe on a hot day and see what happens!

PER SERVING • 74 CALORIES (28% FROM FAT) • 2 G FAT • 3 G PROTEIN
10 G CARBOHYDRATE • 0 MG CHOLESTEROL • 231 MG SODIUM • 2 G FIBER

1 pound fresh asparagus

1 tablespoon unhulled sesame seeds

1 tablespoon distilled white vinegar

1 tablespoon seasoned rice vinegar

1 tablespoon soy sauce

1 tablespoon honey

1 teaspoon toasted sesame oil

Snap the tough ends off the asparagus, then cut it on the diagonal into 1½-inch pieces. Drop into boiling water for 1 minute. Drain and immediately plunge into cold water until chilled. Pat dry.

Toast the sesame seeds in a nonstick skillet over medium heat for 2 to 3 minutes, stirring constantly.

Mix the vinegars, soy sauce, honey, and toasted sesame oil in a bowl. Add the asparagus and 2 teaspoons of the sesame seeds. Toss to mix. Refrigerate 1 to 3 hours, tossing occasionally.

Garnish with the remaining sesame seeds before serving.

Couscous Veggie Salad

SERVES 6

Using whole-wheat couscous gives you optimal nutritional benefits.

PER SERVING • 135 CALORIES (6% FROM FAT) • 1 G FAT • 3 G PROTEIN
28 G CARBOHYDRATE • 0 MG CHOLESTEROL • 153 MG SODIUM • 4 G FIBER

1 cup whole-wheat couscous
1 cup boiling water
½ small red onion, minced
1 red bell pepper, diced
1 carrot, grated
½ cup finely shredded red cabbage
½ cup green peas, fresh or frozen

½ cup raisins or currants
1 tablespoon balsamic vinegar
2 tablespoons seasoned rice vinegar
1 teaspoon toasted sesame oil
1 teaspoon soy sauce
1 teaspoon stone-ground mustard
1 teaspoon curry powder

Place the couscous in a bowl and pour the boiling water over it. Stir to mix, then cover and let stand until cooled. Fluff lightly with a fork.

Add the onion, bell pepper, carrot, cabbage, peas, and raisins or currants to the couscous.

Combine the vinegars, toasted sesame oil, soy sauce, mustard, and curry powder. Mix well. Pour over the salad and toss to mix.

Try this one with Carrot Ginger Soup (page 288) on the side!

Essential Salad

When fresh, edible flowers are added to this potent nutrition mix, it becomes a feast for the soul.

PER SERVING • 10 CALORIES (0% FROM FAT) • 0 G FAT • 0 G PROTEIN
2 G CARBOHYDRATE • 0 MG CHOLESTEROL • 6 MG SODIUM • 2 G FIBER

7 cups light vegetable greens: red leaf, green leaf, or butter lettuce, field greens, baby greens, parsley, celery tops, spinach, radicchio, etc.

3 cups medium vegetable greens and flowers: bok choy, collards, kale, red cabbage, green cabbage, Swiss chard, watercress, mustard greens, endive, etc.

1½ to 2 cups VeggiePack (page 284), chopped in ¼-inch slices

½ cup optional edible decorative flowers (pansy, nasturtium, chive flowers, squash, or cilantro blossoms, only if unsprayed)

Tear or chop into bite-size pieces, wash and spin dry the light greens. Slice the medium vegetable greens and flowers very thin and add. Add the VeggiePack and edible decorative flowers and toss. Pack into 1-pint ziplock or the new "green" bags and store in the refrigerator.

Green Green Papaya Salad

SERVES 6

Garlic and lime uniquely complement the papaya in this easy-to-prepare and delicious salad. Try it as a snack or as a prelude to your main dish.

PER SERVING • 62 CALORIES (34% FROM FAT) • 2 G FAT • 1 G PROTEIN
8 G CARBOHYDRATE • 0 MG CHOLESTEROL • 166 MG SODIUM • 1 G FIBER

1 medium green (unripe) papaya

1 tomato, seeded and sliced into strips

2 tablespoons vegetarian chicken-style seasoning

3 tablespoons fresh lime juice

2 cloves garlic, minced

3 tablespoons ground roasted peanuts

¼ teaspoon crushed red pepper

6 red lettuce or cabbage leaves

1 lime, cut into six wedges

Peel and seed the papaya; shred into long strips. Place in a bowl with the tomato, chicken-style seasoning, lime juice, garlic, peanuts, and crushed red pepper. Toss to mix.

Place the lettuce or cabbage leaves on individual plates and divide the salad among them. Serve with a wedge of lime.

Lentil Salad

SERVES 8

This also makes a great filling for pita bread. It's good to include one of the many varieties of lentils in your diet at least once a week!

PER SERVING • 134 CALORIES (13% FROM FAT) • 2 G FAT • 5 G PROTEIN
23 G CARBOHYDRATE • 0 MG CHOLESTEROL • 177 MG SODIUM • 3 G FIBER

2 cups cooked lentils
2 cups cooked Brown Rice (page 268)
½ cup thinly sliced red onion
1 tomato, diced
2 cucumbers, diced
1 cup finely chopped parsley
Juice of 1 lemon (about 3 tablespoons)

1 tablespoon olive oil
1 tablespoon seasoned rice vinegar
½ teaspoon dry mustard
½ teaspoon paprika
½ teaspoon salt
1 clove garlic, crushed or pressed
½ teaspoon Sucanat

Combine the lentils, rice, onion, tomato, cucumber, and parsley in a salad bowl. Mix the lemon juice, olive oil, seasoned rice vinegar, dry mustard, paprika, salt, crushed garlic, and Sucanat in a small bowl. Pour over the salad and toss gently to mix.

Potato, Apple, and Cabbage Salad

SERVES 6

A new and exciting rendition of Waldorf salad.

PER SERVING • 169 CALORIES (20% FROM FAT) • 4 G FAT • 9 G PROTEIN
25 G CARBOHYDRATE • 0 MG CHOLESTEROL • 273 MG SODIUM • 3 G FIBER

4 red potatoes

1 teaspoon black mustard seeds

2 cups finely shredded green cabbage

1 large green apple, cored and diced

2 tablespoons drained and minced capers

3 tablespoons finely chopped parsley

1 pound firm silken tofu (1½ 10.5-ounce packages)

3 tablespoons lemon juice

2 tablespoons white or yellow miso

2 teaspoons prepared mustard

2 tablespoons roasted peanuts, chopped

2 green onions, sliced

Scrub and dice the potatoes and steam them until just tender. Transfer to a large bowl.

Toast the mustard seeds in a dry skillet, stirring constantly, until they begin to pop. Add them to the potatoes, along with the cabbage, apple, capers, and parsley.

Place the tofu in a blender with the lemon juice, miso, and prepared mustard. Blend until completely smooth. Pour over the salad and toss to mix. Chill thoroughly.

Top with peanuts and green onions before serving.

Spaghetti Squash Veggie Salad

SERVES 8

Spaghetti squash is a delicious alternative to pasta. If cooked just right, it can be used in any recipe that calls for spaghetti.

PER SERVING • 192 CALORIES (25% FROM FAT) • 5 G FAT • 4 G PROTEIN
31 G CARBOHYDRATE • 0 MG CHOLESTEROL • 38 MG SODIUM • 11 G FIBER

1 small spaghetti squash
½ cup pearl barley
1 red bell pepper, cut into 1-inch
   julienne
5 green onions, sliced on the diagonal
1 cup snow peas, sliced on the diagonal
   into bite-sized pieces
2 cups corn, fresh or frozen
1 red chili pepper, seeded and minced
⅓ cup balsamic vinegar
3 tablespoons olive oil

2 tablespoons finely chopped sun-dried
   tomatoes
3 cloves garlic, crushed
1 teaspoon cumin
½ teaspoon coriander
¼ teaspoon black pepper
1 head romaine lettuce
Chopped cilantro, for garnish
Black mustard seeds, for garnish
Cherry tomatoes, for garnish

Cut the spaghetti squash in half and scoop out the seeds with a spoon. Steam the squash in a covered pot until it is just tender when pierced with a fork, about 25 minutes. There should still be a little bit of resistance when you test the squash. It is important not to overcook it. Chill the squash, then tease the strands apart with a fork.

Rinse the barley and simmer it in 2 cups of water until it is tender, about 25 minutes. Rinse with cold water and drain completely. Place it in a large bowl with the bell pepper, green onions, snow peas, corn, and chili pepper. Toss to mix.

Combine the vinegar, olive oil, sun-dried tomatoes, garlic, cumin, coriander, and black pepper in a small bowl.

To assemble the salad, shred enough of the romaine lettuce to cover each plate generously. Top with about ¾ cup of the spaghetti squash, and about 1 cup of the vegetable mixture. Pour the dressing over the salad and garnish with chopped cilantro, black mustard seeds, and 1 or 2 cherry tomatoes.

Spinach and Mandarin Orange Salad
with Sesame Dressing

SERVES 6

An easy but elegant recipe. Has great eye appeal!

PER SERVING • 69 CALORIES (18% FROM FAT) • 1 G FAT • 2 G PROTEIN
12 G CARBOHYDRATE • 0 MG CHOLESTEROL • 49 MG SODIUM • 3 G FIBER

1 bunch fresh spinach

2 mandarin oranges or tangerines, peeled

1 small red onion

2 tablespoons unhulled sesame seeds

¼ cup apple juice concentrate

3 tablespoons balsamic vinegar

Fresh-ground black pepper

Wash and dry the spinach, then remove the stems and tear any large leaves into bite-sized pieces. Place in a salad bowl.

Divide the mandarin oranges or tangerines into segments and add to the spinach.

Peel the onion and cut it in half from top to bottom. Cut enough very thin slices to make ½ cup and toss these with the spinach.

Heat the sesame seeds in a small pan until they are fragrant and begin to pop. Grind them to a fine powder in a blender. Add the apple juice concentrate and balsamic vinegar. Stir to mix.

Just before serving, pour the dressing over the salad and toss to mix. Add fresh-ground black pepper to taste.

Thai Slaw

SERVES 6

*T*he rice and GardenChick'n combined with the cabbage make this a hearty meal all by itself, or a substantial side dish to complement a main course.

PER SERVING • 184 CALORIES (21% FROM FAT) • 4 G FAT • 25 G PROTEIN
12 G CARBOHYDRATE • 0 MG CHOLESTEROL • 352 MG SODIUM • 1 G FIBER

2 tablespoons brown rice
2 tablespoons vegetarian chicken-style
   seasoning
¼ cup distilled water
1 pound GardenChick'n
1 tablespoon toasted sesame oil
1 to 2 stalks lemongrass, finely chopped
3 kaffir lime leaves, finely chopped
   (optional)

⅓ cup fresh lime juice
¼ teaspoon red pepper flakes
3 cups finely shredded red and green
   cabbage, mixed
3 green onions, finely sliced on the
   diagonal
2 to 3 tablespoons finely chopped
   cilantro
Additional cilantro sprigs for garnish

Carefully brown the rice in a heavy pan or skillet until darkened but not burned. When cool, blend to a fine powder in a blender or spice mill and set aside.

In a small bowl, mix chicken-style seasoning with the water, set aside.

Grind the GardenChick'n into small pieces in a food processor or blender. Heat 2 teaspoons of sesame oil in a large nonstick skillet and brown the GardenChick'n over medium-high heat, stirring often. Remove from the heat and refrigerate until completely chilled.

In a separate bowl, combine the chicken-style broth with the remaining teaspoon of sesame oil, lemongrass, kaffir lime leaves, lime juice, and red pepper flakes. Pour over the GardenChick'n, then add the red and green cabbage, green onions, and cilantro. Toss to mix. Sprinkle with the roasted brown rice. Garnish with additional cilantro sprigs.

Whole-Grain Satay Salad

SERVES 8

Wheat berries add crunchiness to this brown rice salad, which is dressed with an Indonesian-style peanut sauce.

PER SERVING • 118 CALORIES (18% FROM FAT) • 2 G FAT • 3 G PROTEIN
21 G CARBOHYDRATE • 0 MG CHOLESTEROL • 417 MG SODIUM • 3 G FIBER

¼ cup wheat berries

2 large onions, thinly sliced

1 cup brown rice

1 15-ounce can Swanson's Vegetable
  Broth

1 teaspoon finely chopped chili pepper,
  or ½ teaspoon red pepper flakes

1 tablespoon finely chopped fresh ginger

2 tablespoons peanut butter

3 tablespoons seasoned rice vinegar

2 teaspoons tamari soy sauce

1 cup chopped cilantro

1 cup sliced green onions

Soak the wheat berries in 2 cups of water overnight. Rinse and drain.

Heat ½ cup of water in a large pot and add the onions. Cook until all the liquid is gone and the onions begin to stick. Stir in another ¼ cup of water and cook until it has evaporated and the onions begin to stick again. Add another ¼ cup of water and repeat the process until the onions are nicely browned.

When the onions are browned, add the soaked wheat berries, the rice, vegetable broth, chili pepper, ginger, and 1 cup of water. Bring to a simmer, then cover and cook, stirring occasionally, until the rice and wheat berries are tender, about 50 minutes.

In a small bowl, mix the peanut butter, vinegar, and soy sauce until smooth. Stir into the rice mixture. Cover and let stand until cool, then stir in most of the cilantro and green onions, reserving about 2 tablespoons of each to sprinkle over the top.

This one goes well with Wendy's Best "Baked" Beans (page 260).

Wild and Brown Rice Salad

SERVES 8

A great addition to any potluck, picnic, or party.

PER SERVING • 189 CALORIES (17% FROM FAT) • 4 G FAT • 4 G PROTEIN
35 G CARBOHYDRATE • 0 MG CHOLESTEROL • 256 MG SODIUM • 3 G FIBER

¼ cup wild rice

1½ cups brown rice

2 to 3 green onions, thinly sliced, including green tops

1 large carrot, grated

1 stalk celery, thinly sliced

1 cup finely shredded green cabbage

¼ cup finely shredded red cabbage

2 tablespoons finely chopped parsley

1 tablespoon olive oil

2 tablespoons Healthful Homemade Mayo (page 334)

1 teaspoon toasted sesame oil

3 tablespoons balsamic vinegar

2 tablespoons seasoned rice vinegar

½ teaspoon salt

½ teaspoon curry powder or garam masala

¼ teaspoon black pepper

1 teaspoon prepared mustard

Rinse the wild rice and place it in a saucepan with 4 cups of water. Bring to a simmer, then cover loosely and cook 20 minutes. Add the brown rice and continue cooking until all the rice is tender, about 45 minutes. Rinse with cold water. Drain, then place in a large bowl and add the onions, carrot, celery, cabbages, and parsley.

Mix the olive oil, Healthful Homemade Mayo, toasted sesame oil, balsamic vinegar, seasoned rice vinegar salt, curry powder, pepper, and prepared mustard. Pour over the salad and toss to mix. Refrigerate 1 to 2 hours before serving.

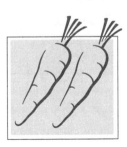

Wild Rice and Asparagus Salad

SERVES 6

Wild, wonderful, and fabulous!

PER SERVING • 126 CALORIES (5% FROM FAT) • 1 G FAT • 6 G PROTEIN
24 G CARBOHYDRATE • 0 MG CHOLESTEROL • 456 MG SODIUM • 4 G FIBER

½ cup wild rice, rinsed

½ cup brown lentils, rinsed

1 15-ounce can Swanson's Vegetable
   Broth

1 onion, chopped

½ pound mushrooms, thinly sliced

1 pound asparagus

3 tablespoons balsamic vinegar

Combine the wild rice and 4 cups of water in a large pan and bring to a simmer. Cover and cook for 30 minutes. Add the lentils and continue to simmer until both the rice and lentils are tender, about 25 minutes longer. Drain, then set aside.

Heat ½ cup of the vegetable broth in a large nonstick frying pan, then add the onion and mushrooms. Cook over medium-high heat, stirring frequently, until the liquid has evaporated and the onion begins to stick to the pan. Add another ¼ cup of the broth, stirring to loosen any vegetable bits, and continue cooking until the mixture begins to stick again. Repeat this process of adding liquid and cooking until it evaporates and the vegetables are well browned.

Snap the tough ends off the asparagus and discard, then cut the stalks on the diagonal into 1-inch lengths. Add to the browned onion-mushroom mixture with ¼ cup of vegetable broth and cook, stirring often, until the asparagus is just tender, about 2 minutes.

Add the lentil-rice mixture to the vegetables along with the balsamic vinegar. Stir gently to mix, then transfer to a serving bowl or platter.

Creamy Cauliflower Soup (page 289) provides a nice side dish for this salad.

Desserts

Apricot-Pineapple Crisp

SERVES 9

Anything that has apricots in it automatically becomes one of my favorites!

PER SERVING • 171 CALORIES (23% FROM FAT) • 4 G FAT • 3 G PROTEIN
29 G CARBOHYDRATE • 0 MG CHOLESTEROL • 63 MG SODIUM • 3 G FIBER

1 cup dried apricots

2 cups chopped fresh pineapple

1 cup rolled oats, quick or regular

½ cup chopped walnuts

¼ cup maple syrup

¼ teaspoon cinnamon

¼ teaspoon ginger

¼ teaspoon salt

1 teaspoon vanilla

Pour 1 cup of boiling water over the dried apricots and let stand until softened, about 30 minutes. Drain, then coarsely chop the apricots. Combine them with the pineapple and spread in a 9-inch square nonstick baking dish.

Preheat the oven to 350°F. Combine the rolled oats, walnuts, maple syrup, cinnamon, ginger, salt, and vanilla. Stir until mixed, then spread evenly over the apricot-pineapple mixture. Bake until the top is lightly browned, about 35 minutes.

CranApple Crisp

SERVES 9

This dessert is sure to win over family and friends.

PER SERVING • 164 CALORIES (17% FROM FAT) • 4 G FAT • 3 G PROTEIN
30 G CARBOHYDRATE • 0 MG CHOLESTEROL • 61 MG SODIUM • 5 G FIBER

3 green apples, cored and peeled

3 tablespoons lemon juice

1 tablespoon Sucanat

1 tablespoon cinnamon

1 cup dried cranberries

1½ cups rolled oats

⅓ cup walnuts, finely chopped (optional)

⅓ cup maple syrup

1 teaspoon vanilla

¼ teaspoon salt

Slice the apples and spread them in a 9-inch square, nonstick baking dish. Sprinkle with lemon juice, Sucanat, cinnamon, and cranberries.

Preheat the oven to 350°F. Combine the rolled oats, walnuts if desired, maple syrup, vanilla, and salt. Stir to mix, then spread evenly over the apples. Bake until the apples are tender when pierced with a knife, about 35 minutes. Let stand 5 to 10 minutes before serving.

Fabulous Fruited Bread Pudding

SERVES 8

Chunks of dried fruit and a sweet white sauce topping make this bread pudding quite special.

PER SERVING • 197 CALORIES (9% FROM FAT) • 2 G FAT • 2 G PROTEIN
42 G CARBOHYDRATE • 0 MG CHOLESTEROL • 226 MG SODIUM • 4 G FIBER

Pudding

4 cups whole-grain bread cubes

2 green apples, cored and grated with
  skin on

⅓ cup chopped dried apricots

⅓ cup chopped dates

⅓ cup golden raisins

2 cups milk, almond, soy, rice, or nonfat
  dairy

⅓ cup Sucanat

1 tablespoon cornstarch

½ teaspoon cinnamon

⅛ teaspoon nutmeg

¼ teaspoon salt

Sweet White Sauce

1 cup milk, almond, soy, rice, or nonfat
  dairy

⅓ cup Sucanat

1 tablespoon cornstarch

⅛ teaspoon salt

2 teaspoons vanilla

Preheat the oven to 350°F. Place the whole-grain bread cubes in a large bowl. Add the grated apple, dried fruits, milk, Sucanat, cornstarch, cinnamon, nutmeg, and salt. Mix well, then spoon into a 9 × 9-inch baking dish. Cover with foil and bake for 35 minutes. Remove from the oven and discard the foil.

To prepare the sweet white sauce, mix the milk, Sucanat, cornstarch, and salt in a saucepan and heat, stirring constantly, until thickened. Stir in the vanilla and pour over the baking pudding before serving.

Apple Custard Fruit Tart

SERVES 12 (MAKES 1 10-INCH TART)

This dessert is delicious and has a captivating visual presence. Great for special occasions!

PER SERVING • 175 CALORIES (19% FROM FAT) • 4 G FAT • 2 G PROTEIN
32 G CARBOHYDRATE • 0 MG CHOLESTEROL • 66 MG SODIUM • 3 G FIBER

Crust

1 cup rolled oats, regular

½ cup chopped walnuts

¼ cup pure maple syrup

¼ teaspoon cinnamon

¼ teaspoon ginger

¼ teaspoon salt

Apple Custard

1 24-ounce jar unsweetened applesauce

½ cup Sucanat

2½ tablespoons agar flakes

¼ teaspoon cinnamon

1 cup milk, almond, soy, rice, or nonfat dairy

1 teaspoon vanilla

Sweet White Sauce

½ cup milk, almond, soy, rice, or nonfat dairy

1 tablespoon Sucanat

2 teaspoons cornstarch

Pinch salt

Glaze

½ cup white grape juice concentrate

2 teaspoons cornstarch

⅛ teaspoon cinnamon

Fruit Topping

1 banana, sliced

10 fresh strawberries, sliced

30 blueberries

1 kiwi, peeled and sliced

Combine the rolled oats, walnuts, maple syrup, cinnamon, ginger, and salt. Press into a 10-inch pie plate and bake 8 minutes. Remove from the oven and set aside.

In a saucepan, mix the applesauce, Sucanat, agar flakes, and cinnamon. Bring to a simmer and cook 5 minutes. Remove from the heat and add the milk and vanilla. Mix well, then pour into the baked crust.

To make the sweet white sauce, combine the milk, Sucanat, cornstarch, and salt in a saucepan. Heat gently, stirring constantly, until thickened. Spread evenly over the tart.

Combine the white grape juice concentrate, cornstarch, and cinnamon in a saucepan and heat, stirring constantly, until clear and thickened. Before serving, spread the glaze evenly over the top of the tart. Chill thoroughly. Top with the sliced banana, strawberries, blueberries, kiwi, or other in-season fresh fruit.

Fresh Apricot Crisp

SERVES 8

A divine dessert that is simple to make.

PER SERVING • 243 CALORIES (29% FROM FAT) • 8 G FAT • 6 G PROTEIN
36 G CARBOHYDRATE • 0 MG CHOLESTEROL • 4 MG SODIUM • 4 G FIBER

4 cups apricots, pitted and coarsely
  chopped
2 tablespoons lemon juice
2 cups rolled oats
¾ cup walnuts, finely chopped

½ cup maple syrup
1 teaspoon vanilla
½ teaspoon salt
Vegetable oil spray

Preheat the oven to 350°F. Toss the chopped apricots with the lemon juice and set aside.

Combine the rolled oats with the chopped walnuts, maple syrup, vanilla, and salt. Mix thoroughly. Spray a 9-inch square baking pan lightly with a nonstick spray. Spread all but 1 cup of the oat mixture in the pan. Spread the apricots evenly over the mixture in the pan. Top with the remaining oat mixture. Bake for 35 to 40 minutes, until the top crust is lightly browned.

Fruit Cake

SERVES 9

A simple holiday treat that was quite popular at my gourmet restaurant.

PER SERVING • 280 CALORIES (13% FROM FAT) • 4 G FAT • 5 G PROTEIN
56 G CARBOHYDRATE • 0 MG CHOLESTEROL • 178 MG SODIUM • 6 G FIBER

1 cup Sucanat

½ cup apple juice concentrate

1 cup grated carrots

1 cup chopped mixed dried fruit

1¼ teaspoons cinnamon

½ teaspoon nutmeg

¼ teaspoon cloves

1½ cups whole-wheat pastry flour

1 teaspoon baking powder

½ teaspoon baking soda

½ teaspoon salt

½ cup walnuts

Combine the Sucanat, apple juice concentrate, carrots, dried fruit, cinnamon, nutmeg, and cloves in a saucepan with 1½ cups of water. Bring to a simmer and cook 10 minutes. Remove from the heat and cool completely.

Preheat the oven to 350°F. In a large mixing bowl, combine the flour, baking powder, baking soda, and salt. Add the cooled fruit mixture and walnuts. Stir to mix. Spread the batter into a 10-inch springform pan. Bake until a toothpick inserted in the center comes out clean, about 50 minutes.

Gingerbread

SERVES 9 (9 × 9-INCH CAKE)

A healthy version of an old-fashioned favorite.

PER SERVING • 207 CALORIES (0% FROM FAT) • 0 G FAT • 4 G PROTEIN
48 G CARBOHYDRATE • 0 MG CHOLESTEROL • 263 MG SODIUM • 2 G FIBER

½ cup raisins

½ cup pitted dates, chopped

1⅓ cups water

½ teaspoon salt

2 teaspoons cinnamon

1½ teaspoons ginger

¾ teaspoon nutmeg

¼ teaspoon cloves

2 cups whole-wheat pastry flour

¾ cup Sucanat

1 teaspoon baking soda

1 teaspoon baking powder

Vegetable oil spray

Combine the dried fruits, water, salt, and spices in a large saucepan. Bring to a boil. Boil for 2 minutes, then remove from heat and cool completely.

Preheat the oven to 350°F. Stir the flour, Sucanat, baking soda, and baking powder together. Add to the cooled fruit mixture and stir just to mix. Spread into a 9 × 9-inch pan that has been sprayed with a nonstick spray. Bake for 30 minutes, or until a toothpick inserted into the center comes out clean.

Healthy Brownies

MAKES 12 BROWNIES

A healthy after-school treat.

PER SERVING • 111 CALORIES (8% FROM FAT) • 1 G FAT • 3 G PROTEIN
22 G CARBOHYDRATE • 0 MG CHOLESTEROL • 153 MG SODIUM • 2 G FIBER

1 cup whole-wheat pastry flour
⅓ cup cocoa powder
¾ teaspoon baking soda
½ teaspoon salt

¼ teaspoon cinnamon
1 10.5-ounce package firm silken tofu
¾ cup Sucanat
1 teaspoon vanilla

Stir the flour, cocoa, baking soda, salt, and cinnamon together in a large mixing bowl.

Puree the tofu in a food processor until completely smooth, then blend in the Sucanat and vanilla.

Preheat the oven to 350°F. Add the tofu mixture to the dry ingredients and stir just enough to mix. Spread into a nonstick or oil-sprayed 9 × 9-inch pan and bake 20 to 25 minutes. The brownies should spring back when pressed lightly in the center. Remove from the oven and allow to cool in the pan 10 minutes.

Spice Cake

SERVES 12

The title is simple, but the flavors are wonderfully complex. Check it out, it's fat-free!

PER SERVING • 275 CALORIES (0% FROM FAT) • 0 G FAT • 4 G PROTEIN
64 G CARBOHYDRATE • 0 MG CHOLESTEROL • 302 MG SODIUM • 2 G FIBER

3 cups whole-wheat pastry flour
1 tablespoon baking soda
½ teaspoon salt
½ teaspoon cardamom
½ teaspoon cinnamon
¼ teaspoon nutmeg
¼ teaspoon cloves

1 cup Sucanat
¾ cup apple juice concentrate
¼ cup orange juice concentrate
½ cup applesauce
1 teaspoon vanilla
1 cup raisins
Additional applesauce, for serving

Preheat the oven to 350°F. Mix the flour, baking soda, salt, cardamom, cinnamon, nutmeg, and cloves. In a separate bowl, mix the Sucanat with the apple juice concentrate, orange juice concentrate, applesauce, and vanilla. Stir in the flour mixture and raisins, then spread the batter in a nonstick or oil-sprayed 13 × 9-inch cake pan. Bake until the top springs back when lightly pressed, about 35 minutes. Top with additional applesauce, when serving.

Very Berry Cobbler

SERVES 8

If you love berries as I do, here is an enjoyable, low-fat way to serve them. Top this off with a scoop of frozen nonfat yogurt or nondairy vanilla dessert.

PER SERVING • 115 CALORIES (3% FROM FAT) • 4 G FAT • 2 G PROTEIN
26 G CARBOHYDRATE • 0 MG CHOLESTEROL • 165 MG SODIUM • 2 G FIBER

⅔ cup whole-wheat pastry flour
½ cup Sucanat
1½ teaspoons baking powder
¼ teaspoon salt

⅔ cup milk: almond, rice, soy, or nonfat dairy
2½ cups berries: boysenberries, blackberries, or raspberries

Preheat the oven to 350°F. In a mixing bowl, stir together the dry ingredients. Add the milk and stir until the batter is smooth. Spread the berries in a 9 × 9-inch baking dish. Pour the batter over the berries. Bake for 45 minutes until lightly browned.

Yummy Yam Pie

SERVES 12 (MAKES 1 10-INCH PIE)

Sweet potatoes or yams make a delicious pie, which most people will assume is pumpkin. Because the sweet potatoes are sweet, very little sugar is needed.

PER SLICE (1/12TH OF PIE) • 188 CALORIES (37% FROM FAT) • 8 G FAT • 2 G PROTEIN
27 G CARBOHYDRATE • 0 MG CHOLESTEROL • 139 MG SODIUM • 3 G FIBER

⅓ cup plus 1 tablespoon Sucanat
5 tablespoons cornstarch
½ teaspoon cinnamon
½ teaspoon ginger
¼ teaspoon nutmeg

¾ teaspoon salt
1½ cups cooked, mashed yams
1½ cups reduced-fat coconut milk
1 cup pecans
⅔ cup whole-wheat pastry flour

Preheat the oven to 350°F. In a large bowl, stir together the ⅓ cup Sucanat, the cornstarch, cinnamon, ginger, nutmeg, and ½ teaspoon of the salt. Blend in the mashed yams and the coconut milk.

Toast the pecans in the oven until they begin to brown, 10 to 15 minutes. Cool. Grind into fine pieces in a food processor, then mix in the flour, 1 tablespoon Sucanat, and remaining ¼ teaspoon salt. Add 2 tablespoons of water and mix thoroughly. The mixture should be just moist enough to hold together. Press into a 10-inch pie pan. Bake for 6 minutes, then pour in the yam filling. Return to the oven and bake until the filling is set, about 45 minutes. Cool before cutting.

Mango-Apricot Bread Pudding

SERVES 8

This may be my favorite dessert in the bunch. Maybe it's because I love mango and apricots.

PER SERVING • 194 CALORIES (17% FROM FAT) • 4 G FAT • 3 G PROTEIN
37 G CARBOHYDRATE • 0 MG CHOLESTEROL • 245 MG SODIUM • 3 G FIBER

Pudding

⅓ cup chopped dried apricots

1 large ripe mango

6 cups bread cubes

2¾ cups milk: almond, rice, soy, or nonfat dairy

⅓ cup Sucanat

¼ cup golden raisins

1 tablespoon cornstarch

½ teaspoon cinnamon

½ teaspoon coriander

¼ teaspoon nutmeg

¼ teaspoon salt

Coconut Sauce

¾ cup light coconut milk

¼ cup Sucanat

1 tablespoon cornstarch

⅛ teaspoon salt

2 teaspoons vanilla

Pour 1 cup of boiling water over the dried apricots and let stand until softened, about 30 minutes. Drain and coarsely chop the apricots, then place them in a large bowl.

Peel the mango and cut the flesh off the pit. Cut any large pieces into ¼-inch chunks and add to the apricots.

Add the bread cubes, milk, Sucanat, golden raisins, cornstarch, cinnamon, coriander, nutmeg, and salt. Stir to mix. Spread in a 9 × 9-inch nonstick or glass baking dish, cover with foil, and let stand 5 minutes.

While the pudding stands, preheat the oven to 350°F.

Bake the pudding for 35 minutes. In the meantime, prepare the coconut sauce: Whisk the coconut milk, Sucanat, cornstarch, and salt together to remove any lumps, then heat in a saucepan, stirring constantly until thickened. Stir in the vanilla. When the pudding comes out of the oven, drizzle it with the coconut sauce.

Dips

Energetic Eggplant Dip

MAKES 2 CUPS

I really "dig" this low-fat eggplant dip!

PER SERVING • 26 CALORIES (33% FROM FAT) • 1 G FAT • 0.5 G PROTEIN
4 G CARBOHYDRATE • 0 MG CHOLESTEROL • 21 MG SODIUM • 1 G FIBER

1 large globe eggplant

⅓ cup seasoned dry whole-wheat bread crumbs

⅓ cup Healthful Homemade Sour Cream (page 334)

2 tablespoons lemon juice

1 teaspoon minced garlic

¼ teaspoon red pepper sauce

3 tablespoons minced parsley

To cook the eggplant in a microwave, cut a 5-inch slit the length of the eggplant and place it on a microwave-safe plate. Cook on high for 10 minutes, or until the eggplant is very soft and has collapsed. Set aside for 5 minutes. To broil the eggplant in a conventional oven, pierce it in several places with a fork and place it on a baking sheet. Broil about 6 inches from the heat until blackened on all sides. Remove from the oven and set aside to cool.

When the eggplant is cool enough to handle, cut it open and spoon the flesh into a large bowl. Mash it with a fork, breaking up any long strands. Stir in the bread crumbs, Healthful Homemade Sour Cream, lemon juice, garlic, and red pepper sauce.

Spread on a decorative plate. Sprinkle with parsley. Chill completely and serve with thin rounds of crisp raw vegetables, such as zucchini, yellow squash, jicama, turnips, or sweet potatoes. It also goes wonderfully with our Crisp Pita Chips (page 224).

Guacabonzo
MAKES 2 CUPS

*P*retty catchy name, don't you think? Try this delicious, reduced-fat version of guacamole with baked tortilla chips or as a topping on burritos or tostadas.

PER 2 TABLESPOONS • 29 CALORIES (33% FROM FAT) • 1 G FAT • 1 G PROTEIN
4 G CARBOHYDRATE • 0 MG CHOLESTEROL • 35 MG SODIUM • 1 G FIBER

1 cup cooked garbanzo beans, drained
1 clove garlic
4 green onions, finely sliced
½ tomato, diced
½ avocado

1½ tablespoons lemon juice
2 teaspoons finely chopped chili peppers
¼ teaspoon salt
Leaf lettuce, for serving

Place the drained garbanzo beans and garlic in a food processor and process until smooth. Add the green onions, tomato, avocado, lemon juice, chili peppers, and salt. Blend in short bursts until chunky. Serve on a bed of fresh leaf lettuce. Pass the chips, please!

Yogurt Dill Dipping Sauce
MAKES 1 CUP

*D*elight in this "dilly" of a sauce! It can be used for a salad dressing, too.

PER TABLESPOON • 17 CALORIES (9% FROM FAT) • 0.2 G FAT • 1 G PROTEIN
2 G CARBOHYDRATE • 1 MG CHOLESTEROL • 51 MG SODIUM • 0.3 G FIBER

3 cloves garlic
1 cucumber, peeled and finely diced
¼ cup fresh dill, finely chopped
½ cup nonfat yogurt, room temperature
¼ teaspoon sea salt

⅛ teaspoon white pepper
½ cup Healthful Homemade Yogurt
    Cheese (page 335), or low-fat/
    nonfat cream cheese at room
    temperature

Puree the garlic, half the cucumber, and dill. Fold in the remaining cucumber, salt, and pepper. Blend the yogurt and softened cheese by hand and mix in. Refrigerate to store.

Not Your Average Hummus

MAKES 2½ CUPS

Serve this beautiful dip with homemade pita chips.

PER 2 TABLESPOONS • 40 CALORIES (4% FROM FAT) • 0.2 G FAT • 1 G PROTEIN
8 G CARBOHYDRATE • 0 MG CHOLESTEROL • 177 MG SODIUM • 2 G FIBER

8 carrots, scrubbed

1 15-ounce can garbanzo beans, drained
and rinsed

4 cloves garlic

¼ cup lemon juice

2 tablespoons balsamic vinegar

1 tablespoon tamari soy sauce

¼ teaspoon cumin

4 drops red pepper sauce

½ teaspoon salt

Roasted red peppers for garnish

Parsley for garnish

Cut the carrots into inch-long pieces and steam them until tender when pierced with a fork, about 20 minutes. Place in a food processor with the garbanzo beans, garlic, lemon juice, vinegar, tamari, cumin, red pepper sauce, and salt. Blend until completely smooth, scraping the sides of the appliance frequently. Spoon into a serving bowl and garnish with strips of roasted red pepper and fresh parsley. Place the bowl on a platter and surround it with pita chips or wedges of fresh pita bread.

Refreshing Cucumber Dip

This easy-to-prepare dip can also double as a sandwich spread.

PER 2 TABLESPOONS • 48 CALORIES (41% FROM FAT) • 2 G FAT • 4 G PROTEIN
3 G CARBOHYDRATE • 0 MG CHOLESTEROL • 81 MG SODIUM • 1 G FIBER

2 cucumbers

¼ cup finely diced red onion

1 pound very fresh firm tofu

3½ tablespoons lemon juice

2 cloves garlic, peeled

½ teaspoon soy sauce

½ teaspoon salt

¼ teaspoon coriander

¼ teaspoon cumin

Pinch cayenne pepper powder

2 tablespoons minced cilantro

Peel, seed, and grate the cucumbers. Place them in a mixing bowl with the red onion.

In a blender, combine the tofu, lemon juice, garlic, soy sauce, salt, coriander, cumin, and cayenne. Blend until completely smooth, then pour over the cucumbers and mix well. Transfer to a serving dish and chill 2 to 3 hours. Garnish with fresh cilantro and serve with Crisp Pita Chips (page 224).

Pea Guacamole

SERVES 6

Enjoy this avocado-free version of a very versatile dip.

PER SERVING • 60 CALORIES (0% FROM FAT) • 0 G FAT • 3 G PROTEIN
10 G CARBOHYDRATE • 0 MG CHOLESTEROL • 65 MG SODIUM • 3 G FIBER

1 cup frozen green peas

2 tablespoons Healthful Homemade
   Yogurt Cheese (page 335)

2 teaspoons lime juice

1 small tomato, peeled, seeded, and diced
   in ¼-inch pieces

¼ cup finely diced red onions, soaked in
   water to reduce acidity

1 clove garlic, chopped

1 jalapeño, seeded and finely diced

2 tablespoons finely chopped
   cilantro

¼ teaspoon cumin

Pinch cayenne pepper powder

Salt (optional)

In a blender or food processor, blend the peas, yogurt cheese, and lime juice. Mix in the rest of the ingredients and serve.

Twins' Fruit Dip

MAKES 1 QUART

I love this sauce folded in a fruit salad or simply for dipping bite-sized pieces of fresh, ripe fruit.

PER 2 TABLESPOONS

WITH TOFU • 30 CALORIES (18% FROM FAT) • 0.6 G FAT • 1 G PROTEIN
5 G CARBOHYDRATE • 0 MG CHOLESTEROL • 2 MG SODIUM • 0 G FIBER

WITH YOGURT CHEESE • 27 CALORIES (0% FROM FAT) • 0 G FAT • 1 G PROTEIN
6 G CARBOHYDRATE • 0 MG CHOLESTEROL • 2 MG SODIUM • 0 G FIBER

1 cup pineapple juice, fresh or
  unsweetened
½ cup orange juice, fresh or from
  concentrate
½ teaspoon orange zest (grated orange
  peel)
¼ cup cornstarch

½ teaspoon lemon zest (grated lemon
  peel)
½ cup Sucanat
1 cup firm tofu, Healthful Homemade
  Yogurt Cheese (page 335), or nonfat
  cream cheese

Place all the ingredients except the tofu or yogurt cheese or cream cheese in a double-boiler or heavy pan. Bring to a light boil on medium heat, stirring constantly with a whisk. When thickened (4 to 5 minutes), remove from the heat and set aside. Whip the firm tofu in a food processor until smooth, or soften the nonfat cream cheese or yogurt cheese to room temperature. Fold either the tofu, cream cheese, or yogurt cheese into the fruit mixture.

Dressings

Balsamic Sprinkled Vinaigrette, 330

Citrus Vinaigrette, 330

Raspberry Vinaigrette, 332

Tangy Grapefruit Vinaigrette, 332

Thousand Island Dressing, 331

Balsamic Sprinkled Vinaigrette

MAKES ½ CUP

An all-around dressing that tastes great sprinkled over our EssentialSalad, or try it as a dipping sauce for our VeggiePack!

PER TABLESPOON • 5 CALORIES (0% FROM FAT) • 0 G FAT • 0 G PROTEIN
1 G CARBOHYDRATE • 0 MG CHOLESTEROL • 75 MG SODIUM • 0 G FIBER

3 tablespoons balsamic vinegar
3 tablespoons seasoned rice vinegar

2 tablespoons distilled water
1 to 2 cloves garlic, crushed

Whisk the vinegars, 2 tablespoons water, and the crushed garlic together. Store in a tightly capped container in the refrigerator.

Citrus Vinaigrette

MAKES ¾ CUP

Another perfect complement to your EssentialSalad—simple yet complex in flavor!

PER TABLESPOON • 12 CALORIES (0% FROM FAT) • 0 G FAT • 0 G PROTEIN
3 G CARBOHYDRATE • 0 MG CHOLESTEROL • 94 MG SODIUM • 0 G FIBER

Juice of 1 large orange
Juice of ½ lime
2 tablespoons seasoned rice vinegar

2 teaspoons Sucanat
¼ teaspoon salt
½ teaspoon dried tarragon

Whisk all the ingredients together in a small bowl. Toss with the salad just before serving.

Thousand Island Dressing

Try this sauce on a grilled Gardenburger for a gastronomical delight!

PER TABLESPOON • 20 CALORIES (21% FROM FAT) • 0.5 G FAT • 1 G PROTEIN
3 G CARBOHYDRATE • 0 MG CHOLESTEROL • 126 MG SODIUM • 0 G FIBER

3 tablespoons Healthful Homemade
   Mayo (page 335)

2 tablespoons ketchup

1 tablespoon sweet pickle relish

1 roasted red pepper, seeded and finely
   diced

2 tablespoons minced celery

2 tablespoons seasoned rice vinegar

Combine all the ingredients and stir well to mix.

Raspberry Vinaigrette

MAKES ½ CUP

This versatile dressing is great over EssentialSalad or even a baked potato.

PER TABLESPOON • 4 CALORIES (0% FROM FAT) • 0 G FAT • 0 G PROTEIN
1 G CARBOHYDRATE • 0 MG CHOLESTEROL • 74 MG SODIUM • 0 G FIBER

2 tablespoons raspberry vinegar

2 tablespoons seasoned rice vinegar

¼ teaspoon crushed dried rosemary

¼ teaspoon dried tarragon

Whisk the vinegars, rosemary, and tarragon together with 2 tablespoons of water. Store in the refrigerator in a tightly capped container.

Tangy Grapefruit Vinaigrette

MAKES 1 CUP

Citrus juices make a tasty base for salad dressings.

PER 2 TABLESPOONS • 10 CALORIES (0% FROM FAT) • 0 G FAT • 0 G PROTEIN
2 G CARBOHYDRATE • 0 MG CHOLESTEROL • 0 MG SODIUM • 0 G FIBER

½ cup fresh grapefruit juice

½ cup rice wine vinegar

¼ cup cold water

1 small clove garlic, finely minced

1 teaspoon finely chopped fresh basil

½ teaspoon finely chopped fresh thyme

½ teaspoon black pepper

½ teaspoon finely chopped parsley

Whisk together the grapefruit juice, vinegar, and water in a small nonreactive bowl. Add the garlic, basil, thyme, pepper, and parsley. Mix well and chill until ready to use. It will keep nicely in the refrigerator for several days.

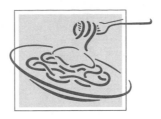

Sauces

Fresh Fruit Syrup

PER ¼-OUNCE SERVING • 12 CALORIES (0% FROM FAT) • 0 G FAT • 0 G PROTEIN
3 G CARBOHYDRATE • 0 MG CHOLESTEROL • 0 MG SODIUM • 0 G FIBER

3 cups fruit (choose one of the following: apricots, black cherries, blueberries, papaya, peaches, pineapple, raspberries, strawberries, or another fruit of choice)

½ to ¾ cup Sucanat
1 teaspoon Fruit Fresh

Place fruit of choice, Sucanat, and Fruit Fresh in a blender. Blend on high until smooth.

Homemade Basics

Healthful Homemade Sour Cream

MAKES 1¼ CUPS

This Sour Cream is delicious with hearty soups and stews, like Hungarian Goulash (page 242) or Wonderful Russian Borscht (page 295). It can also be used as a base for creamy salad dressings and sauces.

PER TABLESPOON • 9 CALORIES (32% FROM FAT) • 0.3 G FAT • 1 G PROTEIN
1 G CARBOHYDRATE • 0 MG CHOLESTEROL • 62 MG SODIUM • 0 G FIBER

1 10.5-ounce package firm silken tofu
1 tablespoon seasoned rice vinegar
1 tablespoon lemon juice

1 teaspoon cider vinegar
1 teaspoon Sucanat
½ teaspoon salt

Combine all the ingredients in a blender or food processor and process until completely smooth.

Healthful Homemade Mayo

MAKES 1½ CUPS

At last, a tasty mayonnaise replacement!

PER TABLESPOON • 26 CALORIES (55% FROM FAT) • 2 G FAT • 2 G PROTEIN
1 G CARBOHYDRATE • 0 MG CHOLESTEROL • 63 MG SODIUM • 0 G FIBER

¾ pound firm tofu
1 tablespoon lemon juice
½ teaspoon salt

1 tablespoon canola oil
4 teaspoons seasoned rice vinegar

Combine all the ingredients in a blender or food processor and process until completely smooth.

Healthful Homemade Yogurt Cheese

MAKES 2 CUPS

Savor this flavorful, nonfat alternative to cream cheese or sour cream.

PER CUP • 238 CALORIES (0% FROM FAT) • 0 G FAT • 24 G PROTEIN
35 G CARBOHYDRATE • 11 MG CHOLESTEROL • 346 MG SODIUM • 0 G FIBER

4 cups nonfat yogurt, plain

Place the yogurt in a strainer inside a container and refrigerate overnight. The liquid will drain off and leave a thickened cheeselike product. Four cups of yogurt makes 2 cups of yogurt cheese.

Simple Marinara Sauce

MAKES 4 CUPS

*S*erve this easily prepared, fat-free marinara with your favorite pasta and steamed vegetables.

PER 1/2 CUP • 41 CALORIES (0% FROM FAT) • 0 G FAT • 1 G PROTEIN
7 G CARBOHYDRATE • 0 MG CHOLESTEROL • 10 MG SODIUM • 2 G FIBER

½ cup sweet white wine

1 onion, chopped

4 cloves garlic, crushed

1 28-ounce can chopped or crushed
  tomatoes

1 tablespoon mixed Italian herbs

1 teaspoon Sucanat

¼ teaspoon black pepper

Heat the wine in a large pot, then add the onion and garlic. Cook over medium heat, stirring often, until the onion begins to brown, about 10 minutes.

Add the tomatoes, Italian herbs, Sucanat, and black pepper. Simmer for 15 to 20 minutes.

Simple Peanut Sauce

MAKES 1 CUP

*T*his sauce is delicious with pasta or with cooked vegetables.

PER TABLESPOON • 38 CALORIES (62% FROM FAT) • 3 G FAT • 1 G PROTEIN
2 G CARBOHYDRATE • 0 MG CHOLESTEROL • 38 MG SODIUM • 0 G FIBER

⅓ cup peanut butter

½ cup hot water

1 tablespoon soy sauce

1 tablespoon seasoned rice vinegar

2 teaspoons Sucanat

2 cloves garlic, minced

2 teaspoons chopped fresh ginger

⅛ teaspoon cayenne pepper powder

Whisk all ingredients together until the sauce is smooth.

RESOURCES

Animal Rights

ORGANIZATIONS

Ark Trust, 5461 Noble Avenue, Sherman Oaks, CA 91411-3519; (818) 786-9990. Founded in 1991 by Gretchen Wyler. It is the only animal-rights group whose primary focus is to facilitate progressive coverage of animal issues by the major media. It is a national, non-profit organization devoted to raising public awareness about the many protection issues facing us today.

Compassion in World Farming, 20 Lavant Street, Petersfield, Hants, England. Write for information.

EarthSave, 706 Frederick Street, Santa Cruz, CA 95062; (408) 423-4069. Founded in late 1988 by John Robbins to educate people about the powerful effects their food choices have on the environment, individual health, and all life on earth, working for a plant-based diet.

Farm Animal Reform Movement, P.O. Box 30654, Bethesda, MD 20824; (301) 530-1737. Educates the public about adverse animal agriculture and its impact on human health and the environment. Slides, videos, and over one hundred books available.

Farm Sanctuary, P.O. Box 150, Watkins Glen, NY 14891; (607) 583-2225. Working to eliminate abusive animal agricultural practices, and to educate the public on factory farming and promote alternatives to factory farm products. Publications available on ethical treatment of animals.

The Fund for Animals, 850 Sligo Avenue, Suite LL2, Silver Spring, MD 20901; (301) 585-2591.

Humane Farming Association, 1550 California Street, Suite 6, San Francisco, CA 94109; (415) 485-1495. Write or call for information.

Humane Society of the United States, 2100 L Street, Washington, DC 20037; (202) 452-1100. A moderate animal welfare organization.

National Audubon Society, 645 Pennsylvania Avenue, SE, Washington, DC 20003. Write for information.

National Wildlife Federation, 1400 16th Street, NW, Washington, DC 20036. Write for information.

North American Vegetarian Society (NAVS), P.O. Box 72, Dolgeville, NY 13329; (518) 568-7970. Educates the public and the media about the nutritional, economical, ecological, and ethical benefits of a vegetarian diet.

People for Ethical Treatment of Animals, 501 Front Street, Norfolk, VA 23510; (757) 622-PETA. Write or call for information.

Progressive Animal Welfare Society, P.O. Box 1037, Lynnwood, WA 98046; (206) 743-3845. Write or call for information.

United Poultry Concerns, P.O. Box 59367, Potomac, MD 20859; (301) 948-2406.

BOOKS/MAGAZINES/NEWSLETTERS

Beyond Beef, by Jeremy Rifkin. New York: Dutton, 1992. Why does a pound of ground beef sell in the supermarket for only a few cents more than a pound of beans, when production of the meat requires up to five thousand gallons of water and sixteen pounds of feed (much of it corn and soybeans)? Explores the devastating effects of the overpopulation of cattle on the earth and the necessity of changing our diet.

Diet for a New America, by John Robbins. Walpole, NH: Stillpoint Publishing, 1987. Nominated for a Pulitzer Prize. This powerful book shows the impact a meat-centered diet has on human health, the global environment, and animal welfare. It has changed many people's lives. If you care about your health or the planet, you can't afford not to read it! Available in paperback.

Shopping Guide for Caring Consumers: A Guide to Products That Are Not Tested on Animals. Summertown, TN: Book Publishing Company, 1993. People for the Ethical Treatment of Animals, 501 Front Street, Norfolk, VA 23510; (757) 622-PETA.

Student Network News, Humane Society of USA, 67 Salem Road, East Haddam, CT 06423; (203) 434-8666.

Environment

Center for Environmental Education (CEE), 881 Alma Real Drive, Suite 300, Pacific Palisades, CA 90272; (310) 454-4585, fax (310) 454-9925. Networks and provides information about services and programs for educators, students, and environmental organizations.

EarthSave, 706 Frederick Street, Santa Cruz, CA 95062; (408) 423-4069. Founded in 1988 by John Robbins to educate people about the powerful effects their food choices have on the environment, individual health, and all life on earth.

Friends of the Earth, 218 D Street, SE, Washington, DC 20003; (202) 544-2600. Global environmental advocates.

Greenpeace USA, 1436 U Street, NW, Washington, DC 20009; (202) 462-1177. One of the most activist-oriented environmental groups.

Kids for a Clean Environment (Kids FACE), P.O. Box 158254, Nashville, TN 37215; (615) 331-7381. An organization created by a child and for children. It has developed environmental projects and programs that have been implemented in classrooms by teachers and school groups across the nation.

Natural Resources Defense Council, 40 West 20th Street, New York, NY 10011; (212) 727-2700. Very effective organization. Write for information.

North American Vegetarian Society (NAVS), P.O. Box 72, Dolgeville, NY 13329; (518) 568-7970. Educates the public and the media about the nutritional, economical, ecological, and ethical benefits of a vegetarian diet.

Ozone Action, 34 Wall Street, Suite 203, Asheville, NC 28801; (704) 254-3811.

Rainforest Action Network, 450 Samsome, Suite 700, San Francisco, CA 94111; (415) 398-4404.

Sierra Club, 730 Polk Street, San Francisco, CA 94109; (415) 776-2211. One of the country's biggest environmental lobbyists.

U.S. Public Interest Research Group, 215 Pennsylvania Avenue, SE, Washington, DC 20003. Researches and fights for consumer and environmental protection.

The Video Project, 5332 College Avenue, Suite 101, Oakland, CA 95476; (510) 655-9050, fax (510) 655-9115.

Worldwatch Institute, 1776 Massachusetts Avenue, Washington, DC 20036; (202) 452-1999. A research group that monitors the whole earth.

Blueprint for a Green School, Center for Environmental Education (CEE), 881 Alma Real Drive, Suite 300, Pacific Palisades, CA 90272; (310) 454-4585, fax (310) 454-9925. Introduces all environmental issues impacting schools and suggests activities and extension resources for further action.

E: The Environmental Magazine, P.O. Box 6667, Syracuse, NY 13217-7934; (800) 825-0061.

Earth First! Journal, P.O. Box 5871, Tucson, AZ 85703; (602) 622-1371.

GAIA: Atlas of Anatomy of Planet Management, by Norman Myers. New York: Anchor Press/Doubleday, 1984. This book explains our place on this planet and the damage we are doing to ourselves. It is, in fact, a sort of blueprint for our survival.

Global Response, P.O. Box 7490, Boulder, CO 80306-7490; phone/fax (303) 444-0306. Brings environmental awareness and activism to concerned people of all ages.

Greenpeace Quarterly, 1436 U Street, NW, Washington, DC 20009; (202) 462-1177. An accessible adult environmental publication.

The Rain Forest Book, by Scott Lewis and the Natural Resources Defense Council. New York: Berkley Books, 1990.

State of the World, published annually by Worldwatch Institute, a research group that monitors the whole earth. 1776 Massachusetts Avenue, NW, Washington, DC 20036; (202) 452-1999.

Vital Signs, Environmental Alert Series, by Worldwatch Institute, 1776 Massachusetts Avenue, NW, Washington, DC 20036; (202) 452-1999.

World Watch magazine, by Worldwatch Institute, 1776 Massachusetts Avenue, NW, Washington, DC 20036; (202) 452-1999.

Health/Nutrition

ORGANIZATIONS

American Vegan Society, 501 Old Harding Highway, Malaga, NJ 08328. Write for information.

Bastyr University, 14500 Juanita Drive, NE, Bothell, WA 98011; (206) 523-9585, fax (206) 527-4763. The university's nutrition program emphasizes the study of physiology, biochemical, socioeconomic, political, and psychological aspects of human nutrition. The program offers an M.S. in nutrition, B.S. in natural health sciences with a major in whole food nutrition, and a didactic program in dietetics.

Beyond Beef, 1130 17th Street, NW, Suite 300, Washington, DC 20036; (202) 775-1132. Write for information.

Center for Science and Public Interest (CSPI), 1875 Connecticut Avenue, NW, Suite 300, Washington, DC 20009-5728; (202) 332-9110. Nutrition advocacy organization that strongly supports school lunch reform. Issues press releases and testifies on school lunches and other nutrition issues before Congress and other governmental bodies. Publishes the *Nutrition Action Newsletter,* one of the most useful nutrition tools available to the general public.

Citizens for Health, P.O. Box 1195, Tacoma, WA 98401; (206) 922-2311, fax (206) 922-7583. A nonprofit consumer advocacy organization dedicated to promoting wellness and preventive health care. Actively engaged in promoting or opposing legislation at state and national levels.

Food and Water, 225 Lafayette Street, Suite 612, New York, NY 10012; (212) 941-9340, (800) EAT-SAFE. Food irradiation. Write or call for further information.

Natural Food Systems, Inc., P.O. Box 1028, Pagosa Springs, CO 81447; (800) U-SHARED. Write or call for information.

North American Vegetarian Society (NAVS), P.O. Box 72, Dolgeville, NY 13329; (518) 568-7970. Educates the public and the media about the nutritional, economical, ecological, and ethical benefits of a vegetarian diet.

Physicians Committee for Responsible Medicine, P.O. Box 6322, Washington, DC 20015; (202) 686-2210. Write or call for information. This is a very dynamic, influential organization.

Sprouting Publications, Box 62, Ashland, OR 97520. Write for information.

Vegetarian Nutrition Dietetic Practice Group, The American Dietetic Association, Suite 800, 216 West Jackson Blvd., Chicago, IL 60606-6995.

Vegetarian Resource Group, P.O. Box 1463, Baltimore, MD 21203; (410) 366-VEGE. Works on both local and national levels to educate the public about vegetarianism and veganism.

BOOKS/MAGAZINES/NEWSLETTERS

American Health, RD Publications, 28 West 23rd Street, New York, NY 10010. Write for magazine.

Becoming Vegetarian, by Vesanto Melina, Brenda Davis, and Victoria Harrison. Summertown, TN: Book Publishing Company, 1995.

Bottom Line, Boardroom Inc., Box 2614, Greenwich, CT 06836-2614; (800) 274-5611.

Choices for Our Future, by Ocean Robbins and Sol Solomon. Summertown, TN: Book Publishing Company, 1994. Student guide to ecological issues of our day. Available through EarthSave, 706 Frederick Street, Santa Cruz, CA 95062; (408) 423-4069.

Citizens for Health and Action Alerts, P.O. Box 1195, Tacoma, WA 98401; (206) 922-3311, fax (206) 922-7583.

Consumer Reports on Health, Consumers Union, 101 Truman Avenue, Yonkers, NY 10703-1057. Note: This publication explicitly states no reproduction without prior written permission.

Cooking Light, P.O. Box 830549, Birmingham, AL 35282. Write for magazine.

Dr. Dean Ornish's Program for Reversing Heart Disease: The Only System Scientifically Proven to Reverse Heart Disease without Drugs or Surgery, by Dr. Dean Ornish, M.D. New York: Random House, 1990. The new federal guidelines for food labeling say a healthy diet is "up to 30% fat." Dr. Ornish says 10 percent can reverse heart disease, when combined with moderate exercise and relaxation/yoga/stress management. The results convinced a major insurance company to offer discounts to followers of the Ornish Program. Can be ordered from EarthSave, 706 Frederick Street, Santa Cruz, CA 95062; (408) 423-4069.

EarthSave, EarthSave International, 706 Frederick Street, Santa Cruz, CA 95062-2205; (408) 423-4069.

East-West Nutrition Newsletter, T. Colin Campbell. Ph.D., Senior Editor, Box 1023, 95 Brown Road, Ithaca, NY 14850.

Eat for Life, by C. Woteki, Ph.D., R.D., Washington, DC: National Academy of Sciences, 1992.

Eat More, Weigh Less, by Dr. Dean Ornish, M.D., New York: HarperCollins, 1993. Very low-fat vegetarian recipes from famous chefs. Now available in paperback. Available from EarthSave, 706 Frederick Street, Santa Cruz, CA 95062; (408) 423-4069.

Eating Well, Ferry Road, P.O. Box 1001, Charlotte, VT 05445. Write for magazine.

The Edell Health Letter, 301 Howard Street, Suite 1800, San Francisco, CA 94105.

Environmental Nutrition, 52 Riverside Dr., Suite 15A, NYC, NY 10024. Write for newsletter.

The Felix Letter. Get your copy by writing to: P.O. Box 7094, Berkeley, CA 94707.

The Food Channel, Noble & Associates, Inc., 515 North State Street, Chicago, IL 60610; (800) 986-6253.

The Food Channel: Hot Bytes—Late Breaking Food Trend News: Same as above.

The Healing Foods, by P. Hausman. New York: Dell, 1989.

Health, P.O. Box 56863, Boulder, CO 80322. Write for magazine.

Health and Fitness Excellence, by R. Cooper, Ph.D. Boston: Houghton Mifflin, 1989.

Health & Healing, Phillips Publishing, Inc., 7811 Montrose Road, Potomac, MD 20854; (800) 539-8219.

Healthy School Lunch Action Guide, by Susan Campbell and Todd Winant, EarthSave, 1994. How to teach and motivate children to make healthy food choices and to bring healthier lunches to the schools in your community. Video available through EarthSave, 706 Frederick Street, Santa Cruz, CA 95062; (408) 423-4069.

Lifeline, Lifestyle Medicine Institute, Better Health, P.O. Box 1761, Loma Linda, CA 92354.

The McDougall Plan, by John McDougall, M.D., and Mary McDougall. Piscataway, NJ: New Century Publishers, 1983. Learn why a grain-based diet is the best for the body, from a nationally recognized authority with his own clinic and radio show (in Los Angeles, 7:00 to 9:00 P.M. Sundays on KABC, 790 AM). Includes recipes.

The McDougall Program: 12 Days to Dynamic Health, by John McDougall, M.D., and Mary McDougall. New York: Penguin Books, 1990. Readers can go through Dr. McDougall's twelve-day hospital program at home. It replaces the disease-causing standard American diet with a starch-based diet free of animal products and added fats, and shows you how to prevent, control, and sometimes reverse degenerative diseases such as atherosclerosis, arthritis, and cancer.

Medical Letter Review, SelfCare Catalog, 5850 Shellmound Street, Suite 390, Emeryville, CA 94608.

The Mount Sinai School of Medicine Complete Book of Nutrition. New York: St. Martin's Press, 1990.

New Century Nutrition, ParaComm, Inc., P.O. Box 4716, Ithaca, NY 14852; (607) 266-0313.

Nutrition Action Healthletter, CSPI, 1875 Connecticut Avenue, NW, Suite 300, Washington, DC 20009-5728; (202) 332-9110.

Nutrition Action's Eating Smart Shopping Guide, CSPI, 1875 Connecticut Avenue, NW, Suite 300, Washington, DC 20009-5728; (202) 332-9110.

Prevention, 33 East Minor Street, Emmaus, PA 18098. Write for subscription.

Simply Vegan, by Debra Wasserman and Reed Mangels, Ph.D., R.D., 1991. An extensive vegan nutrition section, sample meals, food definitions, and suggestions on cruelty-free shopping, all make this book a complete guide to healthy living. Vegetarian Resource Group, P.O. Box 1463, Baltimore, MD 21203; (410) 366-VEGE.

Tufts University Diet & Nutrition Letter, 53 Park Place, New York, NY 10007; (800) 274-7581.

University of California at Berkeley Wellness Letter, P.O. Box 420148, Palm Coast, FL 32142; (904) 445-6414.

Vegetarian Journal, by Vegetarian Resource Group. Available in some natural-food stores, or by mail. VRG, P.O. Box 1463, Baltimore, MD 21203; (410) 366-VEGE.

Vegetarian Journal's Guide to Natural Foods Restaurants in the U.S. and Canada. Avery Publishing Group. Lists two thousand restaurants, vacation spots, camps, and local vegetarian group contacts. Available through Vegetarian Resource Group, P.O. Box 1463, Baltimore, MD 21203; (410) 366-VEGE.

Vegetarian Times. Monthly, $24.95 one-year (12 issues) subscription. Available on newsstands.

Vegetarianism and Veganism. The Vegetarian Resource Group works on both local and national levels to educate the public about vegetarianism and veganism. P.O. Box 1463, Baltimore, MD 21203; (410) 366-VEGE.

The Wellness Encyclopedia, by the authors of the *University of California at Berkeley Wellness Letter.* Boston: Houghton Mifflin, 1991.

The Wellness Encyclopedia of Food and Nutrition, by S. Margen, M.D. New York: Rebus, 1992.

Your Good Health, Creative Promotions and Radio Syndications, 10757 Queensland Street, Los Angeles, CA 90034.

Recommended Tools

EQUIPMENT AND USEFUL ITEMS FOR THE HOME

Health Appliances and Specialty Cookware. Cookers, crushers, food processors, graters, juice extractors, and stainless-steel cookware, etc. Write or call for catalog and prices: Miracle Exclusive, Inc., a division of Flora, Inc., 62 Seaview Boulevard, Port Washington, NY 11050; (516) 484-2121, (800) 645-6360, fax (516) 484-2199.

Vita-Mix. Information, recipes, and instructions available. Vita-Mix Corporation, 8615 Usher Road, Cleveland, OH 44138; (216) 235-4840, (800) 848-2649. "The best blender and food machines I've ever used!" declares author GardenChef Paul Wenner.

Waring food processors and blenders. Appliance stores everywhere.

Real Recycled, catalog of environmentally sensitive products, 1541 Adrian Road, Burlingame, CA 94010-2107; (800) 233-5335.

BIBLIOGRAPHY

Unsigned Reports

"ADA Right in Time" and "No More Meat?" *EarthSave,* Winter 1995–96, p. 3.

"Alcohol: Spirit of Health?: How Alcohol Helps," *Consumer Reports on Health,* April 1996, p. 37.

"Beta Carotene: How It Took Center Stage," *UC Berkeley Wellness Letter,* April 1996, p. 2.

"A Better Burger," *American Health,* October 1994, p. 32.

"Breast Cancer," *Nutrition Action Healthletter,* January/February 1996, Cover Story, p. 4.

"Calcium & Vitamin D," *Nutrition Action Healthletter,* Cover Story, April 1996.

"Diet News: Good Dog," *Bon Appétit,* October 1995, Health News & Views, p. 148.

"Dodging Cancer with Diet," *Nutrition Action Healthletter,* January/February, 1995, Cover.

"Entering a High-Protein Twilight Zone," *Tufts University Diet & Nutrition Letter,* May 1996, "Special Report," p. 4.

"Fatal Disease Sinks Prices of British Beef," *Oregonian,* March 24, 1996, p. 4.

"Feedstuffs: Special Report," *EarthSave,* November 6, 1995, p. 28.

"Fish: What's the Catch?" *EarthSave: Personal Food Choices—Global Results,* Spring 1996, vol. 7, no. 1, p. 1.

"Getting Calcium Without the Fat," *Consumer Reports,* May 1996, p. 48.

"Health," *EarthSave Index,* Winter 1995–96, p. 8.

"Healthy Eating: Demystifying the Daily Value . . . or Whatever Happened to RDA's?" *Consumer Reports on Health,* March 1996, p. 33.

"Lightening Your Weight Management Load: Forget the Negative Self-Talk," *Tufts University Diet & Nutrition Letter,* March 1996, vol. 14, no. 1, p. 1.

"Pork Production Booming, But It's Hardly Hog Heaven," *Sunday Oregonian,* December 31, 1995, sec. A: National/International, p. 12.

"Quick Studies: Carcinogens in Chicken?" and "A Meat & Poultry Primer," *Nutrition Action Healthletter,* November 1995, p. 12.

"Recommended Revisions for Dietary Guidelines for Americans: Plant-Based Diets Get Federal Stamp of Approval!" *EarthSave,* January 31, 1995.

"Related Actions: Suffering Survey," *Farm Report,* Summer/Fall 1995, p. 5.

"Should You Be Eating More Protein—or Less?" *UC Berkeley Wellness Letter,* June 1996, "Special Report," p. 4.

"Substance May Cause Weight Loss in People Suffering from Cancer," *Oregonian,* February 22, 1996, sec. B, p. 7.

"Veggie Invasion," *Vegetarian Times,* January 1996, p. 20.

"The Weighting Game," *Nutrition Action Healthletter,* May 1995, p. 4.

"Weight-Loss News That's Easy to Stomach," *Tufts University Diet & Nutrition Letter,* April 1996, vol. 14, no. 2, p. 17.

"World Hunger," *EarthSave Index,* Spring 1996, p. 7.

"Your Tax Dollars Are Feeding Cattle and Destroying Habitat," *National Wildlife,* December 1995/January 1996, p. 58.

Signed Reports

Barnard, Neal D., M.D., "The Pyramid Crumbles: Rewriting the U.S. Diet Guidelines." *Good Medicine: Prevention & Nutrition* (Summer 1995):16.

———. "The $60 Billion Drum Stick." Physicians Committee For Responsible Medicine, news release, November 20, 1995.

———. "Prevention and Nutrition: Foods That Build Immunity." *Good Medicine* (Winter 1996):18.

———. "Brain-Rot Disease of the Week." *Oregonian,* March 31, 1996.

Barnard Neal, M.D., Andrew Nicholson, M.D., and Jo Lil Howard. "The Medical Costs Attributable to Meat Consumption." *Physicians for Responsible Medicine: Preventive Medicine* 24 (November 20, 1995):3.

Boss, Kit. "Meatless: What Vegetarians Talk about When They Talk about Food." *Seattle Times/Seattle Post-Intelligencer,* November 21, 1993, Northwest Living, p. 14.

Brody, Jane E. "FOODday: Want to Beat Cancer? Cut Back on Those Fats, Eat Your Vegetables." *Oregonian,* November 27, 1996, OP, p. 3.

Challem, Jack. "Vegetarianism: Doesn't Turn You On? Consider Trying It Part Time." *Let's Live* (August 1994): 56.

Conrad, Paul. "Using PR to Build Profits." *In Business,* May/June 1995, p. 26.

Cooper, Dr. Kenneth. "From Aerobics to Antioxidants." *Journal of Longevity Research* 2, no. 2 (1996):43.

Foster, Randy S. "Local Dairy Farmers Find Anti-growth Hormone Arguments Hard to Swallow." *Enterprise Record,* Chico, CA, February 3, 1994.

Gibson, Richard. "Restaurants Beef Up Vegetarian Menus." *Wall Street Journal,* October 15, 1991, Marketing, B6.

Heberlein, Greg. "Northwest 100: Wholesome & Hearty's Healthy Growth Puts It at Top of Menu." *Seattle Times,* June 5, 1994, sec. M., p. 10.

Hochwald, Lambeth. "Reinventing the Vegetable." *Natural Health,* March/April 1996, Special Consumer Guide, p. 105.

Jacobson, Michael F., Ph.D., and Bruce Maxwell. "Best Children's Foods." *What Are We Feeding Our Kids?,* August 1994, Introduction, p. 9.

Jaret, Peter. "Living Colors." *Health,* March/April 1996, p. 91.

Krupp, Fred. "Pollution Prevention Pays." *EDF (Environmental Defense Fund) Letter,* May 1996, vol. 27, no. 3, Director's Message, p. 3.

Lemonick, Michael D. "Fat-Free Fat." *Time,* January 8, 1996, p. 53.

Liebman, Bonnie. "Special Report: Clues to Prostate Cancer." *Nutrition Action Healthletter,* March 1996, p. 12.

Mayer, Nancy. "The Futurist of Food." *Oregonian,* September 25, 1994, Northwest Living, sec. L, p. 1.

Meadows, Donella. "This Land Was Your Land: Three Views of a Theft in Progress." *Amicus Journal,* Winter 1996. Washington Watch, p. 11; and Spring 1996.

Monks, Vicki. "Environmental Regulations: Who Needs Them?" *National Wildlife: Quality of Life* (February/March 1996):25; and "Want to Get Involved" (February/March 1996):29.

O'Connor, Rose Ellen. "Drop in Grazing Fees Due, Hurting Chance of New Law." *Oregonian,* January 23, 1996, sec. A, p. 5.

O'Neill, William, & Co. "The Best Small Companies in America: Making the List." *Forbes,* November 7, 1994, pp. 234–38.

Parfit, Michael. "Diminishing Returns: Exploiting the Ocean's Bounty." *National Geographic,* 188, no. 5 (November 1995):2.

Parr, Jan. "Under the (Veg) Influence." *Vegetarian Times,* September 1995, In the News: Food, p. 22.

Recer, Paul. "Low Calorie Diets Might Slow Aging." *Oregonian,* April 30, 1996, sec. A, p. 7.

Steeley, Robert. "Reports on Cattle Disease Shake British Beef Industry." *Oregonian,* March 22, 1996, sec. A, p. 5.

Stenson, Jacqueline. "New Benefits Found from Dr. Ornish's Heart-Disease Reversal Plan." *Medical Tribune,* October 12, 1995, p. 3.

Strawn, John. "Stolen Future—Too Soon to Panic?," and Ellen Emry Heltzel, "Environmentalist Raps Effects of Chemicals." *Sunday Oregonian,* March 31, 1996, sec. E, p. 6.

Trumbell, Mark. "Good-Tasting Meatless Burger? It's Here and It's Selling." *Christian Science Monitor* 86, no. 50 (February 4, 1994).

Wright, Lawrence. "Silent Sperm." *New Yorker,* January 15, 1996, p. 47.

Wyatt, John, with Joyce E. Davis, Ani Hadjian, Rajiv M. Rao, and Ricardo Sookdeo. "The Best and Worst Stocks of 1993." *Fortune,* January 24, 1994, p. 52.

Books

Abramovitz, Janet N. *Imperiled Water, Impoverished Future.* Washington, D.C.: Worldwatch Institute, 1996.

Airola, Paavo, Ph.D., N.D. *Cancer, The Total Approach.* Phoenix, AZ: Health Plus Publishers, 1972.

American Heart Association. *The Healthy Heart Walking Book.* New York: Simon & Schuster, Macmillan, 1995.

Attwood, Charles R., M.D. *Dr. Attwood's Low-Fat Prescription for Kids.* New York: Penguin Books, 1995.

Bailey, Covert. *The New Fit or Fat.* Boston: Houghton-Mifflin, 1991.

Bailey, Covert, and Rhonda Gates. *Smart Eating.* Boston: Houghton Mifflin, 1996.

Barnard, Neal, M.D. *The Power of Your Plate.* Summertown, TN: Book Publishing Company, 1990.

———. *Live Longer, Live Better.* Audio cassette. Summertown, TN: Book Publishing Company, 1991.

———. *Foods That Cause You to Lose Weight: The Negative Calorie Effect.* McKinney, TX: The Magni Group, Inc., 1992.

———. *Food for Life.* New York: Crown Publishers, 1993.

Barnard, Neal, M.D., with recipes by Jennifer Raymond. *Fit for Life: How the New Four Food Groups Can Save Your Life.* New York: Harmony Books, 1993.

————. *Eat Right/Live Longer.* New York: Harmony Books, 1995.

Batmanghelidj, F., M.D. *Your Body's Many Cries for Water.* Falls Church, VA: Global Health Solutions, Inc., 1995.

Benjamin, James. *Food: Green Grow the Profits.* Monrovia: CA: National Health Federation, 1973.

Blonz, Edward R., Ph.D. *The Really Simple No-Nonsense Nutrition Guide.* Emeryville, CA: Conari Press, 1993.

Bonk, Melinda, ed. *Alternative Medicine Yellow Pages.* Puyallup, WA: Future Medicine Publishing, Inc., 1995.

Brown, Lester R., et al. *State of the World.* New York: W. W. Norton, 1996.

Calborn, Cherie, M.S., C.N. *The Healthy Gourmet.* New York: Random House, 1996.

Campbell, Susan, and Todd Winan. *Healthy School Lunch Action Guide.* Santa Cruz, CA: EarthSave, 1993.

Carper, Jean. *The Food Pharmacy.* New York: Bantam, 1988.

————. *Food—Your Miracle Medicine.* New York: HarperCollins Publishers, 1993.

Chopra, Deepak, M.D. *Ageless Body, Timeless Mind.* New York: Harmony Books, 1991.

————. *Perfect Weight.* New York: Harmony Books, 1991.

Coe, Sue. *Dead Meat.* New York: Four Walls Eight Windows, 1995.

Connor, Sonja L., M.S., R.D., and William E. Connor, M.D. *The New American Diet.* New York: Fireside, 1989.

————. *The New American Diet Cookbook.* New York: Simon & Schuster, 1997.

Davis, Brenda, Victoria Harrison, and Vesanto Melina. *Becoming Vegetarian.* Summertown, TN: Book Publishing Company, 1995.

DeBakey, Michael. *The Living Heart Guide to Eating Out.* New York: MasterMedia Limited, 1993.

Diamond, Harvey, and Marilyn Diamond. *Fit for Life II: Living Health.* New York: Warner Books, 1987.

Donkersloot, Mary, R.D. *The Fast-Food Diet.* New York: Simon & Schuster, 1991.

Duffy, William. *Sugar Blues.* New York: Warner Books, 1975.

Empringham, James, D.Sc., Ph.D. *What to Eat and Why: Pandora's Box of Invisible Foes.* Los Angeles, CA: Health Education Society, 1942.

Evans, William, Ph.D., and Irwin H. Rosenberg, M.D. *Biomarkers: The 10 Keys to Prolonging Vitality.* New York: Simon & Schuster, 1991.

Figtree, Dale, Ph.D. *Eat Smart: A Guide to Good Health for Kids.* Clinton, NJ: New Win Publishing, 1992.

Gallagher, Charlette R., and John B. Allred. *Taking the Fear Out of Eating.* Boston: Cambridge University Press, 1992.

Goldbeck, Nikki, and David Goldbeck. *The Goldbecks' Guide to Good Food.* New York: New American Library, 1987.

Havala, Suzanne, M.S., R.D. *Simple, Low-Fat and Vegetarian.* Baltimore, MD: The Vegetarian Resource Group, 1994.

———. *Shopping for Health.* New York: HarperCollins Publishers, 1996.

Hawken, Paul. *The Ecology of Commerce.* New York: HarperCollins Publishers, 1993.

Hempel, Toby. *Japanese Finger Massage.* New York: Globe Communications Corp., 1980.

Hendler, Sheldon Saul, M.D., Ph.D. *The Doctors' Vitamin and Mineral Encyclopedia.* New York: Simon & Schuster, 1990.

Hills, Christopher, Ph.D., D.Sc. *Light Force.* Boulder Creek, CA: University of the Trees Press, 1979.

Hirsch, David. *The Moosewood Restaurant Kitchen Garden.* New York: Simon & Schuster, 1992.

Hobbs, Christopher. *Ginkgo, Elixir of Youth.* Capitola, CA: Botanica Press, 1994.

Igoe, Robert S. *Dictionary of Food Ingredients.* New York: Van Nostrand Reinhold, 1989.

Igram, Cass, D.O. *Self-Test Nutrition Guide.* Hiawatha, IA: Knowledge House Publishers, 1994.

Jacobi, Dana. *The Natural Health Cookbook.* New York: Simon & Schuster, 1995.

Jacobson, Michael F., Ph.D. *The Complete Eater's Digest and Nutrition Scoreboard.* New York: Anchor Press/Doubleday, 1985.

———. *What Are We Feeding Our Kids?* New York: Workman Publishing Co., 1994.

Jensen, Bernard. *Health Magic Through Chlorophyll.* Provo, UT: BiWorld Publishers, 1973.

Jones, Susan Smith, Ph.D. *Choose to Be Healthy.* Berkeley, CA: Celestial Arts, 1987.

Kilham, Christofer S. *The Bread and Circus Whole Food Bible.* New York: Addison–Wesley, 1991.

Klaper, Michael, M.D. *Pregnancy, Children, and the Vegan Diet.* Umatilla, FL: Gentle World, 1988.

Kradjian, Robert M., M.D. *Save Yourself from Breast Cancer.* New York: Berkley Publishing Group, 1994.

Krizmanic, Judy. *A Teen's Guide to Going Vegetarian.* New York: Penguin Books, 1994.

Lappé, Frances Moore. *Diet for a Small Planet.* Tenth Anniversary Edition. New York: Ballantine Books, 1982.

Lucia, Salvatore Pablo, M.D. *Wine and Your Well-Being.* New York: Popular Library, 1971.

Mabe, Rex. *Gardening with Herbs.* Greensboro, NC: Potpourri Press, 1973.

McDougall, John A., M.D., *McDougall's Medicine: A Challenging Second Opinion*. Hampton, NJ: New Century Publishers, 1986.

McDougall, John A., M.D., and Mary A. McDougall, L.P.N. *The McDougall Plan*. Piscataway, NJ: New Century Publishers, 1983.

———. *The McDougall Program: Twelve Days to Dynamic Health*. New York: Plume, 1990.

———. *The New McDougall Cookbook*. New York: E. P. Dutton, 1993.

———. *The McDougall Program for Maximum Weight Loss*. New York: E. P. Dutton, 1994.

Messinger, Lisa. *Why Should I Eat Better?* Garden City Park, NY: Avery Publishing Group, 1993.

The Moosewood Collective. *Moosewood Restaurant Cooks at Home*. New York: Simon & Schuster, 1994.

Murray, Michael, and Joseph Pizzorno, N.D. *Encyclopedia of Natural Medicine*. Rocklin, CA: Prima Publishing, 1991.

Mycoskie, Pam. *Butter Busters*. New York: Warner Books, 1994.

Napier, Kristine M., M.P.H., R.D. *How Nutrition Works*. Emeryville, CA: Ziff-Davis Press, 1995.

Ornish, Dean, M.D. *Dr. Ornish's Program for Reversing Heart Disease*. New York: Random House, 1990.

———. *Eat More, Weigh Less*. New York: HarperCollins Publishers, 1993.

Perlow, Nat K. *Everything You Need to Know About Cholesterol*. Ft. Lauderdale, FL: Globe Communications Corp., 1987.

Pfeiffer, Carl C., Ph.D., M.D. *Nutrition and Mental Illness*. Rochester, VT: Healing Arts Press, 1987.

Raymond, Jennifer. *The Peaceful Palate: Fine Vegetarian Cuisine*. Palo Alto, CA: Self-published, 1992.

Rifkin, Jeremy. *Beyond Beef*. New York: Penguin Books, 1992.

Robbins, John. *Diet for a New America*. Walpole, NH: Stillpoint Publishing, 1987.

———. *May All Be Fed: Diet For a New World*. New York: William Morrow & Co., 1992.

Robbins, Ocean, and Sol Solomon. *Choices for Our Future*. Summertown, TN: Book Publishing Company, 1994.

Rose, Howard A. *No Bull Diet*. Great Neck, NY: Hart Marketing Co., 1992.

Shelton, Herbert M. *Food Combining Made Easy*. San Antonio, TX: Dr. Shelton's Health School, 1951.

Shintani, Terry, M.D., J.D., M.P.H. *Eat More, Weigh Less Diet*. Honolulu, HI: Halpax Publishing, 1993.

Somer, Elizabeth, M.A., R.D. *Food and Mood*. New York: Henry Holt and Company, 1995.

Sorenson, Marc, Ed.D. *Mega Health*. Ivins, UT: National Institute of Fitness, 1993.

Tennyson, Jeffrey. *Hamburger Heaven*. New York: Hyperion, 1993.

University of California San Diego. *The UCSD Healthy Diet for Diabetes*. Boston: Houghton Mifflin, 1990.

Vegetarian Resource Group. *Guide to Natural Foods and Restaurants*. Garden City Park, NY: Avery Publishing Group, 1995.

Walford, Roy L., M.D. *The Anti-Aging Plan*. New York: Four Walls Eight Windows, 1994.

Wasserman, Debra, and Reed Mangels. *Simply Vegan*. P.O. Box 1463, Baltimore, MD 21203, 1991.

Wasserman, Debra, and Charles Stahler, eds. *Vegetarian Journal Reports*. P.O. Box 1463, Baltimore, MD 21203, Vegetarian Resource Group, 1990.

Webb, Denise, Ph.D., R.D., and Anastasia Schepers, M.S., R.D. *The Complete Brand-Name Guide to Microwaveable Foods*. New York: Bantam Books, 1991.

Weil, Andrew. *Spontaneous Healing*. New York: Knopf, 1995.

Whitaker, Julian, M.D. *Is Heart Surgery Necessary?* Washington, DC: Regnery Publishing, 1995.

Wilkins, F., and D. Wilkins. *Memory Minder: Personal Health Journal*. Eugene, OR: Memory Minder, 1994.

Wittenberg, Margaret M. *Experiencing Quality: A Shopper's Guide to Whole Foods*. Austin, TX: Whole Foods Market, Inc., 1987.

Woteki, Katherine, and Paul Thomas. *Eat for Life*. New York: HarperCollins Publishers, 1992.

ACKNOWLEDGMENTS

I am inspired, humbled, and awed by the creative spirit behind all life. I pay homage to the loving souls of people like Mahatma Gandhi, Albert Einstein, Martin Luther King, Jacques Cousteau, the Kellogg Brothers, Ellen White, Paul Bragg, Nathan Pritikin, Rachel Carson, and others who no longer inhabit this earthly plane, but whose eternal spirits illuminate the path toward planetary peace.

I am grateful for the loving ways of my parents, Dick and Frances, my grandparents Paul and Peggy, and my brothers and sisters, Peggy, Linda, Rick, Marcét, and Dana, who have been a wellspring of support to me over the years.

My life has been deeply touched by many remarkable and talented people who have shared their knowledge, their time, their work energy, or their financial support. I would like to recognize the following individuals who helped nurture my life, my businesses, and helped me fulfill my dreams: John and Madeline Parsons, Joe, Georgine, and Michael Honke, Dr. Frank and Pam Wise, George and Mary Jane Barker, Harry Merlo, Gary Maffei, Cosmos Kapanzos, Tom Mock, Nick Goyak, Karl Mundorff, Bill Hunker, Charles Monahan, Mike Rubic, Doug Kreft, Matt Palmer, David Traxler, Gary Agron, Bill Maris, Charles Diker, Christopher Ann, Liz Dorward, Frank Card, N. D., Rhonda J. Sands, Pat Klinger, Jim Jackson, Ralph Kovel, E. Kay Stepp, Dan and Carol Sinclair, Michael Ray, Rick Cesari, Mike Conkle, Steve Rosendahl, Matt Patsky, Nikki Riddle, Dr. Prasanna and Norma Pati, Rich Dietz, Lyle Hubbard, Mary Dillon, David Gates, Carter Elenz, Claudia Knotek, Stu Reeder, Ted Isaacs, Nancy Johnson, Tina Runcie, Deborah Widener, John Bauer, and some of the early employees, Mary Ann Scott, Elizabeth Hamblin, Tim Swan, Mike Porter, and past and present employees of Wholesome & Hearty Foods too numerous to mention upon whose work the foundation of Wholesome & Hearty Foods, Inc., was built. A special and heartfelt thanks to Allyn B. Smaaland, who made the first few million

Gardenburgers "pretty," and Michael Meek, who knocked on thousands of restaurant doors to make sure that people got to taste those "pretty" Gardenburgers.

The life work of the following individuals has made the world a healthier, safer, and more harmonious place; their work has increased global awareness of the importance of making the right food choices and has impacted the world in a variety of powerful and positive ways. In this context, I'd like to acknowledge these following extraordinary individuals: John Robbins, Deo Robbins, Ocean Robbins, Michael Jacobson, Ph.D., and his exceptional staff, Dean Ornish, M.D., Neil Barnard, M.D., Dr. John and Mary McDougall, Terri Shintani, M.D., J.D., M.P.H., Paul Hawken, Michael Klaper, M.D., Ruth Heindrich, Ph.D., Charles R. Attwood, M.D., Jeremy Rifkin, Peter Burwash, T. Colin Campbell, Ph.D., Robert Krajian, M.D., Howard Lyman, Joe Pizzorno, Jr., N.D., Frances Moore Lappé, Casey Casem, Jai and Linda Kordich, Karla Verbeck, Marr Nealon, Susan Campbell, Gretchen Wyler, Dr. William and Sonja Connor, Linnea Jepson, Paige Powell, Alex Pacheco, Sue Coe, and so many others who are generating global awareness about our food choices.

I am grateful to the hundreds of television, radio, and print media reporters and personalities, photographers, videographers, and public relations people with whom I have had the pleasure to discuss my story, my business, and my adventure over the past decade. Special thanks to Claire Wehrley, Steve Sinovic, Dick Allgire, Faith Popcorn, David Silver, David Wasser, O. C. Budge, Steve Bryant, Woody Harrelson, Paul Gentry, Carol Ladd, whose words, art, photographs, videotape and film have helped to support our mission, and, in turn, help the world.

I would like to salute the following outstanding people whose unique talents made possible the creation of all the recipes and many other parts of this book. Sincere thanks to Jennifer Raymond, M.P.H., Steven Avis, and Wendy Cantor for the long and delightful days and weeks of shopping, food preparation, cooking, food testing, eating, feeding, cleaning, and—the hardest task of all—getting the results of all that on paper. Also, a special thanks to our research and development team at Wholesome and Hearty Foods, especially Sarah Masoni, for the great work she has done over the years. Additional thanks go to the people who helped with the myriad of details: David Wilson Ivy, Chris Tawney, Linda Jones, Mary Worth, Nancy Clawson, John Moore, Maria Stams, and Deb Foster, my personal assistant. You are all very special to me.

In particular, I want to offer everlasting appreciation and gratitude to my close and remarkable friends Karla Jo Renee, Susan Harris, Tamara Swan, and especially Anita A. Pati, all of whom have been a constant inspiration to me. You four have nurtured my spirit during the most challenging times of my life and I treasure the light of your souls.

Special kudos to my very gifted agent, David Rorvik, who brought the idea of this book to me and who has been a real driving force behind it. I am also very grateful to my editor at Simon & Schuster, Bob Bender, who believed in, invested in, and supported the reality of bringing my story to the world. Thanks to everyone else at Simon & Schuster who put forth their best energies in making this book a success.

I also extend my deepest thanks to all who are working to help bring our world back into balance.

A special remembrance to two very special people who left this realm far too soon: John Bauer, good friend and exemplary human being; and Jack Lee, chief of the "Gardenvillage" and trusted mentor. You are both deeply missed.

Finally, to all the nonhuman animals of the world who are such a source of mystery, uniqueness, and unconditional love, and who have made all that we've done so worthwhile, I dedicate this book.

May Mother Earth guide your spirit to peace, health, and a life in balance.

Yours for healthful food choices throughout the world.

GardenChef Paul F. Wenner

GENERAL INDEX

cowboy socialism and, 87–89
grain production and, 69–70, 72
imports and, 71
moral fiber and, 79–86
overgrazing and, 70–71, 87–89
soil erosion and, 70–71, 73
water and, 72, 73
meditation, 129–31
Meek, Michael, 42
Merlo, Harry:
Gardenburger and, 37
L-P and, 36
WHFI and, 38–39, 41, 44
micronutrition, 109, 116–17
milk and milk products:
calcium in, 112, 117
casein in, 123
disease and, 60
fat in, 122
toxins in, 83–84
Miracle of Fasting, The (Bragg), 24–27, 124
molasses, 115
Monks, Vicki, 90–91
Montaigne, Michel Eyquem de, 80
moral fiber, 79–86
More, Sir Thomas, 80
Moseley, Ray, 63
Mt. Hood Jazz Festival, 34–35
muscle, development of, 112

Natural Food Expo Show, 41
natural-food restaurant, 33–35
New American Diet, The (Connor and Connor), 100,
113, 136–37
Nicholson, Andrew, 51–52, 53
nitrous oxide, 74
Nutriclean, 180
nutrition:
resources and information about, 340–44
Wenner's classes on, 32

Ogallala Aquifer, 72
Olestra, 66
omega-3 fatty acids, 78
One Percent for Health Foundation, 48
Ornish, Dean, 100–101, 105, 134
osteoporosis, 60, 112
overexercising, 132
overfishing, 89

overgrazing, 70–71, 87–89
overpopulation, 67–68, 69
ozone layer, 74–76

Paramount Studios, 42
Pati, Anita, 43
pesticides, 62, 68
phytochemicals, 120
pigs, mistreatment of, 84–85
Pimentel, David, 70
plants, medicinal, 71
poultry, mistreatment of, 85–86
prions (proteinacous infectious particles), 63
products:
belief in, 38
extra dimensions of, 32–33
respect for, 33, 40
sales focus on people vs., 32
protein, 55, 111–13
animal, 97–98, 104, 105, 112–13
calcium and, 112
fat from, 112
in vegetarian diets, 105

railroads, GardenPlan and, 168
rain forests, deforestation of, 71
RDAs (Recommended Dietary Allowances), 105
recipes:
Super Sixteen, 198–200
see also Recipe Index
Rees, William E., 68
Regan, Tom, 81
resources, 337–44
resources, natural, misuse of, 51, 67–68, 91–92
restaurants, GardenPlan and, 168–69, 176
Rifkin, Jeremy, 71–72
Robbins, John, 12–13, 82, 84–85, 86
Roberts, William, 105
Roodman, David Malin, 93
Rosendahl, Steve, 45
Ruttan, Vernon, 68

salad dressings, 123
sales:
balance in, 33
communication in, 32
focus on people in, 32
of Gardenburger, 35, 40, 45–46, 47, 48
insights, 31–33, 38, 40

RECIPE INDEX

hot almond cocoa, 207
hot and hearty five-grain cereal, 217
hummus, not your average, 326
Hungarian goulash, 242–43

island salsa, 224–25

juice fizz, orange spice, 208

kale:
    garlicky garbanzos and, 275
    red potatoes with, 280
    with winter squash, 276

lasagna, garden, 240–41
lassi, frozen mango, 206
lentil:
    and barley soup, 294
    salad, 305
lime dressing, citrus salad with, 299
linguine with broccoli and roasted garlic,
    243
lunch, see main courses

Madras tofu "chicken" curry, 239
main courses, 229–62
mandarin orange and spinach salad with sesame
    dressing, 308
mango:
    -apricot bread pudding, 322
    dango cocktail, 207
    frozen lassi, 206
Manoa sunrise smoothie, 208
marinade, sweet ginger, broiled tofu in, 268
marinara sauce, simple, 336
Maui, Gardenburger, 241
mayo, healthful homemade, 335
meditation sushi, 225
Mediterranean vegetables, 276–77
medley, golden potato, 274–75
Middle Eastern pita sandwich, 244
mighty multigrain cereal, 218
milk, almond:
    chai with, 204
    fresh, 205
    hot cocoa, 207
Mom's tamale pie, 245
multigrain cereal, mighty, 218
mushrooms, pan-roasted portobello, over broiled
    polenta, 246

noodles:
    Chinese, and cabbage, 298–99
    soba, black beans and tofu "chicken" over, 233
    soba, parsley pesto with, 247
    Thai peanut, 283
not your average hummus, 326

Olé, Gardenburger, 242
omelette, spinach, 220
onion:
    soup, French, 291
    and spinach turnovers, 227
    zucchini pie, 261
orange, mandarin, and spinach salad with sesame
    dressing, 308
orange juice spice fizz, 208
oven fries, fat-free, 272

pan-roasted portobello mushrooms over broiled
    polenta, 246
papaya salad, green green, 304–5
parsley pesto with soba noodles, 247
pasta:
    black beans and tofu "chicken" over soba
        noodles, 233
    Chinese noodles and cabbage, 298–99
    fettuccine and roasted vegetables, 272–73
    garden lasagna, 240–41
    gone wild, 248
    Hungarian goulash, 242–43
    linguine with broccoli and roasted garlic,
        243
    parsley pesto with soba noodles, 247
    Southwest fettuccine, 238
    Thai peanut noodles, 283
    vegetable stroganoff, 250
pea guacamole, 327
peanut noodles, Thai, 283
peanut sauce, simple, 336
pesto, parsley, with soba noodles, 247
pies:
    Mom's tamale, 245
    yummy yam, 321
    zucchini onion, 261
pilaf:
    basmati and wheat berry, 264–65
    with dried fruits, 278
pineapple:
    -apricot crisp, 314
    -glazed butternut squash, 279

METRIC EQUIVALENCIES

Liquid and Dry Measure Equivalencies

CUSTOMARY	METRIC	
¼ teaspoon	1.25	milliliters
½ teaspoon	2.5	milliliters
1 teaspoon	5	milliliters
1 tablespoon	15	milliliters
1 fluid ounce	30	milliliters
¼ cup	60	milliliters
⅓ cup	80	milliliters
½ cup	120	milliliters
1 cup	240	milliliters
1 pint (2 cups)	480	milliliters
1 quart (4 cups, 32 ounces)	960	milliliters (.96 liter)
1 gallon (4 quarts)	3.84	liters
1 ounce (by weight)	28	grams
¼ pound (4 ounces)	114	grams
1 pound (16 ounces)	454	grams
2.2 pounds	1	kilogram (1000 grams)

Oven Temperature Equivalencies

DESCRIPTION	°FAHRENHEIT	°CELSIUS
Cool	200	90
Very slow	250	120
Slow	300–325	150–160
Moderately slow	325–350	160–180
Moderate	350–375	180–190
Moderatly hot	375–400	190–200
Hot	400–450	200–230
Very hot	450–500	230–260

GARDENINFORMATION

Call us toll free or see our home page on the World Wide Web.

The Original Gardenburger® veggie patty, as well as many other Gardenproducts™, are available in the freezer case of your grocery or natural food store. Keep your eyes open for the original Gardenburger® veggie patty on restaurant menus across America.

For information about where to find our products, call toll free: **1-800-636-0109** or see our website at: **http://www.gardenburger.com**